MW01259141

As a global brand, McDonald's relies heavily on our suppliers across the world to embed sustainability in order for us to achieve our ambitious goals. This handbook is a highly practical manual to help our suppliers and tens of thousands of other companies like them become better businesses.
Francesca DeBiase, Executive Vice President, Chief Global Supply Chain Officer, McDonald's

This is the book for anyone who wants to turn their interest in being a responsible business into tangible action. The book is packed with practical advice and proven case studies, which together constitute a how-to guide for any responsible business leader.
Ben Fletcher, Group CFO, the Very Group

Family businesses have a particularly strong sense of stewardship and desire to be a force for good. For those family businesses who are young or just starting to more consciously realise their social impact, this book is a very practical, easy-to-use guide that can help companies turn those aspirations into action.
Sir James Wates CBE, Chairman, Wates Group and Chair, the Institute of Family Business

The Sustainable Business Handbook is required reading for executives who are looking to better understand and respond to one of the most important issues facing business today: sustainability (ESG).
Siddharth Sharma, Group Chief Sustainability Officer, Tata Sons, India

This is the practical 'how to' of sustainability that so many businesses urgently need. Drawing on years of practical, hands-on experience, the authors demystify the language of sustainability and provide plain-language guidance for action – now. This book is great news for any leader of any small or medium-sized business looking for the 'how to do it' of sustainability. In clear, simple and, above all, business-focused language, the authors have provided a much-needed tool that will enable a more sustainable, resilient and, yes, profitable future.
Rob Cameron, Global Head of Public Affairs at Nestlé SA.

This is the go-to manual for how to futureproof your business.
Steve Howard, Chief Sustainability Officer, Singapore's Temasek International and Co-chair, the We Mean Business coalition.

We all *know* where we need to be by 2050: a net zero economy. Even better, we all *want* to be there. After all, it is very difficult to raise our families and do business on a dead planet. But, as always, most of us struggle to figure out how to get there; even when pressured. This is where David, Chris and Mark come in. In this book, they break down the challenges and provide clear insights into how to become a more sustainable organization.
Peter Paul van de Wijs, Chief of External Affairs, GRI

If we are to address the climate, nature and inequality crises, we need companies of all sizes to become sustainable. That is why *The Sustainable Business Handbook* is such a timely gift for executives everywhere. Direct and pragmatic, it lays out the framework for initiating or continuing a company's sustainability journey.
Andrea Figueiredo Teixeira Alvares, Chief Marketing, Innovation and Sustainability Officer, Natura &Co, Brazil

A book that comes not a moment too soon. If you are just starting out on your sustainability journey and struggling to mainstream it in your business strategy, operations and culture, *The Sustainable Business Handbook* is the guidebook for you. Engaging and Insightful, the book synthesizes best practice and advice from scores of innovators and early adopters, and it provides clear and practical steps that will help you embed sustainability in your business to make it more successful, profitable and resilient over the long term.

Amita Chaudhury, Group Head of Sustainability (ESG) at AIA, Singapore

It is critical to build bridges connecting well-intentioned commitments to make change happen with the actions needed to make these changes real. Practical handbooks like this – with a focus on the tools and real-life stories of both strategies that work and those that don't – are precious to people who are harnessing the power of business as a force for good.

Charmian Love, Co-founder, B Lab UK

This book, with three authors on three continents, adopts a practical and international approach to the over-familiar, but poorly understood topic of sustainability. It addresses all the roadblocks that hinder companies from taking the steps needed to ensure their own and our planet's survival. It starts with purpose of a company – why is it in business and who is it here to serve. Dig deeply into this and from there it is plain sailing.

Katie Hill, Executive Director, B Lab Europe

Climate change, the loss of nature and rising inequality represent the biggest crises facing businesses today, while sustainability and purpose have become mainstream levers of performance. That is why addressing them effectively has become key determinants of business success. And yet few companies know where to start. How do you put principles into practice? This comprehensive, step-by-step guide has the answers, skilfully navigating business through the big questions of our time.

Alan Jope, CEO, Unilever plc

David, Chris and Mark invite readers to suggest content for the second edition of this handbook. My hope is that dynamic businesses across Africa will use this handbook and thus make sure that we have many more examples from Africa in that second edition.

Dr Ndidi Nnoli-Edozien, Chair, Circular Economy Innovation Partnership (CEIP) Africa and Chair, Afrikairos

Sustainability is not a luxury but a must for all businesses. Large firms are changing and small ones need to catch up quickly in order to survive and grow. *The Sustainable Business Handbook* comes at a perfect time.

Dr Guo Peiyuan, Co-founder and General Manager of SynTao Co., Ltd, Beijing

Business leaders are facing an unprecedented shift in expectations from their stakeholders to embrace ESG. *The Sustainable Business Handbook* provides practical measures for companies of all sizes and from all geographies to respond to these expectations and become better businesses through the integration of sustainability.

Mark Cutifani, Chief Executive, Anglo American

Sustainability is an important value-driver for all businesses. For those executives running companies that have yet to embrace sustainability, I highly recommend you read this book as it is an actionable primer to get your company up to speed on this critical business imperative.

Frank Ravndal, CEO, HAVI

For the corporate manager who is tasked with bringing sustainability to their company, this handbook provides a wealth of useful advice on everything from assessing ESG materiality to building a culture of sustainability. The authors' experience with executing sustainability strategies provides readers with very practical ways to position their company to manage ESG risks and explore related business opportunities.

Tensie Whelan, Clinical Professor, Business and Society and Director, NYU Stern Center for Sustainable Business, USA

There is a growing wave of companies everywhere needing to begin their sustainability journeys and *The Sustainable Business Handbook* is a critical tool to help them do it effectively.

Feroz Koor, Group Head of Sustainability, Woolworths, South Africa

Sustainability is now mission critical. David, Chris and Mark deliver a timely and pragmatic guide to help organizations move from intent to action. We welcome this roadmap to accelerate the sustainability agenda and usher in a new era of stakeholder capitalism.

Sarah Galloway, Co-leader, Global Sustainability Sector, Russell Reynolds Associates

It is clear that we need many more companies ramping up their sustainability efforts in the coming years if we are going to achieve the UN Sustainable Development Goals by 2030. *The Sustainable Business Handbook* provides a perfectly timed and well-thought-through roadmap for companies beginning their sustainability journey.

Dr Mark Watson, Group Head of Sustainability, John Swire & Sons (H.K.) Ltd, Hong Kong

There has never been a greater need for a 'how-to' book on sustainable business and *The Sustainable Business Handbook* delivers. It provides both the context for why businesses must seize the opportunity of sustainability and a practical guide for transforming your company.

Amanda MacKenzie, CEO, Business in the Community, The Prince's Responsible Business Network, UK

The Sustainable Business Handbook

A Guide to Becoming More Innovative, Resilient and Successful

David Grayson

Chris Coulter

Mark Lee

Publisher's note

Every possible effort has been made to ensure that the information contained in this book is accurate at the time of going to press, and the publishers and authors cannot accept responsibility for any errors or omissions, however caused. No responsibility for loss or damage occasioned to any person acting, or refraining from action, as a result of the material in this publication can be accepted by the editor, the publisher or the author.

First published in Great Britain and the United States in 2022 by Kogan Page Limited

2nd Floor, 45 Gee Street	8 W 38th Street, Suite 902	4737/23 Ansari Road
London	New York, NY 10018	Daryaganj
EC1V 3RS	USA	New Delhi 110002
United Kingdom		India

www.koganpage.com

Kogan Page books are printed on paper from sustainable forests.

ISBNs

Hardback	978 1 3986 0406 3
Paperback	978 1 3986 0404 9
Ebook	978 1 3986 0405 6

British Library Cataloguing-in-Publication Data

A CIP record for this book is available from the British Library.

Library of Congress Control Number

2021055790

Typeset by Integra Software Services, Pondicherry
Print production managed by Jellyfish
Printed and bound by CPI Group (UK) Ltd, Croydon, CR0 4YY

CONTENTS

LIST OF FIGURES AND TABLES

ABOUT THE AUTHORS

David Grayson CBE is Emeritus Professor of Corporate Responsibility at Cranfield School of Management. From 2007 to 2017 he was Professor and Director of the Doughty Centre for Corporate Responsibility at Cranfield. He is chair of the Institute of Business Ethics and has worked with businesses and responsible business coalitions across the world. David is based in London and Sheffield, UK.
www.DavidGrayson.net

Chris Coulter is CEO of GlobeScan, an international insights and advisory consultancy working at the intersection of brand purpose, sustainability and trust, and he is based in Toronto, Canada. Chris is a member of B Lab's Multinational Standards Advisory Council and is Chair of Canadian Business for Social Responsibility (CBSR).
www.GlobeScan.com

Mark Lee is an ERM Partner and the Director of the SustainAbility Institute by ERM, and he is based in Berkeley, California. The Institute's purpose is to define, accelerate and scale sustainability performance by developing actionable insight for business. Mark is a member of both the Advisory Board of Sustainable Brands and the Senior Advisory Board of the Centre for Responsible Business at the Haas Business School at UC Berkeley.
www.SustainAbility.com

FOREWORD

We have no option but to address the greatest planetary and social challenges facing us, as quickly as science says is necessary. This takes tremendous effort and collaboration from the entire private sector and an eco-system of partners across policymakers, NGOs, civil society and academia. With *The Sustainable Business Handbook*, more companies will be able to make a contribution, and our chances of collective success are increased.

Corporate sustainability has developed tremendously over the last few decades, especially in recent years. The conversation has moved from why and what to *how*. But, if we are honest, there are far too few players in the game, and many are struggling with how to get started or how to have bigger impact. One of the biggest opportunities I see relates to how to move companies from a risk-minimizing mindset to an opportunity and innovation mindset.

The timing of *The Sustainable Business Handbook* could therefore not be better, as it offers a clear *how* for everyone and every organization. The *Handbook* invites all companies, large and small, upstream and downstream, from all sectors, to take up one of the greatest opportunities in business today – to build a successful business by addressing the world's most urgent economic, environmental and social challenges.

The Sustainable Business Handbook presents 13 chapters covering topics essential to improving corporate sustainability performance. These cover how companies can get started, how they can build up a sustainable business and how to best take it to the world. The book is designed to guide business decision-makers and leaders through any and all parts of their sustainability journey, enabling a genuine positive difference for people and the environment.

The book's authors – David Grayson, Chris Coulter and Mark Lee – are on a mission to engage the most companies possible, as immediately as practical, in ensuring a just transition to a net zero economy by 2050. However, while 2050 goals are essential to set a clear direction, what happens in the years leading up to 2030 will determine if we have a chance of creating a society and environment where many people can thrive.

The Sustainable Business Handbook fulfils this purpose by developing chapters that can be absorbed on their own or in concert with others. In addition to the authors' own considerable experience and their research on best practices, each chapter presents two examples of companies that have already embraced the topic at hand, creating case studies that are both encouraging and applicable.

Based on my experience, having been in the corporate sustainability field for the last 25 years, there are 'Six As' that I perceive essential to successfully implementing sustainable business performance: Ambition; Accountability and Ability; Agency and Agility; and Advocacy. David, Chris and Mark use other words, but, in essence, we outline the same key success factors.

It is fundamentally about being clear on how your company can positively contribute to the biggest challenges facing humankind using your know-how, offer and value chain. It requires change management and courageous leadership at every level of the organization. It is full of complexity and hardship, to be sure, but also delivers rich rewards that include a more future-fit and successful business. Becoming a sustainable business meets the moment of growing shareholder expectations for ESG, employee expectations for purposeful companies, customer expectations for products and services that do not harm people or the planet and societal expectations for responsible businesses.

I wish you, dear reader, a wonderful journey on the road to a more sustainable business. You won't regret the decision to begin or accelerate this voyage. And remember, if you don't do it, who will? And if not now, when?

Pia Heidenmark Cook
Senior Adviser to, and former Chief Sustainability Officer of, IKEA
(Ingka Group)

ACKNOWLEDGEMENTS

The memory of certain conversations lingers with you. Among the 50 or so interviews we did with business leaders and sustainability experts across the world for our previous book, *All In: The Future of Business Leadership*, one with Mike Barry continued to stick out. Mike was then head of sustainability at the UK retailer Marks & Spencer. He told us that he wasn't so interested in making corporate sustainability leaders – the current 'gold medallists' – a little bit better. He was, however, intensely interested in helping create tens of thousands of 'silver and bronze medallists'. In other words, Mike wanted to see many, many more businesses get serious about embedding sustainability and quickly.

So do we! This is why, when Kogan Page approached us about collaborating on *The Sustainable Business Handbook*, we needed little persuasion. Kogan Page have a well-earned reputation for understanding the marketplace and saw the need for something practical that busy managers could pick up and use quickly. As authors, we have appreciated the constructive challenges and suggestions from Amy Minshull and Ryan Norman, our editors, and the work of the design team who responded so well to our suggestions for a book cover that hinted at regeneration and the positivity that can be unleashed by embedding sustainability in business.

We have shamelessly badgered friends and colleagues to help us, often asking them to read a chapter (or two!) and/or respond to specific queries at very short notice. We are truly humbled and grateful for the encouragement and support we have received from so many people. This has often been accompanied by encouragement from them to 'get the handbook published as it is now really needed'. We hope so, and we hope that we have done justice to everyone's wise suggestions.

Our thanks go to Alvaro Almeida, Raphael Bemporad, Dan Bena, Ruth Bender, Marianne Bogle, Perrine Bouhana, Saulius Buivys, Lainey Chambers, Mark Chambers, Gareth Chick, Lester Coupland, Sally Davis, Christine Diamente, Sonsoles Diaz Castano, Sue Garrard, Chris Guenther, Richard Hamilton, Sarah Hansen, Pia Heidenmark-Cook, Adrian Hodges, Anita Hoffmann, Steve Howard, Andrew Kakabadse, Kevin Keith, Gail Klintworth, Michael Kobori, Soulla Kyriacou, David Lear, Gerrit Loots, Amanda Mackenzie, Momo Mahadav, Doc McKerr, James Morris, Margo Mosher, Mzila Mthenjane, Kathy Mulvany, Jane Nelson, Jan Noterdaeme, John O'Brien, Ian Olson, Mark Spears, Bernando Teixera-Dinez, Peter Truesdale, Mike Tuffrey, Peter Paul van de Wijs, Sarah Volkman, Rosina Watson, Robert Wigley and Charles Wookey.

We also appreciate individuals in profiled companies who have responded incredibly fast to last-minute queries: Esther An, Rob Cameron, Cristiano Resende De Oliveira, Suzanne Fallender, Tim Favori, Idit Jankelovicius, Anik Michaud, Miguel Pestana, Amanda Porter, Siddharth Sharma, Manjula Sriram, Vincent Stanley, Pendragon Stuart, Annette Stubbe and Mark Watson.

Thanks also to colleagues who have helped with producing the 'In practice profiles' of companies: Hayley Constable, Anneke Greyling, Anup Guruvugari, Caroline Holme, Heni Kenserii and Sarah Schoorl. And to colleagues who have helped us to develop visuals for the handbook: Francis Cowan, Terri Newman and Alexandra Stevenson.

Finally, we thank our loved ones, who have supported us through this writing project – as they do every day.

David thanks Sue and Jane and Pawel – and also wants to tell Pawel also that he is 'writing a book'!

Chris thanks his marvellous wife, Maggie, and amazing daughter, Clare, for all their support, and he hopes they know how much he loves them.

Mark thanks his wife, Valerie, and his three kids, Norah, Cormac and Eamon, for their patience and care. He couldn't love and appreciate you more.

The usual disclaimers apply: apologies for any accidental errors and omissions.

LIST OF ABBREVIATIONS

B2B	Business to Business
B2C	Business to Consumers
BITC	Business in the Community: UK-headquartered responsible business coalition
BSR	International business coalition and sustainability consultancy originally known as Business for Social Responsibility – now just BSR
CDP	Formerly known as Climate Disclosure Project but now just CDP as extended to water and forestry
CDSB	The Climate Disclosure Standards Board – working to provide material information for investors and financial markets through the integration of climate change-related information into mainstream financial reporting. Linked to CDP
CEO	Chief Executive Officer
CFO	Chief Finance Officer
CR&S	Corporate Responsibility and Sustainability
CSO	Chief Sustainability Officer – most senior executive in the business responsible directly for sustainability
CSR	Corporate Social Responsibility
CSRD	Corporate Sustainability Reporting Directive – proposed EU replacement for NFRD
DE&I	Diversity, Equity and Inclusion
EPR	Extended Producer Responsibility
ESG	Environmental, Social and Corporate Governance
FASB	Financial Accounting Standards Board – sets US financial standards
GRI	Global Reporting Initiative
GSSB	Global Sustainability Standards Board – responsible for the development of the GRI standards

IASB	International Accounting Standards Board
IBE	Institute of Business Ethics
IFRS	International Financial Reporting Standards
IIRC	International Integrated Reporting Council
IPCC	Inter-Governmental Panel on Climate Change
ISSB	International Sustainability Standards Board – proposed new body under IFRS
NFRD	Non-financial reporting directive of European Union
NGOs	Non-governmental organizations
SASB	Sustainability Accounting Standards Board – financial focused standards based on a sector approach
SDGs	Sustainable Development Goals of the United Nations
TCFD	Taskforce Climate Financial Disclosures – how companies should report on their climate impacts
TNFD	Taskforce on Nature-related Financial Disclosures – how companies should report on their nature impacts
UNGC	United Nations Global Compact
VRF	Value Reporting Foundation – merger of SASB and IIRC

Introduction

The Unipart Group (UG) is a successful, UK-headquartered group which brings together digital, manufacturing, logistics and consultancy in a set of products and services that create imaginative solutions for their customers.

UG's roots are in manufacturing within the automotive sector, but market changes have required the business to reinvent itself several times over the last four decades in order to remain competitive. Today, Unipart serves some of the world's largest companies, such as Jaguar Land Rover, Sky and Vodafone, as well as the UK rail industry and the British National Health Service.

Recently, one of UG's customers raised concerns about single-use plastic and packaging used in the transportation of their products. They wanted Unipart to find a more sustainable solution at no extra cost. UG employees did intensive investigations and experimentation – often in their own time – to find a cost-effective answer, a far more sustainable pallet and packaging solution. The solution *saved* considerable sums of money that, under the terms of their service contract, Unipart shared with the client.

HAVI was founded in 1974, originally serving only McDonald's restaurants in Chicago. Today, HAVI partners with a variety of foodservice and high-care brands including McDonald's, Shell and Coca-Cola in over 100 countries, each of whom relies on HAVI to help deliver their own quality and sustainability promises. In September 2021, HAVI announced a new partnership with

McDonald's to innovate and create more sustainable Happy Meal toys. By 2025, McDonald's goal is for every Happy Meal toy to be made from renewable, recycled or bio-based and plant-derived materials. Using a baseline from 2018, this goal could result in around a 90 per cent reduction of fossil fuel-based plastics used in the Happy Meal giveaways. HAVI assisted McDonald's in initiating this transition and will be a key player in making this goal actionable.

Created in 1987, MAS is a widely recognized design-to-delivery provider in the apparel, textile and footwear industries. The group is headquartered in Sri Lanka and has 52 manufacturing plants across 17 countries. MAS partners with some of the world's largest apparel and textile brands including Gap, H&M, Calvin Klein and Patagonia. One area of concern that customers have highlighted to MAS is deforestation. MAS understands that land procured and built on by MAS contributes to this issue. Thus, the group has a goal to replace habitats at 100 times the space MAS occupies by 2025, equating to over 25,000 acres.

These anecdotes illustrate several points relevant to this *Sustainable Business Handbook*:

- Often, pressure on companies like Unipart, HAVI and MAS comes when their big customers make ambitious sustainability commitments, which they need their global value chain partners to help them deliver. Such pressures are increasing.
- Sustainability needs innovation at speed and at scale.
- With ingenuity and creativity, sustainability does not have to cost money. It can help a business *save* or even *make* money.
- There is no shortage of employees keen to take initiative and find solutions that are good for society and the planet and for business. It is not a zero-sum game. Done well, it is win–win!

This is very much the approach of *The Sustainable Business Handbook*, which aims to help businesses become more successful by embracing and addressing the risks and the opportunities presented by sustainability.

Why this handbook

We wrote *The Sustainable Business Handbook* because, while a growing number of businesses are taking sustainability seriously and making great progress, many don't know where to begin, and some who have begun the journey don't have the skills and resources required to advance.

In response, we have tried to collect, synthesize and summarize the best advice and knowledge on how to embed sustainability in business in ways that make it more successful, profitable and resilient over the long term.

Applying the classic Innovation Adoption Curve, we distil learning from innovators and early adopters and try to make it accessible and usable for others. Our goal is to reach beyond today's established sustainability leaders and help others ready to treat sustainability as a business imperative to join the race for sustainability and up their game. Our collective experience, honed working globally on sustainability for many decades, tells us that this is a marathon and not a sprint, demanding that businesses be in peak condition if they are to compete and thrive in a world where sustainability is increasingly central to all systems, including commerce.

After COVID-19

We wrote this handbook during the COVID-19 pandemic. Reflecting a new operating reality, all our authors' meetings and all our interviews have been virtual.

It's unclear which aspects of this new mode of operating will persist. Some predict a lurch back to business as usual. Others, including the EU and the Biden Administration, aspire to 'build back better' by ensuring pandemic recovery efforts accelerate development of a more sustainable economy.

We are firmly in the second camp, for example believing that workplaces will not – and should not – revert to pre-pandemic type. More remote and hybrid working and workplaces will be the norm. This will reduce commuter and office environmental impact, and create opportunities to build more flexible, inclusive and welcoming work-forces – for example, by better accommodating disabled employees and employees with caring responsibilities from childcare to eldercare to looking after loved ones with a disability. Redesigned workspaces will bring new leadership challenges as well. Building shared vision and culture and inculcating desired behaviours and ways of operating will demand new approaches and new skills from employers and managers at all levels.

The pandemic has threatened our lives and our way of life. It also showed how quickly massive change and innovation can occur. His Royal Highness The Prince of Wales, who has championed responsible business and sustainability for nearly half a century, told leaders at the G7 Summit in Cornwall in June 2021 that:

> The fight against this terrible pandemic provides, if ever one was needed, a crystal-clear example of the scale, and sheer speed, at which the global community can tackle crises when we combine political will with business ingenuity and public mobilization. We are doing it for the pandemic... we must also do it for the planet.

COVID-19 adds to other powerful forces that have come together to intensify pressure on businesses to become more serious about embedding sustainability. This is evident in the results of a 2021 survey of corporate chief executive officers (CEOs) conducted by the global consultancy Accenture in partnership with the United Nations Global Compact. It reveals that 79 per cent of CEOs believe that the pandemic has highlighted the need to transition to more sustainable business models. Additionally, 62 per cent of CEOs said the pressure to act on sustainability grew significantly over the last three years, while 73 per cent said they expect pressure to act on sustainability to grow significantly over the next three years.[1] While COVID-19 was unforeseen, its impact has accelerated other sustainability trends reshaping markets and society.

The latest GlobeScan / SustainAbility Leaders Survey of sustainability experts conducted by two of the current authors' organizations, GlobeScan and the SustainAbility Institute by ERM in July 2021, found widespread consensus on the urgency of a basket of pressing global issues (see Figure 0.1).

FIGURE 0.1 Growing urgency of sustainable development challenges

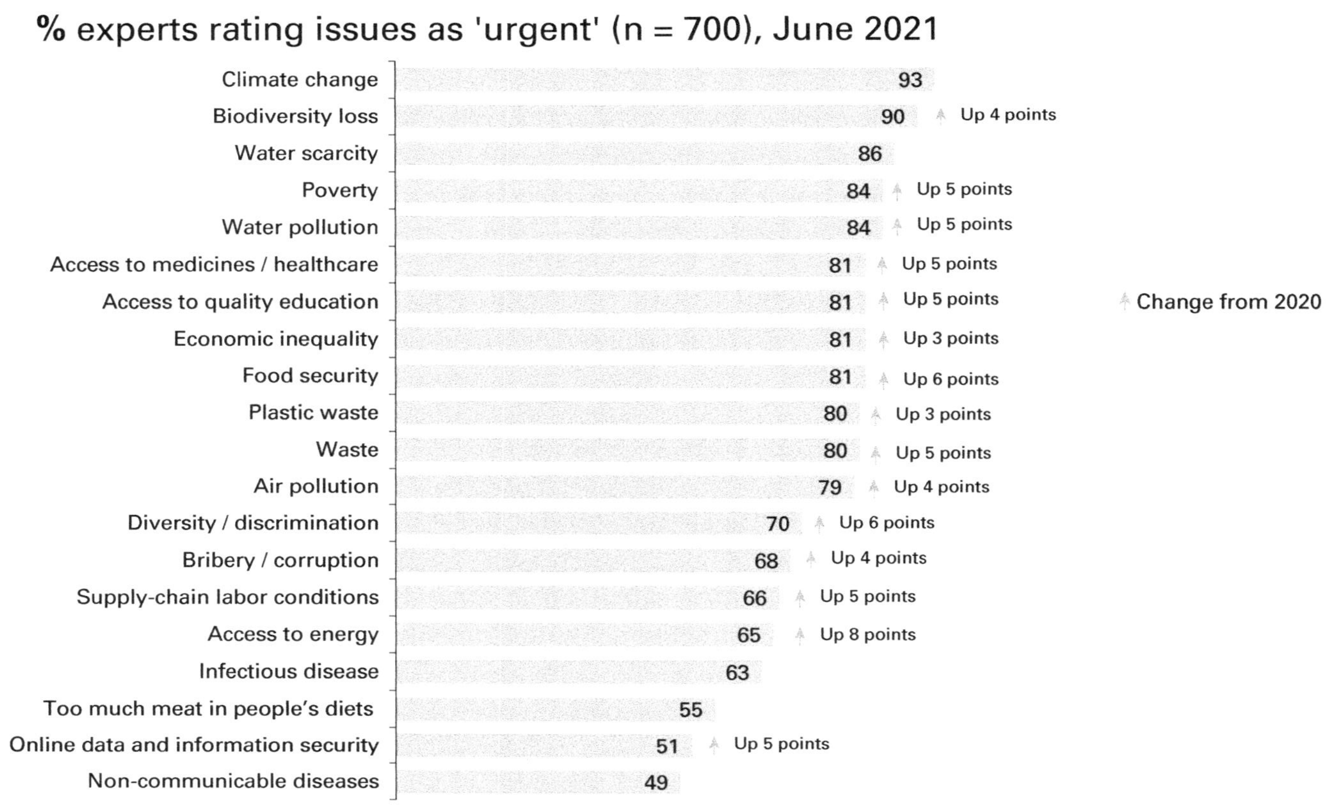

% experts rating issues as 'urgent' (n = 700), June 2021

Issue	%	Change from 2020
Climate change	93	
Biodiversity loss	90	Up 4 points
Water scarcity	86	
Poverty	84	Up 5 points
Water pollution	84	Up 5 points
Access to medicines / healthcare	81	Up 5 points
Access to quality education	81	Up 5 points
Economic inequality	81	Up 3 points
Food security	81	Up 6 points
Plastic waste	80	Up 3 points
Waste	80	Up 5 points
Air pollution	79	Up 4 points
Diversity / discrimination	70	Up 6 points
Bribery / corruption	68	Up 4 points
Supply-chain labor conditions	66	Up 5 points
Access to energy	65	Up 8 points
Infectious disease	63	
Too much meat in people's diets	55	
Online data and information security	51	Up 5 points
Non-communicable diseases	49	

Reproduced with the kind permission of GlobeScan and the SustainAbility Institute by ERM.[2]

Climate crisis

The reality of the climate emergency is becoming ever more apparent, with more frequent extreme weather globally bringing wildfires, severe flooding and record-breaking temperatures and scientists highlighting the dangers of irreversible changes in regions such as the Arctic. The speed and extent of action undertaken to tackle COVID-19 has undermined some of the remaining arguments against moving decisively and quickly towards a net zero carbon future. The pandemic has demonstrated that, in an extreme global emergency, it is possible for the public and private sectors to move radically and at speed. Many expect nothing less to address the climate crisis.

Hyper global inequalities

The pandemic also exposed harsh inequalities between and within countries relating to health, education, income and more. We have seen significant rises in extreme poverty across the world. This has created pressure on business to look more deeply at issues such as the living wage. In China, for example, President Xi Jinping is emphasizing 'common prosperity' and wanting to 'encourage high-income groups and enterprises to return more to society'.[3]

The brutal murder of George Floyd in the USA, captured on a cell phone camera, attracted global media attention and sparked outrage across the world. The cruelty of his killing helped make his death a stand-out and a stand-up moment. Floyd's murder gave renewed energy to #BlackLivesMatter and led sports stars and others to 'take the knee'. This has led to wider calls to address systemic racism, compelling business leaders to help confront racial and other inequalities like those related to gender, disability, age and sexual orientation. All this helps to elevate awareness of the importance of diversity, equity and inclusion (DE&I) strategy, as well as programmes in companies and in society broadly. As with climate, the pandemic amplified existing trends, making them central and permanent on the agenda.

Globalization and its discontents

The pandemic also intensified debates about the course of globalization, especially regarding the conditions faced by those who may have lost out or been left behind by the changes it has brought. Companies are reconsidering 'just in time' supply chain management approaches and looking to build more 'just in case' resilience. In parallel, politicians have to manage surges of populism driven by immigration, inequalities and identity. Politicians struggling to be 'tough on populism, tough on the causes of populism' have been developing ideas of #BuildBackBetter or #BuildForwardTogether, often combined with tackling climate change. These political currents will put new requirements on business while creating new business opportunities.

Investor awakening

All the trends above have contributed to an explosion of investor interest in sustainability or ESG (Environmental, Social, Governance) performance. This interest has been growing for more than a decade (Goldman Sachs coined the term 'ESG' in 2007), but now it has critical mass, a phenomenon well captured in an amusing cartoon circulating on social media in early 2021, showing the fastest things on earth in ascending order of speed: from the cheetah to an aeroplane, to 'people becoming specialists in ESG'.

Overall, ESG focus is pressuring global businesses to embed sustainability themselves and to put more ESG requirements into contracts with their suppliers, who in turn require more from their suppliers and so on.

Whether climate, inequality, globalization or other issues, these are not challenges for business alone, but businesses will be on the front line, and the winners will be those that get on the front foot on sustainability. In short, anyone who imagined that sustainability was just a management fad that would soon go away needs to think again – and fast.

How to use this handbook

There is no easy, one-size-fits-all approach to making a business more sustainable. While we have tried to present our material in a logical flow, and you can read the handbook from start to finish, each chapter is meant to be free standing so that readers can dip in selectively.

The first section of the book, Getting started, explores *purpose:* what a business exists for and how to define it (Chapter 1); *materiality:* the priority sustainability issues facing a business (Chapter 2); and the *business case* for embedding sustainability (Chapter 3).

The second section of the handbook, Building it up, looks at developing a comprehensive sustainability *strategy* (Chapter 4); *operationalizing* the strategy across the business (Chapter 5); and building a sustainable *culture* (Chapter 6). This section also looks at developing *leadership* at all levels of the business (Chapter 7); *reporting* (Chapter 8); and how to ensure effective *governance* of a company's commitments to sustainability (Chapter 9).

The third section of the handbook, Taking it to the world, examines stakeholder *engagement* (Chapter 10); *communications* and storytelling (Chapter 11); *partnering* (Chapter 12); and *advocacy* for sustainability (Chapter 13).

We follow a similar structure for each chapter, first defining the subject matter, then explaining why it matters and how to do it. Each chapter has profiles of businesses we consider good examples, a summary of the chapter's content and an action checklist, and each chapter finishes with a list of further resources. Jargon is avoided where possible and defined in the Glossary when used.

What we hope you will think, feel and do after reading this

After reading *The Sustainable Business Handbook*, we hope you will:

- Be more convinced that sustainability is a business imperative.
- Feel more confident about getting started and initiating a more strategic approach to making your business more sustainable.
- Be clearer about the key things you must do.

- Have a better understanding of the range and depth of help and expertise that is now available.
- Have a better idea of the methods and approaches that will suit your business.

Terminology

We define a **sustainable business** as one that operates with minimal negative impacts and helps solve societal and planetary challenges. Many people (especially investors and those dealing with investors) refer to this nowadays as ESG.

We know some people distinguish between sustainability and ESG, but we are going to be using sustainability and ESG interchangeably in this handbook. We do this because sustainability is about aspiring to continue the business into the indefinite future. Nowadays that means managing risks and opportunities associated with the social, environmental and economic *impacts* that a business has, which requires the good governance and leadership at all levels of an organization as emphasized under ESG.

Sustainability covers a very broad range of issues. In recent years, issues such as bio-diversity, corporate tax strategy, employee health and well-being, artificial intelligence, gender, ethnicity and disability pay ratios, healthy diet and obesity, living wage, mental health, responsibility for mass redundancies caused by automation and single-use plastic, to name just some, have been added to an already formidable sustainability agenda. See the Wordle in Figure 0.2 for an illustrative list of sustainability-related topics.

Our credentials

Between the three of us we have almost 100 person years working in this field. (Yes! We all started very young and have been at this for most of our adult lives!)

FIGURE 0.2   Wordle with an illustrative list of sustainability-related topics generated by the authors

- Each of us, and the colleagues in the organizations we run or are associated with, are talking constantly to people in leadership roles in businesses around the world.

- Our respective organizations advise and/or work with and teach businesses and businesspeople around the world.

- We have also advised, worked with or helped to lead coalitions championing responsible business and corporate sustainability globally.

- Each of us works on many of the core sustainability issues facing business in the 2020s, including climate change, diversity, equity and inclusion and business ethics.

We hope you enjoy reading this handbook as much as we enjoyed writing it. We are keen to get your feedback, including suggestions for anything we should plan to add to the second edition!

David, Chris and Mark

Endnotes

1 UN Global Compact (2021) Accenture Strategy CEOs survey 2021, press release 13 June 2021, www.globenewswire.com/en/news-release/2021/06/13/2246179/0/en/Business-leaders-and-companies-meeting-at-this-week-s-UN-Global-Compact-Leaders-Summit-report-growing-pressure-to-act-on-sustainability.html (archived at https://perma.cc/BM77-86EQ)

2 *The 2021 GlobeScan/SustainAbility Leaders Survey* by GlobeScan and the SustainAbility Institute by ERM

3 Kynge, J (2021) Xi Jinping takes aim at the gross inequalities of China's 'gilded age', *The Financial Times*, 20 August

PART ONE

Getting started

01

Purpose

What is it?

In the span of just a few years, purpose has galvanized the world's largest investor, America's largest corporate association and the planet's premium annual gathering of influencers, along with thousands of companies worldwide.

In 2018, BlackRock's CEO, Larry Fink, titled his Annual Letter to CEOs 'A Sense of Purpose'. In it, the founder and leader of the world's largest institutional investor asked companies to embrace the notion of having a long-term strategy bigger than simply making a profit.[1]

In 2019, the Business Roundtable (BR), a Washington-based business lobby organization, adopted a new 'Statement on the Purpose of a Corporation' expressing signatories' 'fundamental commitment to *all* stakeholders', who they defined as customers, employees, suppliers, communities and shareholders, which many interpreted as a powerful boost to the concept of stakeholder capitalism.[2] Nearly 200 of the largest companies in the United States signed on to this revised statement of purpose but not without controversy (some have charged the Business Roundtable with purpose washing – that is, not matching rhetoric with action).[3]

In 2020, the World Economic Forum (WEF) launched *The Davos Manifesto: The universal purpose of a company in the fourth industrial revolution*, which states that 'The purpose of a company is to engage all its stakeholders in shared and sustainable value creation.'[4]

Defining an organization's purpose is a good place to begin the sustainability journey. By purpose, we mean why a company exists – the authentic, inspiring and practical expression of how it can make the world better through its business success (see Figure 1.1).

Colin Mayer of the Saïd Business School at the University of Oxford defines corporate purpose as producing 'profitable solutions to the problems of people and planet and not to profit from producing problems for people or planet'.[5]

Purpose as a key element for business is not new; it has been part of many corporate cultures for decades, even centuries in some cases. For instance, Lord Lever founded Unilever in 1885 with a societal purpose expressed as follows: 'To make hygiene commonplace'. What is different now is that purpose has evolved an explicit connection to sustainability, helping express a company's commitment to society and the environment. Many leading companies today have updated their purpose to reflect this, while others have created new statements. To again use the Unilever example, in 2010 the company refreshed Lord Lever's original purpose, evolving it to 'To make sustainable living commonplace'.

Indeed, many companies – both incumbents and start-ups – have formalized their purpose in ways that provide a North Star for how the enterprise can be successful in the marketplace and contribute to a better future.

FIGURE 1.1   Visualizing purpose

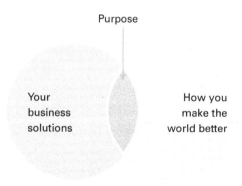

Purpose applies not just to companies, but also to brands. Brands with purpose have become an important pursuit for many corporate brand houses including Clorox, Nestlé, PepsiCo, Procter & Gamble, Reckitt, SC Johnson, Unilever and others.

Some examples of corporate purpose from across the world are outlined in the table below.

TABLE 1.1 Examples of corporate purpose around the world

AIA	To help millions of people live healthier, longer, better lives.
GlaxoSmithKline	To improve the quality of human life by enabling people to do more, feel better and live longer.
IKEA	To create a better everyday life for the many people.
Mahindra	We've made humanity's innate desire to Rise our driving purpose. We challenge conventional thinking and innovatively use our resources to drive positive change in the lives of our stakeholders and communities across the world, to enable them to Rise.
Maple Leaf Foods	To raise the good in food.
Natura &Co	To nurture beauty and relationships for a better way of living and doing business.
Nestlé	Unlocking the power of food to enhance quality of life for everyone, today and for future generations to come.
Nike	To bring inspiration and innovation to every athlete in the world.
Old Mutual	Our purpose is to help our customers thrive by enabling them to achieve their lifetime financial goals, while investing their funds in ways that will create a positive future for them, their families, their communities and broader society.
Patagonia	We're in business to save our home planet.
Suzano	Renewing life inspired by trees.
Tesla	To accelerate the world's transition to sustainable energy.
Tiger Brands	We nourish and nurture more lives every day.
Unilever	To make sustainable living commonplace.
Walmart	To save people money and help them live better.

Why it matters

Purpose has always been an important asset for companies, and it has become more so as sustainability has become a recognized value driver for business. Purpose provides a framework for a company's actions and its approach to sustainability. The most effective purpose is often one that simply and authentically defines the company's commitment to sustainability, and the most effective sustainability strategy is one that operationalizes the company's purpose.

Purpose matters to business in a number of fundamental ways:

- It clarifies a company's business focus and coordinates its actions in a unifying way.
- It helps integrate sustainability and ethics into a company's decisions and actions.
- It creates a North Star that attracts and retains talent.
- It inspires employees to see greater meaning in their day-to-day work.
- It inspires and motivates customers, investors, governments, civil society, suppliers and communities to support and contribute to the company's success and the positive impact on people and planet envisaged by the purpose.
- It allows a company to differentiate itself in the marketplace with an authentic narrative that goes beyond the functional and speaks to how it cares about people and planet, which provides a platform for storytelling and engagement.
- It helps guide decision-making across the enterprise, thereby embedding sustainability considerations into a wide range of behaviours, choices and commitments.

How to do it

We have identified six steps to becoming a purpose-led business.

Step 1: Review corporate assets and history

A great deal of inspiration and insight can be gleaned from existing corporate assets including the company's mission, vision and values.

- **Mission:** What ultimately drives people in the company. It's what the company wants to achieve with the purpose.
- **Vision:** What type of change the company wants to see in the business and in the world at large. This is what the purpose will help deliver.
- **Values:** What describes company culture and forms the core set of principles for how the company behaves. These guide the purpose and the behaviours required to support it.

This review of existing assets can help identify possible themes and form building blocks for the company's purpose.

For example, Walmart's current purpose – 'to save people money and help them live better' – is inspired by the company's vision to 'be the destination for customers to save money, no matter how they want to shop' and a direct reflection of the company's values: service to the customer, respect for the individual, strive for excellence and act with integrity.

Walmart's purpose also is an authentic reflection of the company's founder, Sam Walton, and his original intentions in starting the company. As Doug McMillon, Walmart's CEO, has written: 'Our multi-stakeholder approach is rooted in the purpose Sam Walton articulated nearly three decades ago when he said we have the chance to give the world an opportunity to see what it's like to live a better life… "a better life for all".'[6]

Step 2: Engage

Engaging stakeholders internally and externally is a key part of developing an inspiring and impactful purpose statement. Ideas flow from listening to stakeholders inside and outside the business.

Employee engagement (via surveys, focus groups, townhalls, etc) is critical to uncover ideas for the company's purpose and to build a sense of shared ownership for it. Such a bottom-up approach helps ensure that the purpose is authentic and feels genuine to everyone in the firm.

Engaging external stakeholders such as customers, investors, civil society, government and communities is also vital to purpose development. Interviews with or surveys of these audiences provide insight into your company's reason to exist and help inform ways it can provide the greatest societal benefits and create a better world.

Examples of possible discussion questions for stakeholder engagement include:

• When have we been at our best or most purposeful?

• What motivates you to work for us or partner with us?

• What are the biggest challenges facing our business today?

• What are the most significant ESG impacts of our business, and how can we address these?

• In what ways can we make the biggest contribution to sustainability via our business?

• What new products or services would have the greatest positive impact on people and planet?

• What can we do better than anyone else?

Step 3: Craft the purpose statement

An effective purpose statement describes why the business exists and how it can make a meaningful impact in the world. After undertaking the discovery and engagement phases described in Steps 1 and 2 above, you should now have multiple options for constituent elements of the purpose statement.

Crafting a number of potential purpose statements is often useful. John O'Brien, Managing Partner EMEA at Omnicom's One Hundred Agency Group, described the process he employs with clients: 'The analogy I would use would be tributaries to a river. Various creative streams, both visually and narratively, will emerge from our workshops and research, but they will tend to all head in the same direction and eventually flow together, towards forming a strong all-encompassing approach.'[7]

You can vet the resonance and implications of each draft potential purpose statement with internal and external stakeholders to gain their perspectives on its clarity, fit and ambition, and then use their feedback as a guard against purpose washing (that is, allowing a purpose statement to be grander than actual performance). Further, you can test each statement against a list of criteria for a successful purpose, including:

- Is it clear and easy to understand?
- Will it inspire and motivate current and future employees?
- Does it inspire external stakeholders to partner with and/or support the organization?
- Does it align with and guide the business and its operations?
- Is it practical and does it help facilitate decision-making?
- Is it authentic to the company's values, culture and brand?
- Does it build trust inside and outside the organization?
- Does it differentiate the company?

Finally, the wordsmithing of the final purpose statement should be done in concert with communications specialists inside or outside the company to optimize the language.

Step 4: Ensure core business strategy is aligned to the purpose

Getting the language of your purpose right is important, but the true value of purpose is in improving or even changing the way you do business.

One approach to bringing purpose to life is to engage each of the company's key functions and business units and have them explore what they will do differently going forward to live up to the company's purpose. This can be done via workshops in which each function or business unit develops goals and targets aligned with the purpose and/or by ensuring that purpose alignment is part of the annual planning, review and budgeting processes undertaken across various parts of the business.

One of the most important ways to bring the purpose to life is via an ambitious sustainability strategy that can concretely translate the promise of the purpose into a positive impact on people and the planet (see Chapter 4).

Step 5: Socialize and communicate the purpose

The return on investment (ROI) of corporate purpose depends upon people inside and outside the firm knowing about it, understanding it and embracing it – to truly engage with all those on which the success of the business depends. This requires an engagement plan designed to socialize and communicate the purpose with key audiences, beginning with employees and the board.

Unveiling the purpose to all employees is an effective way to get people engaged. This is often done via a townhall event led by the CEO and other members of senior leadership including the board. Talking through how the purpose was developed and the implications of it for the company going forward are effective ways to get employees excited and thinking differently about their roles. Some companies have taken this further and encouraged people across the company to develop a personal purpose and to consider how this aligns with the purpose of the company.

In addition to broad employee engagement, it is good practice to empower leaders at all levels to more deeply understand the organization's purpose and its implications for them and their teams. This can be done via training and development processes that already exist in the company, as well as workshops to discuss how things might be done differently in a particular function or business unit because of the new purpose.

Some companies intentionally communicate their purpose externally, while others focus mostly on internal stakeholders. Externally, purpose can be communicated to key audiences including investors (during investor calls and at annual general meetings), customers (via account leads, marketing or branding channels), suppliers (through direct engagement as well as procurement questionnaires used to screen suppliers) and broader society (using press releases, social media, advertising and relevant partnerships). But, ideally, a company communicates its purpose internally and externally through everything it does, from how it makes its products to customer service and everything in between.

Socializing and communicating purpose is best done based on a detailed communications plan clearly mapping objectives, target audiences, content and messaging, channels and timings. Well-planned and well-resourced communication of the company's purpose is worth the investment, as this will deliver better ROI, build trust and differentiate the company (see Chapter 11).

Step 6: Measure impact

The final aspect of a well-rounded purpose strategy is to monitor and measure its outcomes and impacts. This might include an annual employee survey to assess levels of understanding of and affinity for the purpose, as well as perceived company performance in terms of living up to it. The same can be done for external stakeholders via customer satisfaction or reputation surveys, and, of course, both internal and external stakeholders can be engaged directly in discussions and focus groups.

Measuring the impact of purpose is also important. Identifying the right metrics to measure the purpose journey is critical: what sort of inputs and outcomes reflect embedding purpose in the company, and how do these connect to the broader business case for sustainability?[8]

Purpose remains a work in progress in many companies. The *2021 Oxford–GlobeScan Corporate Affairs Survey* captured how much additional work is required to effectively embed purpose and measure its impact across the 228 companies surveyed worldwide. While over 4 in 10 (42 per cent) reported that they have been successful in setting a clear purpose, only 25 per cent said they have been successful in identifying the metrics required to enact and measure progress on their purpose, and an even smaller proportion (12 per cent) said they are confident in their ability to monetize the impacts of purpose.[9]

In practice

Anglo American

Anglo American is one of the world's largest mining companies with over 95,000 employees, operations in 15 countries and a 2020 revenue of $30.9 billion. The company was founded in 1917, and it is a significant producer of a range of metals and minerals, including platinum, diamonds, copper, nickel, iron ore and metallurgical coal. The London-headquartered company has been committed to sustainable development for decades and has an established sustainability strategy, The Sustainable Mining Plan.

Anglo American's purpose, 'Re-imagining mining to improve people's lives', was developed in 2018 to help the company redefine what it stands for after a difficult and disruptive few years in the mining sector, which included a great deal of restructuring. The company developed the purpose through an involved process of employee, stakeholder and board engagement over an extended period.

Thousands of employees were engaged to help inform the purpose and also to bring it to life within the business. Similarly, deep listening, dialogues and surveys of hundreds of stakeholders from suppliers, customers, civil society, government, investors and communities were key parts of not only developing the purpose statement but also creating policies, commitments and approaches to mining that try to improve people's lives at scale. This inclusive approach ensured the purpose Anglo American developed was deeply authentic to the company, had shared ownership among the leadership and employees and had external credibility with stakeholders.

Anik Michaud, Anglo American's Group Director, Corporate Relations & Sustainable Impact, describes the intention behind becoming a more purposeful company: 'Our purpose is very much rooted in how Anglo American sees its role in society and how we can and do create value for all stakeholders: shareholders, employees, communities, governments, civil society and others.'[10]

Anglo American has embraced its purpose fully. The purpose is used to frame nearly every board document to set the context for various committee meetings. It is valued by human resources as a proven aid, helpful in attracting top talent, and it directly informs the company's FutureSmart Mining innovation programme. As Michaud notes:

> Our FutureSmart Mining program, informed by our purpose, sees us take a differentiated leadership position, will help us get to our sustainability goals for 2030 and allows us to be sustainably successful as a business as well as make a positive and meaningful impact on the world.[11]

Intel

Intel is a global technology company that was founded in 1968. It is the world's largest semi-conductor manufacturer, with 110,000 employees worldwide and a 2020 revenue of $77.87 billion. The Californian, Santa Clara-headquartered company has a long track record of responsibility, transparency and sustainability reporting.

In 2020 Intel developed a new purpose: 'We create world-changing technology that improves the lives of every human on the planet.' In creating this purpose Intel also chose to design a new sustainability vision and strategy at the same time, making both integral to the new purpose and helping to bring the purpose to life in goals and concrete actions.

Intel's new global impact strategy, RISE, draws upon the inspiration of the company's purpose to articulate and drive its sustainability ambition. Intel's RISE strategy commits the company to 'raising the bar for ourselves and evolving our corporate responsibility strategy to increase the scale of our work with others to create a more responsible, inclusive, sustainable world enabled through technology and our collective actions'.[12]

The company's 2030 goals reflect an innovative approach focused not only on the company's ESG performance and impacts but also on how the company can best move the industry forward on sustainability and address global challenges that affect everyone.

The 2030 goals focus on both Intel's *footprint*, tackling issues such as energy, water, waste, human and labour rights in the supply chain, and employee diversity and inclusion, and on what the company refers to as its *handprint* – that is, utilizing Intel's technology, its expertise and experience, its role as a leading manufacturer and its ability to collaborate and convene in ways to help multiply the positive impact it can have around the world.

This commitment from Intel to act on important issues where it has control and to lead and inspire change through the power of its business provides a great example of purpose in action.

Suzanne Fallender, Global Director, Corporate Responsibility at Intel, comments:

> The launch of Intel's new 2030 goals has enabled us to further increase the level of integration and engagement of more teams and technologists across Intel. It has also resulted in the creation of new collaborative impact models with our customers, NGOs, and policymakers to accelerate the application of technology to help solve some of the world's greatest challenges.

Summary

There is a powerful and growing business case for purpose. It signals to stakeholders what the company stands for and its level of sustainability understanding and ambition. It helps orient the company's overall sustainability strategy and provides inspiration for a company's overall impact on people and the planet.

Finally, purpose provides inspiration and innovation to create a better business. It energizes employees and helps them to get out of bed in the morning to come to work. Externally, it helps motivate, engage and deepen relations with stakeholders.

Action checklist

1 Review the company's history, business and assets to uncover possible building blocks for the company's purpose.

2 Engage people inside the company and external stakeholders to explore why the company exists and to understand how they see its unique value.

3 Develop an inspired, authentic, directional and compelling purpose statement that expresses how the company will make a positive impact in the world.

4 Integrate the purpose into everything the company does.

5 Socialize and communicate the purpose to key stakeholders.

6 Measure how the purpose is being understood by internal and external stakeholders and the overall impact of your purpose.

Further resources

- Blueprint for Better Business (2021) Business as a force for good, www.blueprintforbusiness.org/
- Izzo, J (2018) *The Purpose Revolution*, Berrett-Koehler Publishers
- O'Brien, J and Cave, A (2017) *The Power of Purpose*, Pearson Business
- O'Brien, J and Gallagher, D (2021) *Truth Be Told*, Kogan Page
- Sinek, S (2011) *Start With Why*, Penguin
- The British Academy Future of the Corporation (2019) *Principles for Purposeful Business*, www.thebritishacademy.ac.uk/documents/224/future-of-the-corporation-principles-purposeful-business.pdf
- University of Cambridge Institute for Sustainability Leadership (CISL) (2020, November) University Leading With a Sustainable Purpose: Leaders' insights for the development, alignment and integration of a sustainable corporate purpose, University of Cambridge Institute for Sustainability Leadership

Endnotes

1 Fink, L (2018) Larry Fink's 2018 letter to CEOs: A sense of purpose. BlackRock, 17 January. www.blackrock.com/corporate/investor-relations/2018-larry-fink-ceo-letter (archived at https://perma.cc/43Y7-TCM6)

2 Business Roundtable (2019) Business Roundtable redefines the purpose of a corporation to promote 'an economy that serves all Americans', Business Roundtable, 19 August, www.businessroundtable.org/business-roundtable-redefines-the-purpose-of-a-corporation-to-promote-an-economy-that-serves-all-americans (archived at https://perma.cc/8L65-4NLZ)

3 TCP and KKS Advisors (2020) COVID-19 and inequality: A test of corporate purpose, https://c6a26163-5098-4e74-89da-9f6c9cc2e20c.filesusr.com/ugd/f64551_63f016a989db4dfeaa636d5a659d691a.pdf (archived at https://perma.cc/4MYK-HH2G)

4 Schwab, K (2019) Davos Manifesto 2020: The universal purpose of a company in the fourth industrial revolution, World Economic Forum, 2 December, www.weforum.org/agenda/2019/12/davos-manifesto-2020-the-universal-purpose-of-a-company-in-the-fourth-industrial-revolution/ (archived at https://perma.cc/37S4-NLNS)

5 Mayer, C (2020) It's time to redefine the purpose of business. Here's a roadmap, World Economic Forum, 7 January, www.weforum.org/agenda/2020/01/its-time-for-a-radical-rethink-of-corporate-purpose/ (archived at https://perma.cc/EYH7-9HDF)

6 Walmart (2021) Environmental, Social and Governance FY2021 Summary, https://corporate.walmart.com/esgreport/media-library/document/walmart-2021-esg-annual-summary/_proxyDocument?id=0000017a-82c5-d7dc-ad7a-bac574130000 (archived at https://perma.cc/GKB8-E6UZ)

7 Authors' exchange with John O'Brien, September 2021

8 Barby, C et al. (2021) Measuring purpose: An integrated framework, SSRN, 23 January, https://papers.ssrn.com/sol3/papers.cfm?abstract_id=3771892 (archived at https://perma.cc/SH3R-FRUF)

9 University of Oxford and GlobeScan (2021) Oxford–GlobeScan global corporate affairs survey, https://globescan.com/wp-content/uploads/2021/07/Oxford-GlobeScan_Corporate_Affairs_Survey_Report_2021.pdf (archived at https://perma.cc/DZ8N-4FY7)

10 Coulter, C (2019) Recognizing leaders: Anik Michaud on Anglo American's purpose, GlobeScan, 18 June, globescan.com/recognizing-leaders-anik-michaud-anglo-american/ (archived at https://perma.cc/EX8M-F97G)

11 Coulter, C (2019) Recognizing Leaders: Anik Michaud on Anglo American's Purpose, GlobeScan, 18 June, globescan.com/2019/06/18/recognizing-leaders-anik-michaud-anglo-american/ (archived at https://perma.cc/AHN7-M3YK)

12 Intel (2021) Toward a new era of shared corporate responsibility, Intel, www.intel.com/content/www/us/en/corporate-responsibility/2030-goals.html (archived at https://perma.cc/AK86-B5HF)

02

Materiality

What is it?

One of the first things companies need to do as they embark on the sustainability journey is to conduct a materiality analysis. The term materiality comes from the accounting industry, where financial materiality is an established concept relating to the disclosure or omission of information that can have important consequences on the financial value of an organization.

When it comes to materiality in a sustainability context, it is the process of identifying, defining and prioritizing sustainability or ESG issues for a business.

Materiality helps identify which issues are the most important, helping both to reduce risks to the business and to optimize its positive social, environmental and economic impacts. Materiality helps you figure out which sustainability issues you should focus on throughout your value chain. This prioritization is critical to help guide attention, resources, disclosure, policies and subject-matter expertise, and, ultimately, to inform a strong sustainability strategy.

It should also be noted that materiality will only take you so far. It tells you what your company's top issues are, but it does not tell you what to do about them, how to manage them or what goals to set around them. This is where building an effective sustainability strategy comes in (see Chapter 4).

The Global Reporting Initiative (GRI), the most commonly used sustainability reporting standard in the world, with over 10,000 companies reporting in accordance with it, and the Sustainability Accounting Standards Board (SASB), a standards organization guiding financially material corporate sustainability disclosure, together defined a material issue in a 2021 paper as follows:

> For SASB, material topics are those that are 'reasonably likely to impact the financial performance of a typical company in an industry' – i.e. sustainability issues that impact the long-term value of the company… The GRI reporting framework guides organizations to select topics that reflect their most significant economic, environmental, and social impacts in consultation with stakeholders. The impacts considered should be external-facing – topics that impact people and the environment outside the organization, such as greenhouse gas emissions, human rights and supply chain practices.[1]

Materiality is an often-required input for companies wanting to meet sustainability reporting standards. For instance, GRI makes materiality a mandatory element of its reporting requirements (see Chapter 8).

Given the growing expectations for transparency and disclosure from a range of stakeholders including investors, governments and civil society, it is not surprising to see debates around how materiality is evolving. For instance, in 2020 there was a movement among stakeholders for adoption of 'double materiality', a concept first introduced by the EU Non-financial Reporting Directive,[2] and an important requirement for many European companies because of the EU's Corporate Sustainability Reporting Directive (more on double materiality below).[3]

There are different approaches to materiality, and we should expect new ideas and methodologies in the coming years. It is a dynamic space with lots of options, which is good news for companies as you can often find a solution that fits a company's needs, capacity and scope.

Why it matters

There are many reasons why materiality is a critical part of the sustainability journey and a value driver for companies.

First, materiality allows you to **identify and understand ESG issues** in relation to your business in a comprehensive way. It highlights which issues can have the most impact from a risk and opportunity perspective and allows you to then focus and devote resources to create more value for the company. Identifying risks early can protect the business from unforeseen costs, regulatory demands or business model transformation. Doing materiality well can uncover new areas for growth by creating solutions to pressing challenges or innovating products and services in ways that reduce regulatory, social, environmental or economic risks.

Second, materiality is a potent way to **engage stakeholders** inside and outside your firm (see Chapter 10). A core part of a good materiality analysis involves dialogue and feedback from internal and external stakeholders. This process of understanding expectations and concerns around ESG impacts is an important way to build stronger relations with your stakeholders. Understanding what your stakeholders think and care about when it comes to your company's impacts provides insight into how you can more effectively engage your most important audiences. For instance, if your customers express high degrees of concern over your company's impact on a certain issue, knowing this can help you build a stronger social licence to operate by acknowledging and addressing some of these concerns.

Third, an effective materiality analysis can help **align your company** in ways that allow for stronger performance. Materiality can help educate and inform your colleagues across the business as to what sustainability means for the company, identifying which issues are most pressing and opportune and how you can reduce risk on these issues or innovate to create value from them. This helps align the company and facilitate internal collaboration – both critical ingredients to create a high-performing sustainability culture (see Chapter 6).

Fourth, materiality can improve **reporting and disclosure** (see Chapter 8). As there are growing expectations and demands for transparency (and facilitative technologies to allow this to happen), the need for companies to report on their sustainability performance is likely to grow. Materiality is often a requirement for high-quality reporting (again, see GRI, SASB and other guidelines). Companies, even the largest ones, find it very difficult and costly to report on everything. Having a ranking of ESG issues allows for a much more pragmatic and meaningful approach to disclosure. Materiality helps businesses identify a discrete set of issues on which to focus effort and where it matters most to develop metrics and key performance indicators (KPIs).

Finally, materiality is a valuable input into **sustainability strategy** development (see Chapter 4). A good strategy is innately about focus, and materiality provides a lens to inform your company's sustainability strategy. Materiality helps identify the biggest risks and the greatest opportunities across the many aspects of ESG that need to be the building blocks of your company's sustainability strategy. This all helps you reduce your company's negative impacts on society and the environment and drive stronger sustainability performance, which will ultimately make you a more successful business.

How to do it

There is a wide range of approaches to conducting a materiality analysis. The scope can be large or small, it can focus on stakeholder feedback or digital listening, it can be quantitative or qualitative in nature, or it can be all of these things. What is most important is designing a materiality analysis that is right for you.

As a result, you should design your materiality approach with your company's culture in mind. If your company is a very evidence-based, data-driven, engineering-type culture, then a quantitative approach will likely have more impact. If you are a highly consultative culture, it will be important to design a more qualitative approach.

Materiality can be done in-house or it can be conducted in part-nership with an external consultant. Regardless of how you choose to conduct your materiality analysis, the steps outlined below will help with your process.

Step 1: Understand the operating context to inform the process

One important input into understanding which issues to prioritize in the ESG landscape is to understand the contextual trends that are shaping this agenda. What are the trajectories of various issues? How are governments changing policies around ESG? What are seminal reports such as the World Economic Forum's annual Global Risks Report[4] telling us about the agenda? This type of discovery work helps identify possible material issues and informs the drivers behind them.

In addition, many industry sectors provide good guidance for materiality and reporting (for instance, the International Council for Mining and Minerals (ICMM) and the International Petroleum Industry Environmental Conservation Association (IPIECA). In addition, scanning what your peer companies are doing in your sector and reviewing any published materiality analyses can be valuable to help identify a range of possible issues to test. Similarly, if you are a B2B company, reviewing your customers' materiality assessments can help identify possible material issues for your business.

Reviewing regulatory changes in the ESG landscape in your key markets is valuable, as well as guidance coming from regions with global regulatory influence (for example China, the EU and the USA); this provides additional contextual insight into shifts in your oper-ating environment. Internally, it is important to review any sustainability issues that might already be a part of your company's enterprise risk management (ERM) function, as these can feed the materiality analysis as well.

There is a growing trend for materiality to employ Big Data to better understand priority issues. There are a number of agencies specializing in the use of artificial intelligence to comb and make sense of online information that can be helpful to better visualize the issues connected with your industry (or even your company) and how these topics are being written about, discussed and assessed.

Finally, conducting open-ended interviews with internal and external stakeholders can also help identify the range of possible material issues. Even a half-dozen interviews can be valuable to learn which ESG issues stakeholders are most concerned about.

All of the above possible inputs help provide the context and create a comprehensive list of possible material issues.

Step 2: Engage your stakeholders

Stakeholder engagement is at the heart of materiality analysis. What are stakeholders most concerned about when it comes to your company's impacts? What are their expectations of you on key issues? How can you find ways to build more trust with stakeholders by being responsive to this feedback?

Stakeholder engagement initially entails determining which audiences or stakeholder groups are most important for your company. These can include employees, investors, customers / consumers, suppliers, business partners, civil society, government, academics, local communities and unions. Do all these audiences matter, or do you prioritize a shorter list?

Going beyond employees, investors and customers is a sign of best practice, ensuring the voices, including critical ones, of a broader array of stakeholders (especially those on the front lines of sustainability such as NGOs, academics and scientists) are heard. This can help ensure you don't get surprised by emerging issues and that you are addressing them early. It is important to note that, for certain stakeholders, there is an inherent bias on the types of issues that will be most important to them. For instance, an animal welfare NGO will highlight issues related to treatment of animals in the supply chain, while a community leader working on homelessness will focus on housing.

You can engage your stakeholders using a combination of approaches to assess the importance of key issues. Options may include quantitatively via surveys and/or qualitatively via one-on-one interviews, roundtables or other engagements. A quantitative methodology can help provide more robust, precise and trackable insights for prioritization but can be more costly; a qualitative methodology can provide richer and deeper insights yet deliver more limited representation of stakeholder views. It is possible to use one or both approaches for various stakeholder groups (see Tables 2.1 and 2.2).

TABLE 2.1   Ideas for *qualitative* questions in discussions with your stakeholders

External	Internal
Considering all environmental, social, and governance issues that a company like [INSERT COMPANY] might encounter, which issues stand out as being most important for [INSERT COMPANY] to focus on over the **next five years**?	
What do you consider to be the most significant **environmental** impacts that a company like [INSERT COMPANY] has? Why?	What **environmental issues** can have the most significant business impact on [INSERT COMPANY]? Think financially, reputationally, operationally, etc.
What do you consider to be the most significant **social** or **socio-economic** impacts that a company like [INSERT COMPANY] has? Why?	What **social** or **socio-economic issues** can have the most significant business impact on [INSERT COMPANY]? Think financially, reputationally, operationally, etc.
What are the most important **governance** issues that a company like [INSERT COMPANY] needs to address?	What **governance issues** can have the most significant business impact on [INSERT COMPANY]? Think financially, reputationally, operationally, etc.
What are [INSERT COMPANY]'s biggest opportunities to drive positive environmental or social change?	What are [INSERT COMPANY]'s biggest opportunities to drive business growth by addressing environmental or social issues?

TABLE 2.2   Ideas for *quantitative* questions in discussions with your stakeholders

Environmental / social impact	Business impact
Q. Please rate the importance of each of the following issues for **[INSERT COMPANY] to address** over the next 5 years. Is [ISSUE]...	Q1. Please rate the impact each of the following issues can have on **[INSERT COMPANY]'s business / financial success** over the next five years. Will [ISSUE] have a...
01 – mildly important	01 – minor impact
02 – moderately important	02 – moderate impact
03 – very important	03 – large impact
04 – among the most important	04 – among the biggest impacts
In asking you to answer, we recognize that all these issues are important. We are seeking your input into which ones are relatively more important than others.	*In asking you to answer, we recognize that all these issues are important. We are seeking your input into which ones are relatively more important than others.*

Step 3: Define the dimensions of your materiality matrix

Before you engage your stakeholders, you should think through how you want to showcase your materiality analysis. There are several ways to plot the issues' prioritization. Deciding which option is best for your company is important as it has implications on the questions you ask your stakeholders.

The prioritization of your issues is often rendered into a 2×2 materiality matrix, with one dimension (usually the y-axis) showcasing relative importance of each issue to society. The other dimension (often plotted on the x-axis) relates to importance to the business. Occasionally, companies also include a third dimension (the z-axis), capturing the influence that the business has on each particular issue. The use of this type of matrix is not essential, however. Some companies choose instead to have a list of issues prioritized by different dimensions. It once again depends on what will be most effective within your company.

There has been growing discussion on making the x-axis not just about the importance of each issue to the business but to make it

FIGURE 2.1   Double materiality visual

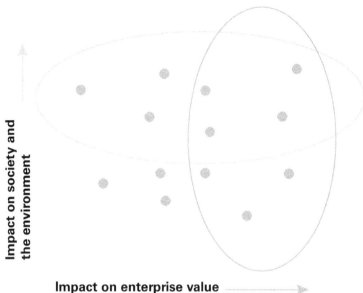

Impact on society and the environment

- considers the company's impacts outwards;
- uses the GRI definition: 'topics that reflect its most significant impacts on the economy, environment and people, including impacts on human rights' (draft);
- presented in the sustainability report;
- for multiple stakeholders.

Impact on enterprise value

- considers the company's impacts inwards;
- uses the SASB definition: 'expected to influence investment or lending decisions that users make on the basis of their assessments of short-, medium- and long-term financial performance and enterprise value' (draft);
- presented in the annual report;
- for investors, lenders and other creditors.

Reproduced with kind permission of BSR.[5]

more sharply focused on financial impacts. This so-called double materiality builds on the traditional approach by not only prioritizing possible ESG issues from the perspective of what matters most to stakeholders but also emphasizing how these issues could potentially impact the company's financial success. Consequently, double materiality has a similar y-axis to traditional materiality (that is, impacts on society) but the x-axis is focused on impacts on the financial value of the enterprise rather than wider or more general impacts on the business (see Figure 2.1).

There is flexibility on which dimensions you choose. We recommend having a short discussion with your internal team and external consultant (if you have engaged one) to think through which dimensions will be most useful to your company. If your company does pursue a double materiality approach, this will mean you need to ensure that the perspectives of investors and other financially minded stakeholders inside and outside the organization are given even more weight in the process.

Step 4: Prioritize and plot the issues

The overarching objective of materiality is to identify the most important issues facing your business and then to prioritize them. All of the work in the preceding steps brings us to this point where we rate the issues. Through the process of reviewing the context and getting feedback from stakeholders on the importance of issues, we can begin to score or weight them.

The scoring of issues can be done quite literally in a quantitative survey (this can be done by rating issues on 5-or 10-point scales or by using more sophisticated mathematical techniques such as maximum differentiation or conjoint analysis, statistical analyses common in survey research to help prioritize choices and preferences over a large number of variables) or in a more subjective approach with a structured assessment (for instance, where criteria are developed across several dimensions leading to an aggregated score for each issue).

An important aspect of this rating is to be clear on the timescale you are assessing. Are we assessing material issues today or are we trying to understand what will be most critical in the coming years? Asking people to predict the future is difficult, but it is reasonable and smart to get people to prioritize issues based on a three- to five-year timescale.

Whichever approach you choose, it is important to document the methodology so you can disclose the approach internally and in reporting, and so you can replicate it in future years. This is important for comparability over time – especially if you are in a high-profile industry or otherwise have a significant degree of critical stakeholder interest in your business.

After scoring and ranking, the next step is to visualize the prioritization. This involves plotting the issues along two or three axes. You will need to decide on the scale for each axis based on the scores for each issue. Once all of the issues are rendered onto the two-by-two matrix, it is useful to tier the issues (see Figure 2.2). The issues that are highest on both the x-axis (impact on the business) and the y-axis

FIGURE 2.2   Example materiality matrix

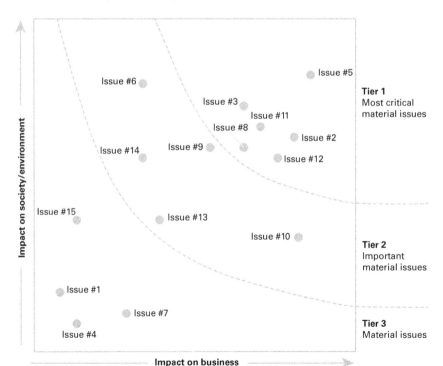

(impact on society) are Tier 1 material issues, followed by a widening grouping of priorities for Tier 2 issues and Tier 3 issues, as outlined in Figure 2.2.

It is important to note that all issues can be highly important at different times according to different stakeholder audiences, so issues in lower Tiers are not unimportant – they are just relatively less important than Tier 1 and 2 issues at a given point in time. Remember, too, that Tier 1, 2 and 3 issues are all important: If an issue warrants being part of the analysis and inclusion on the matrix, then it is material and the company has an obligation to manage it in some form.

Step 5: Socialize and validate materiality

With the materiality matrix in hand, or a simpler ranking of issues, it is time to shift efforts to engaging the business to help inform and ultimately guide sustainability efforts. Finding the right medium to socialize the materiality insights (via presentations, workshops or one-on-one conversations) is a critical next step. These briefings should include the objectives and value of materiality, the methodology (showcasing the rigor and inclusiveness of the process) and the outcomes.

Internally, this engagement should help align the company on top risks and opportunities and lead to positive discussions on new, better and different approaches to improve the impacts of the business on top material issues. Ideally, materiality should be presented to the board to ensure they have visibility on top issues and the corporate plans to manage these issues in ways that reduce risk and exposure for the company. This is crucial if the board is subsequently to own the sustainability strategy.

Externally and internally, the materiality analysis is core to your corporate sustainability reporting. It could be included right at the front of your next report, guiding the structure and disclosure so that your performance and future commitments on these material issues are visible to stakeholders. Or it could be something you use internally to help inform your broader sustainability strategy.

Finally, it is useful to keep in mind the fact that materiality is not a static thing. The context, events, expectations and other inputs are all dynamic, which means that priorities will change. As a result, planning to conduct a materiality analysis every two to three years is recommended.

In practice

Nestlé

Nestlé is the world's largest food and beverage company, with 273,000 employees, over 2000 brands and 2020 annual revenue of more than $93 billion. The corporation, headquartered in Vevey, Switzerland, was founded in 1866 and now operates in 186 countries worldwide.

The company has a long history of corporate sustainability effort. It has been doing a materiality analysis every two years for more than a decade, and it publishes its materiality analysis in its sustainability report during those years.

Nestlé conducts materiality to identify issues for its sustainability reporting and to help focus resource allocation internally and keep up with evolving stakeholder expectations. In 2020 Nestlé evolved its approach to integrate it more fully with the company's Enterprise Risk Management process.

The company uses an independent third party to conduct that materiality analysis and ensure impartial and confidential engagement with stakeholders. A total of 72 internal and external stakeholders were engaged for Nestlé's 2020 analysis.

From Nestlé's materiality matrix below, one can see that climate and decarbonization is viewed as one of the most material issues on both axes: importance to stakeholders and impact on Nestlé's success.

According to Rob Cameron, VP Global Head of Public Affairs & ESG Engagement, 'Integrating our materiality analysis with our Enterprise Risk Management process has substantially increased its profile in the company. As a result, our materiality analysis is, as it should, influencing our planning and decision making at the highest levels.'

FIGURE 2.3 Nestlé materiality matrix

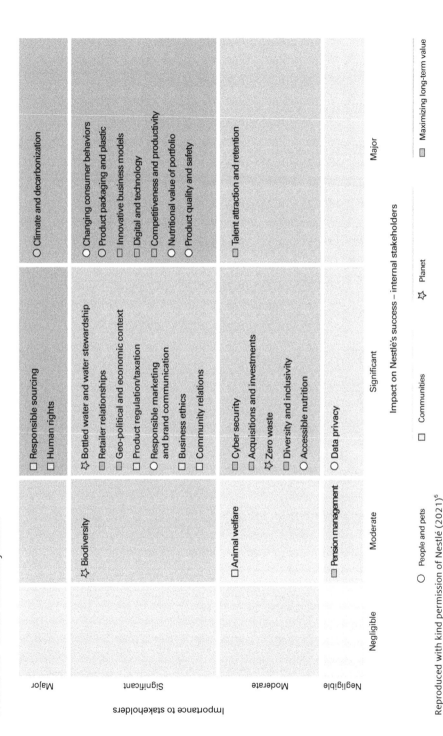

Reproduced with kind permission of Nestlé (2021)[6]

ServiceNow

ServiceNow is a technology company focused on the world of work. The company's cloud-based platform solutions deliver digital workflows that unlock productivity for employees and the enterprise. The company was founded in 2004. In 2020, it had more than 13,000 employees and its revenues were over $4.5 billion.

While the company has conducted an ESG materiality assessment in the past, its 2020 analysis was conducted with the explicit purpose of having it inform the development of ServiceNow's sustainability strategy, or what the company refers to as Global Impact.

Through its materiality analysis, ServiceNow identified a set of top-tier issues that formed the basis for its sustainability strategy development. These Tier 1 issues are wide ranging, from data security and privacy to diversity and inclusion to climate and energy, and are seen by the company as areas where the greatest opportunities exist to create more value for the business and society.

FIGURE 2.4   ServiceNow materiality analysis

ESG materiality	
Tier 1 issues (High importance to stakeholders and high importance to business success)	Data security and privacy
	Diversity, inclusion and belonging
	Future of work
	Corporate governance and business ethics
	Business continuity risks
	Climate and energy
	Digital divide
	Talent
	Emerging technology and ethics
Tier 2 issues (High importance to stakeholders or high importance to business success)	Workflow for good
	Employee and workplace health and safety
	Community engagement
Tier 3 issues (Moderate importance to stakeholders and moderate importance to business success)	Sustainable procurement
	Waste
	Water

Reproduced with kind permission of ServiceNow (2021)[7]

According to Kathy Mulvany, Head of Global Impact at ServiceNow, the company's 2020 materiality assessment had a significant impact on its Global Impact vision. She explains:

> Guided by our Global Impact vision to workflow a better world, we're committed to creating impact and changing the way the world works by focusing on sustaining our planet, creating equitable opportunity and acting with integrity. The ESG materiality assessment that we conducted with third-party sustainability advisor, BSR, in 2020 has been foundational to establishing our strategy and baseline for enhancing our performance as well as empowering our employees and communities and focusing our initiatives and investments on the areas where we have the greatest potential to create value for our business and stakeholders long term.

Summary

Materiality is a foundational part of a company's sustainability journey. It helps inform the company about its greatest sustainability impacts. The process of materiality, largely predicated upon understanding the shifting operating context and stakeholder engagement, is highly valuable to help companies better understand and respond to sustainability risks and opportunities.

In the end, materiality is one of the cornerstones of a successful sustainability strategy as it helps focus resources in ways that address the most significant impacts that a company has on society and the planet and, in doing so, allows the company to be much more future fit.

Action checklist

1 Review the external operating context including societal and regulatory trends.
2 Look to peer companies and see how they define material issues in your sector or value chain.
3 Choose an approach to materiality that fits your corporate culture.

4 Develop a list of possible sustainability issues for prioritization.

5 Engage your stakeholders to help rate and prioritize which issues are most material to your business.

6 Analyse the results of the materiality, prioritize or rank them and present the result visually in a materiality matrix or otherwise.

7 Socialize the outcomes of your materiality analysis with senior executives and colleagues across the business and use it to inform your broader sustainability strategy, including your reporting and disclosure.

Further resources

- Datamaran (2021) Materiality definition: The ultimate guide, www.datamaran.com/materiality-definition/

- Datamaran (2021) The non-financial reporting directive: What you need to know, www.datamaran.com/non-financial-reporting-directive/

- Eccles, R (2020) Dynamic materiality and core materiality: A primer for companies and investors, Forbes, www.forbes.com/sites/bobeccles/2020/01/17/dynamic-materiality-and-core-materiality-a-primer-for-companies-and-investors/?sh=11772b6e2e6a

- European Commission (2021) Corporate sustainability reporting, ec.europa.eu/info/business-economy-euro/company-reporting-and-auditing/company-reporting/corporate-sustainability-reporting_en

- Harrison, D and Bancilhon, C (2021) Double and dynamic: How to enhance the value of your materiality assessment, BSR, www.bsr.org/en/our-insights/blog-view/double-and-dynamic-how-to-enhance-the-value-of-your-materiality-assessment

- TCFD Knowledge Hub (2018) Materiality and the TCFD, www.tcfdhub.org/resource/materiality-and-the-tcfd/

- The online SASB Materiality Map® is an interactive tool that identifies and compares disclosure topics across different industries and sectors, www.sasb.org/standards/materiality-map/

- The SASB Foundation and the Global Reporting Initiative (GRI) (2021) A practical guide to sustainability reporting using GRI and SASB standards, www.globalreporting.org/about-gri/news-center/gri-and-sasb-reporting-complement-each-other/
- WBCSD (2021) The reality of materiality: Insights from real-world applications of ESG materiality assessments, www.wbcsd.org/Programs/Redefining-Value/Redesigning-capital-market-engagement/Resources/The-reality-of-materiality-insights-from-real-world-applications-of-ESG-materiality-assessments

Endnotes

1 The SASB Foundation and the Global Reporting Initiative (GRI) (2021) A practical guide to sustainability reporting using GRI and SASB standards, www.globalreporting.org/media/mlkjpn1i/gri-sasb-joint-publication-april-2021.pdf (archived at https://perma.cc/ZYB8-88J6)

2 Dombrovskis, V (2020) Letter to Jean-Paul Gauzès, 25 June, www.efrag.org/Assets/Download?assetUrl=%2Fsites%2Fwebpublishing%2FSiteAssets%2FLetter%2520EVP%2520annexNFRD%2520%2520technical%2520mandate%25202020.pdf&AspxAutoDetectCookieSupport=1 (archived at https://perma.cc/EB8E-SUEG)

3 European Commission (2021) Corporate sustainability reporting, ec.europa.eu/info/business-economy-euro/company-reporting-and-auditing/company-reporting/corporate-sustainability-reporting_en (archived at https://perma.cc/5442-UGRA)

4 The World Economic Forum (2021) *The Global Risks Report 2021*, www.weforum.org/reports/the-global-risks-report-2021 (archived at https://perma.cc/M4L7-UE2T)

5 Bancilhon, C (2021) Why companies should assess double materiality [blog], BSR, 9 February, www.bsr.org/en/our-insights/blog-view/why-companies-should-assess-double-materiality (archived at https://perma.cc/3BHB-JA4P)

6 SOURCE: www.nestle.com/csv/what-is-csv/materiality (archived at https://perma.cc/Y6J7-DX38)

7 SOURCE: www.servicenow.com/content/dam/servicenow-assets/public/en-us/doc-type/other-document/servicenow-global-impact-report-2021.pdf (archived at https://perma.cc/3UTG-P4UE)

03

Business case

What is it?

In general terms, a business case is defined as 'a justification for a proposed project or undertaking on the basis of its expected commercial benefit'[1] or as 'a written document or verbal presentation which contains the reasons for initiating a task or project'.[2]

The business case for sustainability or ESG does these things and encompasses a greater and more complex picture. Although expected commercial benefit remains an essential element, the business case for sustainability extends beyond financial or economic aspects to consider social and environmental outcomes as well. Schaltegger et al. describe this as 'a situation where economic success is increased while performing in environmental and social issues'.[3] In our interpretation, the business case for sustainability means *addressing short- and long-term risks and opportunities in ways that minimize harm and maximize social, environmental and economic value.*

While each organization must determine what to include in its business case for sustainability, most will employ common elements in its creation. These include:

- the priority issues identified by the company's materiality process (see Chapter 2), which set the boundaries for action by determining an organization's greatest impacts and guiding choices about which actions to take;

- the particular risks and opportunities presented to it by sustainability or ESG, which help guide the allocation of resources and the determination of timelines;

- the company's purpose (see Chapter 1), culture (see Chapter 6) and level of ambition, which will determine the types of goals it sets, the metrics it uses to assess performance and the way it communicates results (see Chapters 8 and 11).

In addition to these components, it is essential to ensure that the business case for sustainability aligns with the overall strategy of the firm.

Whelan and Fink, in an article in the *Harvard Business Review*, talk about the business case for sustainability practices, which they define as those that:

> 1) at minimum do not harm people or the planet and at best create value for stakeholders and 2) focus on improving environmental, social, and governance (ESG) performance in the areas in which the company or brand has a material environmental or social impact (such as in their operations, value chain, or customers). We exclude companies with a traditional CSR program that supports employee volunteering in the community – this does not by itself qualify as sustainability.[4]

Regardless of the ingredients, defining the business case for sustainability is ultimately about creating the most value possible for the enterprise and society. From the business perspective, it will be some combination of reducing costs and avoiding costs, increasing returns at the same time as delivering societal value, minimizing risks and maximizing opportunities, plus building trust and improving reputation.[5]

While complicated to capture and difficult to execute, it is worth the effort. For instance, there is increasing evidence that strong ESG performance on issues such as diversity, equity and inclusion (such as gender diversity on a company's board of directors) and climate preparedness (which can help a company avoid both transition and physical risks associated with climate change and provide direct benefits like lowering an organization's cost of capital) improves governance, saves money, boosts reputation and helps attract and retain employees. A strong business case for sustainability also helps a company avoid greenwashing, committing it to evidence- and science-based factual information and increasing its readiness to communicate credibly on performance against its stated ambitions. This 'case for the business case' is expanded to show how it applies to all companies in the Why it matters section.

Why it matters

In past years, strong sustainability performance was often considered a proxy for good management. In today's business environment, no company can manage well without addressing sustainability as part of its business plan and operations

Part of what has driven the growth in importance of the business case for sustainability and strong performance on priority sustainability issues is the rise of the ESG agenda. While stakeholder pressure has always been a factor, the rapid increase in investor and government interest in ESG performance seen in recent years – plus employee focus on the sustainability performance of their employers or potential employers and consumer focus on the sustainability of the products and services they buy – has increased demand on companies to demonstrate an understanding of and performance on ESG issues. This demand is shaped by bespoke investor analysis of corporate ESG performance, the proliferation and wide use of ESG ratings, political pressure and, increasingly, regulatory standards codifying required ESG performance and/or disclosure. It is partly because of the strength of the ESG movement that this *Sustainable Business Handbook* uses 'sustainability' and 'ESG' as synonyms.

In his 2018 article in *MIT Sloan Management Review* on the business case for sustainability, Andrew Winston says:

> The battle to get companies interested in sustainability is basically over. No large company seriously debates whether environmental and social issues affect the company's bottom line. At the very least, executives recognize that key stakeholders, like their customers and employees, do care about these issues. So, sustainability is on the strategic agenda to stay.[6]

We agree, but, even several years later, many business leaders express doubt about the business case. Perhaps they just do not know where to begin. We believe the first step is understanding the benefits.

Thankfully, there are numerous reasons for committing the time and effort needed to develop a sound business case for sustainability for your company. The more these can be tailored to your organization's specific circumstances, the better.

A compelling business case will have many of the following attributes:

- Helps explain and overcome any internal concerns, doubts or questions regarding sustainability integration and investment, especially those of senior leaders.

- Communicates the benefits of ESG by identifying and making it possible to pursue many types of returns, from profit to reputation, from cost savings to trust, through competitiveness and resilience.

- Supports strategy development by setting out a framework for making sustainability or ESG choices based on their ability to reduce risk and create value.

- Organizes the priority sustainability issues identified in materiality and guides investment in them by making clear where the greatest environmental, social and economic returns lie.

- Demands understanding of those same material issues, which helps connect them to company purpose, strategy and operations as well as enhancing ESG disclosure and communication.

- Meets the expectations of employees, investors, customers, regulators, NGOs and other stakeholders for evidence as to how sustainability ambitions are turned into viable operational pathways.

- Highlights development needs in that the key elements in a business case require adequate senior leader and employee knowledge and skills to support implementation.

- Fosters internal collaboration by making clear which teams (for instance, strategy, sustainability, product development and marketing) need to work together to achieve certain ambitions (like the selection of new materials to use in lower-carbon product design and launch) – and clarifies when external collaboration is needed.

- Demonstrates how company sustainability strategy and performance benefit both company and stakeholders by helping to enhance everything from investor returns to community relations, through employee attraction and retention, customer loyalty and competitiveness.

- Strengthens supply chains by making investment and outcome priorities clear and focusing value chain partnerships on minimizing harm while maximizing social, environmental and economic benefits for all participants.
- Shapes and sharpens advocacy positions and improves public policy engagement because the business has the evidence to substantiate its own sustainability performance and credentials.
- Prepares an organization for a range of future scenarios, which increases long-term business resilience.

The list above is long but still not exhaustive. Companies generally have more reasons to develop and implement a robust business case for sustainability, and individual organizations will, over time, find the factors that are best tailored to their circumstances as well as those most motivating and rewarding. Overall, a sustainability or ESG business case does not just address short- and long-term risks and opportunities in ways that minimize harm and maximize value; done right, it removes sustainability from the realm of 'important' or 'nice to do' and makes it so compelling that an organization could not choose to proceed without it.

How to do it

While there is no question that developing a business case for sustainability is the right thing to do, that does not make it simple. Capturing and quantifying the value of sustainability by looking at different ways it might contribute financial or non-financial value creates the best opportunity to increase long-term business resilience and give your organization the greatest chance of thriving now and in the future. Future business growth will be influenced greatly by sustainability performance and the degree to which internal and external stakeholders understand and buy into it.

Here is a breakdown of key steps to consider taking – one at a time or all at once – when developing a business case or cases for sustainability:

Step 1: Apply existing, external data and evidence

While the business case for sustainability is bespoke for every organization, each company can and should build on existing materials and platforms. It's not about reinventing the wheel, but about determining and doing everything necessary to make a business case that is appropriately specific and customized to your organization.

Thankfully, there are many useful guidelines, standards and frameworks available, including some we believe are relevant to every organization such as the Global Reporting Initiative (GRI), the Science Based Targets initiative (SBTi), the Sustainability Accounting Standards Board (SASB), the Task Force on Climate-related Financial Disclosures (TCFD), the United Nations Global Compact (UNGC) and the United Nations Sustainable Development Goals (the SDGS or the Global Goals). There are also more specific resources, for instance the enormous and growing universe of ESG ratings and rankings and sector-focused tools sometimes developed by industry trade groups, such as the guidance on materiality, reporting and disclosure developed by IPIECA for the energy industry.[7]

Similarly, businesses can learn from the work of others including leadership companies, industry associations and standards bodies, many of whom publish a tremendous amount of valuable guidance material and make it freely available for others' education and use. You can put the tools, frameworks, guidelines and approaches others have developed – like the Greenhouse Gas Protocol, SBTi, Scenarios Planning, Systems Thinking and TCFD – to use for your purposes.

What this means in practice is that we might see, for instance, a company:

- whose strategy is informed by the SDGs;
- signatory to the UNGC and subject to UNGC member sustainability reporting obligations;
- aggressively trying to improve its climate-and water-related performance in part by participating in the CDP Climate and CDP Water ratings;

- with science-based targets to support pursuit of its net zero ambitions;
- which undertakes sustainability reporting and disclosure in a manner aligned with GRI, SASB and TCFD;
- and which judges its ESG performance against peers and, overall, based on its ranking in the MSCI Global Sustainability Indexes and using Bloomberg Terminal ESG data.

While this hypothetical example is complicated, it's increasingly common to see approaches like this, and they are not as difficult to manage as might appear at first glance. This is in part due to some resources becoming more universally accepted (e.g. the UN SDGs provide a global framework for sustainable development, and companies applying the SDGs use them to inform their own strategy by considering which of the issues covered by the 17 Global Goals are most relevant to them) and/or standardized (like the more structured guidance on setting science-based targets being produced by SBTi to help fulfil its objective to drive 'ambitious climate action in the private sector by enabling companies to set science-based emissions reduction targets').

Still, we only recommend a broad, blended approach like the example above to bigger, more global companies and/or more mature sustainability practitioners. Others might choose to join membership organizations such as BSR, CSR Europe, the UNGC or WBCSD (the World Business Academy for Sustainable Development), where member companies share best practices on sustainability and the organizations provide member guidance. For example, the B Corp Certification requires companies (often, but not exclusively, smaller companies) to 'consider the impact of their decisions on their workers, customers, suppliers, community, and the environment' and the certification process provides scores and feedback relevant to sustainability performance and ways to improve it.[8]

Step 2: Examine company-specific evidence and benchmark your peers

It is important to consider your current business model, including the key drivers for profitability in your organization and your key material issues. This will help you assess how sustainable your business model is and begin to plan how to evolve it to minimize harm and maximize environmental, social and economic value in the future. This can mean embracing disruption, such as has occurred in the automobile industry with efforts to transition from internal combustion engines to electric vehicles. You will also want to connect the business model review to the outcomes of your materiality process. Your company's business case for sustainability must address the priority sustainability topics faced by your organization – and stakeholder expectations regarding performance and communication on those issues.

As you are building your company's business case, be sure to use all the already-available data possible. There is now so much quantitative and qualitative information in the market on sustainability topics, including rates of ESG investment growth, potential and current employee interest in sustainability performance, the increasing relevance of sustainability to scenario and risk planning, the manner in which ESG boosts resilience, customer demand for more sustainable products and services and the number of procurement questionnaires referencing ESG and impacting competitiveness.

Pick what is most relevant to your business and package it appropriately for your core audiences. The insurance industry, for example, is one of those particularly affected by high risks from climate change and much greater frequency and severity of extreme weather conditions such as wild fires and flooding. Unsurprisingly, therefore, some of the major insurance companies and particularly the re-insurers have been developing increasingly sophisticated climate risk models and incorporating these in their overall risk frameworks.

It is also useful to benchmark your peers and competitors to understand how they have defined their material sustainability issues and the scale of their ambition and investment. Understanding their focus and their progress can help determine how aggressive to make your own goals and what kind of resources to invest in order to realize them.

Finally, tie the data and evidence you find and the design of your business case to your sustainability strategy, ensuring it articulates how sustainability or ESG planning and action will benefit the business. It is essential that the business case supports your key strategic pillars. One company that does a good job articulating how achieving its strategy will benefit the organization is IKEA. IKEA's People & Planet Positive strategy has three pillars – healthy and sustainable living, circular and climate positive, and fair and equal (which refers to human rights and equity for all the people and communities in IKEA's value chain) – each of which has clear business benefits behind it.[9]

Step 3: Create cross-functional teams to provide relevant business case data to different stakeholders

Bringing the business case fully alive requires packaging and repackaging of business cases to meet the needs of different stakeholders. Combining the diverse skills of internal teams by mixing people from corporate sustainability, strategy, risk, investor relations, brand, communications, government affairs, product development, marketing and so on, and then stretching outside your organization and building appropriate collaborations with external stakeholders and partners, will help in your business case development.

There is value in tailoring elements of the business case to different stakeholders. Every stakeholder group places different value on different outcomes. For example, your Chief Financial Officer may care most about direct financial benefits, while the risk function inside your company is more concerned about reputation impact, and any prospective employees look most closely at your company's climate-related performance and policies relating to diversity, equity and inclusion. By ensuring each stakeholder group gets information about how the sustainability strategy's execution will benefit them, the value of sustainability performance can truly be greater than the sum of the parts.

As you build your business case, quantify everything possible, for instance potential renewable energy investment savings over time and evidence of alpha realized by companies with more diverse boards of directors. In addition, capture qualitative impacts like trust and reputation value, which can be measured – and changes tracked over time – using, for example, employee, supplier and consumer surveys.

Articulating the business case for sustainability is an ongoing task. It is important to recognize that this is an evergreen process area where continuous improvement is required. Consider that even Unilever, one of the most recognized sustainability leaders, on webinars held to announce the company's new 'Unilever Compass' sustainability strategy in the spring of 2021, stated that it still has not completely proved the business case for sustainability and is determined to keep working to illuminate, quantify and conclusively prove what it is certain, based on empirical evidence, is true. The best business cases today and in future, the ones that will be integrated and scale, will be those grounded in solving ESG challenges in ways that save money, make money and/ or create new business opportunities.

In practice

Unilever

Unilever is one of the world's largest consumer goods companies, with over 149,000 employees and 2020 annual revenue of $51 billion.[10] Founded in 1871, Unilever is headquartered in London and operates worldwide.[11]

Unilever holds a portfolio of over 400 brands spanning a variety of sectors including beauty and personal care, foods and refreshments, and home care. Unilever's purpose, to 'make sustainable living commonplace', exists alongside and supports its vision to become the global leader in sustainable business. It is Unilever's ambition to demonstrate how its 'purpose-led, future-fit business model drives superior performance' while 'consistently delivering financial results' within the industry.[12]

In 2010, Unilever rolled out its Sustainable Living Plan (USLP), a framework that became a benchmark for corporate sustainability strategy and performance. The USLP covered a variety of topics aligned with the UN's Sustainable Development Goals (SDGs). The topics were grouped under three banners: improving health and well-being for more than 1 billion people, reducing the company's environmental impact by half and enhancing the livelihoods of millions of individuals.

After a decade spent executing against the USLP, Unilever reimagined its sustainability ambitions, releasing the Unilever Compass in 2021. The Compass is an updated sustainable business strategy, which builds on everything accomplished under the USLP.[13] The Unilever Compass prioritizes five strategic pillars and actions including 'winning with its brands as a force for good, powered by purpose and innovation'. To support this ambition, Unilever created 35 goals encompassing topics from climate action to the future of work, with human rights underlining all the other issues.

It is Unilever's belief that innovation and purpose are the key to sustainable business growth. Additionally, Unilever places a strong emphasis on sustainability governance. With a wide array of complementary governing structures, Unilever seeks to ensure and demonstrate that its business strategy is thorough and subject to appropriate oversight. While the Unilever Compass framework stresses the importance of corporate responsibility to sustainable, long-term financial growth, Unilever's approach to corporate governance ensures that the points laid out in this framework are accomplished, highlighting Unilever's understanding of the business case for sustainability as well as the methods to make it actionable.[14]

At a global virtual event in 2020 celebrating the 10 years of the Sustainable Living Plan, Rebecca Marmot, Unilever's Chief Sustainability Officer, stated:

> There are many highlights from the last ten years. Unilever's Sustainable Living Brands – which include brands like Dove, Hellmann's and Domestos – have consistently outperformed the average growth rate of the rest of the portfolio since the metric was introduced in 2014. We have avoided over €1bn in costs, by improving water and energy efficiency in our factories, and using less material and producing less waste. The USLP has also become a decisive factor to attract the best talent; and has been instrumental to forging strong partnerships with NGOs, government organisations and other businesses.[15]

Maple Leaf

Maple Leaf Foods is a Canadian consumer food company with more than 13,500 employees and 2020 annual revenue of $3.4 billion.[16]

The Mississauga-headquartered organization was formed in 1991 and today operates across Canada, the US and much of Asia.[17]

Maple Leaf is Canada's largest prepared meats and poultry producer, with a portfolio of prepared meats, ready-to-cook and ready-to-serve meals and fresh pork, poultry and plant protein products. The company's vision is to be the most sustainable protein company on earth, and it is actively working to transform the world's food system so that it can survive, and thrive, for generations to come.

Maple Leaf's vision has helped define the four sustainability pillars of the company: Better Food, Better Care (for animals), Better Communities and Better Planet. Maple Leaf is currently focusing on sustainable food production and helping develop a more sustainable protein industry in order to reduce the significant environmental and social footprint of the sector. One outcome of its efforts to date is that it is now the North American leader in Raised Without Antibiotics (RWA) pork.

Maple Leaf is slowly offloading its non-protein portfolio to focus on its sustainable meat product line and offering more plant-based proteins. The company has created a new subsidiary, Greenleaf Foods, which, helped by acquisitions of brands like Lightlife and Field Roast, is accelerating expansion of Maple Leaf's footprint in the conscious food segment. This shift is a result of a clear understanding of the business case for sustainability and is in line with the goals and the ambitious vision the company has set for itself. One example of how focused Maple Leaf is on getting the business case right can be seen in the fact that it undertook the most extensive consumer research in the history of the US plant protein category before relaunching the Lightlife brand with a focus on simple and recognizable ingredients to help it appeal to consumers who want natural, healthy alternatives.

In 2019, Maple Leaf became the first major food company in the world to go carbon neutral and the first Canadian food company to adopt science-based targets, sending a message to consumers and other stakeholders about how it is putting its sustainability vision into action.

Michael McCain, CEO of Maple Leaf, in his message for the company's most recent sustainability report, says:

> Producing food took on an even deeper meaning as our disrupted nation needed nourishment. And we provided high-quality protein made with simple ingredients that people understand. In 2020, products that bear a 'Carbon Zero – Made by a Carbon Neutral Company' logo became available to our consumers to help them choose products that reflect their values.[18]

Summary

A good business case for sustainability has to be short term as well as long term, tactical as well as strategic.

The business case for sustainability matters because:

- More sustainable companies better anticipate, prioritize and address emerging risks and opportunities including new standards and regulations, while deep trust reservoirs make them more attractive to suppliers, customers and partners, improving competitiveness.
- Strong stakeholder relationships lead to deeper engagement, better access to information and enhanced understanding of societal expectations, supporting better strategy and accelerating research and development, innovation and growth.
- Reducing waste and increasing efficiency cuts costs and saves money, while better products, more satisfied customers, improved market position and greater ease attracting investment (from both equity investors and lenders) boost profit.
- Enhanced status as an employer of choice improves a company's ability to attract and retain employees, who increasingly factor in sustainability performance when choosing where to work.
- Overall risk and opportunity awareness improves risk management (including supply chain risk management) and increases marketplace differentiation, boosting reputation and brand equity.

Action checklist

1 Define the most pressing sustainability issues for your organization (the outcomes of your materiality process) and calibrate how they affect performance and profit.

2 Translate this insight into different parts of the business and the activities of the business.

3 Define how these issues create risk and opportunity for your business today and how risks and opportunities may evolve in the future.

4 Identify which stakeholders care most about which issues and what they expect you to do about them, especially the demands of employees, investors and regulators.

5 Determine how addressing your most pressing sustainability issues decreases risks and increases opportunities for your business, satisfies business needs, increases value / returns / profits and boosts long-term business resilience. Include the cost savings that come with choices / actions such as decreased energy or materials use, as well as cost avoidance.

6 Explore how sustainability helps simplify things and reduces the volatility, uncertainty, complexity and ambiguity facing businesses today.

7 Compare your business case to the business case of competitors and sector leaders in sustainability.

Further resources

- Cote, C (2021) Making the business case for sustainability, *Harvard Business Review*
- KPMG (2021) Valuing your impacts on society: How KPMG true value can help measure and manage your impacts, www.kpmg.com/sustainability

- Li, S (2020) The business case for ESGs: Why companies adopt environmental values beyond social responsibility, Forbes, www.forbes.com/sites/stevenli1/2020/04/06/esg-environmental-values-business-case/?sh=663a8b2e708f
- Whelan, T (2020) Making a better business case for ESG, *Stanford Social Innovation Review*
- Willard, R (2012) *The New Sustainability Advantage, 10th anniversary edition,* New Society Publishers

Endnotes

1   'Business case', *Oxford English Dictionary*, Oxford University Press
2   Market Business News (2021) Business case – definition and meaning, *Market Business News*, marketbusinessnews.com/financial-glossary/business-case/ (archived at https://perma.cc/GX3H-77QS)
3   Schaltegger, S, Lüdeke-Freund, F and Hansen, E G (2012) Business Cases for Sustainability: The role of business model innovation for corporate sustainability, *International Journal of Innovation and Sustainable Development*, Vol. 6, No. 2, pp. 95–119
4   Whelan, T and Fink, C (2016) The comprehensive business case for sustainability. *Harvard Business Review*, everestenergy.nl/new/wp-content/uploads/HBR-Article-The-comprehensive-business-case-for-sustainability.pdf (archived at https://perma.cc/6DNG-LUHJ)
5   A formulation articulated by Sue Garrard, chair of Blueprint for Better Business in presentations at Cranfield School of Management, 2019
6   Winston, A (2018) Explaining the business case for sustainability again... and again... and again, *MIT Sloan Management Review*, 7 August, sloanreview.mit.edu/article/explaining-the-business-case-for-sustainability-again-and-again-and-again/ (archived at https://perma.cc/X4YV-NMMB)
7   IPIECA, API and IOGP (2020) *Sustainability Reporting Guidance for the Oil and Gas Industry*, 4th edition, www.ipieca.org/media/5115/ipieca_sustainability-guide-2020.pdf (archived at https://perma.cc/6RYA-RNL6)
8   B Lab (2021) A global community of leaders, https://bcorporation.net/ (archived at https://perma.cc/8WLF-RY7X)
9   IKEA (2020) *IKEA Sustainability Report FY20*, gbl-sc9u2-prd-cdn.azureedge.net/-/media/aboutikea/pdfs/ikea-sustainability-reports/ikea_sustainability-report_fy20_.pdf?rev=51556c50bb594d1391e8a56f5ca05bed&hash=DFE0FADC2F7827888B421CACD310BB44 (archived at https://perma.cc/HGB5-WYL5)

10 Unilever (2020) *Unilever Annual Report and Accounts 2020*, www.unilever.
com/Images/annual-report-and-accounts-2020_tcm244-559824_en.pdf
(archived at https://perma.cc/BL9C-JHVA)

11 Unilever (2021) Unilever at a glance, www.unilever.com/our-company/
at-a-glance/ (archived at https://perma.cc/MX6X-LT7B)

12 Unilever (2021) The Unilever Compass, assets.unilever.com/files/92ui5egz/
production/ebc4f41bd9e39901ea4ae5bec7519d1b606adf8b.pdf/Compass-
Strategy.pdf (archived at https://perma.cc/Z9MC-TPH8)

13 Unilever (2021) Unilever sustainable living plan 2010 to 2020: Summary of 10
years' progress, assets.unilever.com/files/92ui5egz/production/16cb778e4d31b
81509dc5937001559f1f5c863ab.pdf/USLP-summary-of-10-years-progress.pdf
(archived at https://perma.cc/TS7L-D6DK)

14 Unilever (2021) The Unilever Compass, assets.unilever.com/files/92ui5egz/
production/ebc4f41bd9e39901ea4ae5bec7519d1b606adf8b.pdf/Compass-
Strategy.pdf (archived at https://perma.cc/D98U-Z8US)

15 Unilever (2020) Unilever celebrates 10 years of the Sustainable Living Plan,
Unilever, 5 June, www.unilever.com/news/press-releases/2020/unilever-
celebrates-10-years-of-the-sustainable-living-plan.html (archived at https://
perma.cc/YB2V-7RJJ)

16 Sourced from www.mapleleaffoods.com/wp-content/uploads/2021/05/
MLF_WHO_WE_ARE_FACTSHEET_APRIL_29_2021_EN.pdf (archived at
https://perma.cc/6YV8-DCN4)

17 Maple Leaf Foods (2021) Maple Leaf Foods at a glance, www.mapleleaffoods.
com/wp-content/uploads/2021/05/MLF_WHO_WE_ARE_FACTSHEET_
APRIL_29_2021_EN.pdf (archived at https://perma.cc/6YV8-DCN4)

18 McCain, Michael (2021) A message from our CEO, Michael McCain,
www.mapleleaffoods.com/sustainability/our-approach/ceo-message/
(archived at https://perma.cc/U9L8-837U)

PART TWO

Building it up

04

Strategy

What is it?

Management consultants EY argue that sustainability requires 'a redesigning and redefining of strategy and operational processes that meet the changes, needs and expectations of the market and society alike to support long-term value'.[1]

A sustainability strategy is a prioritized set of actions and commitments designed to manage social, environmental and economic or ESG impacts, in order to optimize value to the business and to society by minimizing negative impacts and maximizing positive ones. It provides an agreed framework the business can use to focus investment and drive performance and to engage and guide internal and external stakeholders.[2] As discussed in Chapter 10, stakeholders have a key role in helping to define sustainability strategy and in operationalizing strategy (Chapter 5). It is increasingly a key element of leadership, as described in more detail in Chapter 7. Strategy needs effective governance (Chapter 9) and effective measurement and reporting (Chapter 8).

In our previous book, *All In: The Future of Business Leadership*, we outlined five interlinking attributes essential to building a sustainable business: Purpose, Plan (or Strategy), Culture, Collaboration and Advocacy. All five attributes are crucial, and each reinforces and strengthens the others; in fact, each *needs* the others to work fully. Together, they allow for effective sustainability leadership. For example, a good strategy for sustainability is supported by an appropriate organizational purpose. The culture of the business determines how well the strategy is accepted and implemented as well as whether employees and other stakeholders really get behind it. And a robust sustainability strategy requires a range of collaboration with a variety of partners and involves persuading others to embrace and address sustainability challenges via advocacy.

Why it matters

An ambitious, credible and comprehensive sustainability strategy:

- ensures you know what you intend to do and what you are doing;
- provides focus and enables prioritization (see Chapter 2);
- establishes the basis for investment and the allocation of capitals (human, financial, etc.);
- supports long-term value creation;
- enhances reputation;
- preserves licence to operate;
- increases staff buy-in at all levels;
- guides effort in different parts of the business and fosters inclusion;
- shapes external stakeholder engagement;
- helps assess potential opportunities and determine whether they are in scope.

How to do it

It may be helpful to think of sustainability strategy development in three phases (see Figure 4.1):

- Ideation.
- Prioritization and refinement.
- Promotion.

FIGURE 4.1   Sustainability strategy development

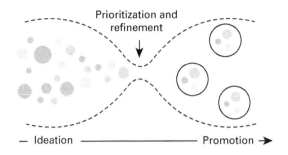

Phase I: Ideation

STEP 1: STOCKTAKE – ASSESS WHAT THE BUSINESS IS DOING ALREADY

A strategy is unlikely to come out of nowhere with no antecedents. While companies may not have an explicit sustainability strategy, most will have a number of specific projects and initiatives to build upon, such as waste reduction, health and wellness programmes, or policies designed to attract and promote more diverse staff. Turning these into a systemic strategic framework signals a more serious intent, identifies gaps and weaknesses, gives a focus and raised profile to sustainability, guides the allocation of resources and generates wider interest and support.

In all likelihood, there will be no shortage of ideas from inside the business about what would constitute a more ambitious sustainability strategy and where the business is currently falling short. A good sustainability strategy will benefit from engaging stakeholders (see Chapter 10) intensely through the process of review, identification of options, clarification, prioritization and refinement, as well as in implementation and further adaptation.

Experienced sustainability professionals recommend engaging senior management at an early stage. This might involve the senior leadership having a facilitated and frank conversation about what is happening in the world, megatrends and their world view. The business might also assess each leader's confidence about / competence in / commitment to sustainability by asking them to rate these on a scale of 1–10. This is typically followed or complemented by a materiality mapping exercise. While an experienced sustainability leader in the business or a consultant might be able to produce a reasonably accurate materiality matrix very quickly, there is value in engaging people at different levels of the business in this exercise. Taking the time to do this helps build awareness and understanding and socializes the idea that ambitious action is needed.

STEP 2: REALITY CHECK – CONDUCT A GAP ANALYSIS BETWEEN CURRENT STATE AND SUSTAINABILITY

Good strategy aligns with organizational vision and purpose and also informs them. While it is certainly possible to have a sustainability strategy without having a purpose, each can enhance the other. An effective sustainability strategy addresses the top issues identified through the materiality assessment process, and as the business considers strategy, it must consider its level of ambition. Is the aspiration to be middle of the pack or a leader? To be a leader on sustainability generally or on a particular aspect such as diversity, equity and inclusion or environmental and labour conditions in the supply chain?

Various business school academics and many sustainability practitioners have developed models of corporate responsibility or sustainability maturity to help boards and senior management teams clarify their sustainability ambition (see Table 4.1).[3] It can be helpful to use a maturity model to provoke debate in the business's leadership and to generate a response to questions including:

- Where is your organization located on the model now?
- Where would you like it to be?
- When do you want to get there?

TABLE 4.1   Stages of sustainability maturity model

	Comply	Compete: Risk-mitigator to opportunity-maximizer	Champion
Purpose and culture	Resists idea of responsibilities beyond profit Its existence is its social contribution	Existing business models Requires business case for sustainability	Finding profitable solutions to problems of people and planet and not profiting from doing harm Every global problem and social issue is a business opportunity in disguise
Strategy	All resources as means to profit More ignorant than oppositional to ESG	Introduces more proactive environmental and social policies to reduce risk	Sustainability integrated into strategy Full ecosystem and social costs and subsidies accounted for

Where a business has both a dedicated sustainability and strategy function, it is ideal for them to work together to develop the sustainability strategy, which otherwise risks being a bolt on to operations rather than integrated with the purpose and overall strategy of the business. It is important that sustainability and business ambitions align. Otherwise, sustainability will forever be on the sidelines of business and not fully integrated. Ensuring the senior management team is engaged minimizes risks of inconsistencies between the sustainability strategy and the direction of the business as a whole. As the authors of a 2020 report from Deloitte Australia write:

> To elevate sustainability objectives means they need to be incorporated into the strategic dialogue at both the executive and board level. Evaluating sustainability objectives inherent in strategic options and incorporating the cascading implications of those choices into business plans and operations, is the most tangible action that leaders can take.[4]

The objective should be to make sustainability and corporate strategies synonymous or at least synchronized. However, unless you are a new start-up business with sustainability baked into vision and purpose from the outset, it takes time to achieve this. Businesses that already employ an Enterprise Risk Management process could extend this to help achieve alignment.

The sustainability consultancy Corporate Citizenship Company notes in a report on how to develop sustainability strategy:

> It is simply not enough to aggregate up existing activities and brand them a strategy. Good strategy requires a process of ruthless decision-making to continue with some activities, scale down or stop others, and start new ones. A good strategy needs to have a hierarchy and a focus. The focus needs to be on the right issues that are most material for the company. Having arrived at the right priorities, the company should be able to channel its investment into a small number of key areas. An effective framework should group together the different issues and explain how the company plans to address them. This not only helps with implementation and the targeting of resources, but also makes engagement and communication of the strategy much more effective.[5]

Phase II: Prioritization and refinement

STEP 3: BENCHMARK – MAP YOUR EMERGING STRATEGY AGAINST LEADING BUSINESSES AND ESTABLISHED SUSTAINABILITY FRAMEWORKS

Particularly when first pulling together a sustainability strategy, it's important to check comprehensiveness with reference to industry leaders and/or against proven sustainability frameworks.

Many corporate sustainability leaders publish considerable information about their sustainability strategy, ambitions, key themes and major goals on their websites and in publicly available sustainability reports or integrated reports that combine the elements of a traditional annual report together with sustainability disclosures. This provides rich material for benchmarking your company's approach. Details of which businesses are regarded as sustainability leaders can be found, for example, in:

- The annual GlobeScan–SustainAbility Leaders Survey of international experts.

- The Dow Jones Sustainability™ World Index, which comprises global sustainability leaders as identified by S&P Global. (It represents the top 10 per cent of the largest 2,500 companies in the S&P Global based on long-term economic, environmental and social criteria.)[6]
- **Corporate Knights'** annual Global 100 index of the world's most sustainable corporations.[7]

Additionally, throughout this handbook, we profile businesses that we think are worth looking at.

When it comes to mapping a sustainability strategy against some external framework, one of the simplest that companies have found useful over the last two decades is to look at actions to minimize negative and increase positive impacts in four broad areas:

- workplace;
- marketplace;
- environment;
- society.

Dr Geoff Kendall, creator of the Future-Fit Business Benchmark, talks of extending Harvard Business School's Professor Michael Porter's Five Forces Framework, which is instinctively recognized by business school-trained managers across the world. Five Forces analysis looks at five key areas: the threat of new market entrants, the power of buyers, the power of suppliers, the threat of substitutes and competitive rivalry. Kendall proposes to extend the Five Forces into eight, adding social, environmental and technological forces to the mix.[8] The Future-Fit Benchmark is a comprehensive and very operational checklist, with very detailed guidance on each of the 23 'break-even goals'. Larger businesses such as The Body Shop and Novo Nordisk have used Future-Fit.

Other frameworks include the Good Business Charter,[9] a British initiative endorsed by the Confederation of British Industry and the

Trade Union Congress. The Good Business Charter commits organizations to:

- real living wage;
- fairer hours and contracts;
- employee well-being;
- employee representation;
- diversity and inclusion;
- environmental responsibility;
- pay fair tax;
- commitment to customers;
- ethical sourcing;
- prompt payment to suppliers.

There is also a version of the charter for smaller firms, developed in partnership with the UK's Federation of Small Businesses.[10]

Another, extensive, framework is the international certification scheme for B Corps (or Benefit Corporations) around the world.[11] The B Corp certification of social and environmental performance is a private certification of for-profit companies.

B Corporations are a kind of business that balance purpose and profit. In order to be certified, companies are required to consider the impact of their decisions on their workers, customers, suppliers, community and the environment. They include businesses like Ben and Jerry's, The Body Shop, Danone, Natura & Co. and Patagonia. B Corps see themselves as 'a community of leaders, driving a global movement of people using business as a force for good'.[12] B Corp certification involves answering and providing supporting evidence in response to 300 questions and typically takes some months to complete. It is a very comprehensive process. The company of Chris Coulter (one of this book's authors), GlobeScan, is a certified B Corp.

Some businesses build their sustainability strategy around the United Nations Sustainable Development Goals (SDGs) adopted in

2015 for the period 2015–2030. One of our friends and colleagues, and a leading sustainability thinker, John Elkington, describes the SDGs as being like 'a purchase order from the future'. In other words, the SDGs represent a blueprint for a more sustainable future where 9–10 billion people can live at least moderately well, within the constraints of one planet by mid-century.[13] Other businesses, while not building their entire strategy around the SDGs, use them to lift the scale of their ambition. Unsurprisingly, the UN Global Compact has designed its strategy around helping businesses and other Compact signatories implement the global goals, providing how-to guidance.[14] Research by accountants Grant Thornton suggests that medium-sized businesses (typically 50–500 employees) in emerging markets are prioritizing sustainability issues to a greater extent than their counterparts in developed economies, but also that these businesses expect a greater positive financial impact from integrating sustainability.[15]

Each of these (Future-Fit, the Good Business Charter, B Corp certification and others) have their protagonists and champions. We recommend talking to businesses in your sector who have successfully used whichever framework you are considering. The key point is that these frameworks can offer a structure and process for refining a sustainability strategy and verifying independently how well the business is actually performing.

STEP 4: TEST – ENSURE PROPOSED SUSTAINABILITY STRATEGY IS RESILIENT AGAINST FUTURE SHOCKS

Resilience in an organizational context is 'the ability of an organization to anticipate, prepare for, respond and adapt to change and sudden disruptions in order to survive and prosper'.[16] It reaches beyond risk management towards a more holistic view of business health and success. So many organizations face catastrophic failures of imagination as to what could happen to them because of a lack of resilience planning. After COVID-19, it seems that more organizations are appointing dedicated resilience staff and launching or upgrading resilience planning.

Cranfield University collaborated with the UK's National Preparedness Commission and Deloitte to develop the *Resilience Reimagined Handbook*.[17] The handbook presents a suite of tools and practices that organizations can use sequentially or from which they can pick and choose to improve their resilience.

These include:

- Anticipating and discussing potential future failures ahead of time.
- Considering connected impacts through the lens of the 'five capitals' of natural, human, social, built and financial capitals.
- Understanding essential outcomes of a project, which can help to identify potential vulnerabilities and alternative ways of delivering essential outcomes if necessary.
- Defining impact thresholds and then stress testing against these under severe but plausible scenarios.[18]

Greater focus on resilience can be combined with deeper focus on sustainability to the advantage of both. As Cranfield's Professor David Denyer, one of the authors of the resilience handbook, explains:

> I see sustainability as addressing causes whilst resilience is also
> addressing symptoms, e.g. if we can't address climate change (through
> adaptation) we had better enhance our ability to cope with disruption,
> e.g. extreme weather events (through mitigation). Of course, society
> has to get better at stopping the source of the problem, such as climate
> change – and then we have less disruptive events.[19]

STEP 5: STRETCH – SET AMBITIOUS SUSTAINABILITY GOALS THAT THE BUSINESS CAN COALESCE AROUND

Whatever frameworks and other tools are used to help to build up the strategy, it is important that the strategy contains clear, measurable goals. Leading companies are increasingly using evidence- or science-based targets such as the Science Based Targets initiative[20] and some companies are committing to become net zero.[21] Such commitments must be backed by credible action plans. Bold, public commitments supported with sound plans can galvanize the company and encourage others to follow suit. For example, in 2019, the online retailer Amazon co-founded The Climate Pledge, a commitment to achieve net zero carbon status by 2040, 10 years ahead of the Paris Agreement timetable. At the time of writing, more than 200 other organizations had signed the Pledge.[22]

A tiny number of companies have committed to go even further and become carbon negative. Microsoft, for example, has promised that by 2030 it will be carbon negative and that by 2050 it will remove from the environment the equivalent of all the carbon the company has emitted, either directly or by electrical consumption, since it was founded in 1975.[23] These are – and are intended to be – the kind of dramatic, game-changing commitments that businesses will not fully know how they will achieve when they first launch them. They are betting that the very fact of making such bold commitments will spur innovation. This is where having trust and goodwill in the bank becomes important. Do stakeholders believe that the business is genuine and honestly committed to do their best to achieve the ambitious stretch targets?

Many businesses won't have the appetite, profile or capacity for such boldness. It is still possible, however, to identify the company's most material issues and develop S.M.A.R.T targets, i.e. goals that are specific, measurable, achievable, relevant and timely. This might mean, for example, radically increasing the number of disabled employees or paying a Living Wage to all employees. It is important to identify who in the business has specific accountabilities for delivering on such targets or at least contributing to them, and to ensure that key performance indicators, appraisals, promotions, rewards, recognition and bonuses are all aligned with these organization-wide goals. More broadly, the business needs to check that it has (or has a plan to acquire) the requisite capabilities to deliver on its promises so that there is not a failure to transition from strategy development to strategy integration.

Phase III: Promotion

STEP 6: COMMUNICATE – DEVELOP A COMPELLING NARRATIVE

Joining together the myriad information and data from existing programmes and initiatives and materiality enables a business to determine its current position and its future ambition. This is the scientific or left-brain approach to strategy development, drawing on the business-case techniques described in Chapter 3.

Inspirational plans also need a right-brain element that is more intuitive and emotional. It is not a coincidence that there is growing interest in the art of storytelling for business, not least in the context of embracing sustainability. Numbers alone can numb us. It is hard for most people to grasp the significance of avoiding x tons of waste to landfill or preventing the release of x tons of CO_2-equivalent emissions into the atmosphere. That is why most of us need analogies such as 'that's the equivalent of four football pitches' or 'that's enough to light up New York city for a year'. Businesses need to win hearts as well as minds. A successful sustainability strategy needs an effective selling job. An important component of business success is communicating progress, so that the organization feels a sense of momentum and advancement towards a wider purposeful goal. As in any other successful sales campaign, you must communicate repeatedly to ensure that staff, customers, suppliers, investors, etc:

- Hear the messages.
- Understand the messages.
- Accept the messages.
- Internalize the messages.
- Act on the messages.
- Enable others to take action on the messages.

Leading companies often use a few key words or an overarching phrase to bring their sustainability strategy to life:

- Netflix talk of their **Net Zero + Nature** strategy.[24]

- Kering, the luxury goods group that pioneered environmental profit and loss accounting, speaks of Care, Collaborate, Create: three pillars to develop more sustainable and more responsible luxury.[25]

- HAVI, the Chicago-based logistics business that is a major supplier to global companies such as McDonald's, has 'Our Better Future Blueprint'.

- The US retailer Target adopted a new sustainability strategy in 2021 called 'Target Forward' built around ambitions to: design and elevate sustainable brands; innovate to eliminate waste and to accelerate opportunity and equity.[26]

- IKEA describes its sustainability strategy as 'caring for people and the planet'.[27]

Great sustainability strategies don't just set a direction and establish key performance indicators, they also tell inspiring stories. One of the best corporate sustainability storytellers was the late, great Ray Anderson, the founder of Interface, the floor coverings business that he set up in Georgia, USA in the 1970s. Anderson built Interface into a billion-dollar business before realizing in 1994 that he had to make a 'mid-course correction' and committing to run Interface sustainably. Successive iterations of the Interface sustainability plan told stories, using the metaphor of climbing a mountain, in this case 'Mount Sustainability', in order to reach Mission Zero.[28] In 2016, Interface launched Climate Take Back, an attempt to reverse global warming with the mantra: 'If humanity changed the climate by mistake... we can change it with intent.'[29]

In many companies, it would be good practice at this stage of strategy development to test the proposed strategy update with key stakeholders by asking:

- Does the overall strategy make sense?

- Is it compelling and motivating?

- Is it explained as clearly as it can be?

In any event, communication of the sustainability strategy needs the support of the board and senior management. Some companies have found it helpful to have executive sponsors for different parts of the sustainability strategy lead its launch, perhaps through an online webinar or at a leadership conference. Senior leaders must champion the strategy both inside and outside the business to create buzz and build enthusiasm and engagement.

STEP 7: ADAPT AND MAINTAIN – BE ALERT TO THE NEED FOR MID-COURSE CORRECTIONS AND ENSURE ALIGNMENT WITH OVERALL CORPORATE STRATEGY

All three of us authors have been involved in sustainability for a long time. Writing this in early autumn 2021, none of us can remember a time of such rapid and comprehensive innovation and development in business and sustainability as today. Sustainability strategy needs to be kept under review and constantly updated to take account of new challenges, new opportunities and new legal and stakeholder expectations. For example, new technologies and techniques like the use of artificial intelligence, machine learning and Big Data to capture and measure performance on different pillars of sustainability are emerging rapidly and becoming widely available.

After the shocks of the COVID-19 pandemic and the global restrictions, more businesses are seeing strategy as a dynamic, living document, subject to regular review and refinement in the face of external developments. This has been likened to a move from maps-based navigation to real-time sat-nav, which means more agile and fast interpretation of new data and insights![30] This makes it even more important that there are no major inconsistencies between overall corporate and sustainability strategies. Equally, it makes it even more redundant to wait for all the answers before implementing sustainability strategy.

It is essential, therefore, that regular reviews are built in to the strategy, so the business can adjust and improve. An important part of regular review is oversight of the business's product or service portfolio. Typically, a business will need to segment the portfolio and identify high-risk products which, if they cannot be reformulated or repositioned, may need to be exited. Similarly, professional services firms such as accountants, advertising agencies, bankers, lawyers and management consultants working with the firm need regular vetting to assess whether their work and approach are compatible with the firm's own commitments to doing business ethically and responsibly and being committed to sustainability.

Some sustainability leaders hold regular 'report-backs' with key stakeholders and sustainability influencers to share details of how they are performing on their sustainability strategy, explain any areas where they are struggling and to invite feedback. Such sessions are both a useful discipline to check regularly on progress to deliver the strategy and a potential source of fresh insight. They can supplement regular reviews of performance versus strategy with the board.

In practice

Ørsted

Ørsted A/S is a multinational power company with more than 6,300 employees and a 2020 annual revenue of over $8 billion. The company, headquartered in Fredericia, Denmark, was founded in 2006, taking the name Ørsted in 2017. Today it operates mostly in Denmark, Sweden, the UK, Germany and the Netherlands, and it has limited operations in the United States.

Ørsted develops, constructs and operates offshore and onshore wind farms, solar farms, energy storage facilities and bioenergy plants, and it provides energy products to customers. It is one of the largest renewable energy companies by capacity globally and the leading offshore wind company.

The company has a simple sounding but profound vision 'To create a world that runs entirely on green energy'. Ørsted is listed as the world's most sustainable energy company in Corporate Knights' 2021 Global 100 ranking of the most sustainable corporations in the world (the third year in a row that it has held this position) and is also on the CDP Climate Change 'A List' recognizing global leaders on climate action.

In the late 2000s, Ørsted was one of the most coal-intensive power generators in Europe and had an expanding oil and gas production business. However, convinced it was the right approach strategically, financially and environmentally, the company decided to become a green energy company. Going green, it realized, is a huge competitive differentiator. In about 10 years, Ørsted has gone from being one of the most fossil fuel-intensive utilities in Europe to the most sustainable energy company in the world. This staggering transformation and complete overhaul of strategy wasn't easy, but the company felt it was necessary to put the planet before anything else.

To drive the transformation, the company invested heavily in renewable energy, particularly offshore wind. It exited the fossil fuel businesses and formulated a vision of creating a world that runs entirely on green energy. Ørsted plans to completely phase out the use of coal in 2023 and will generate nearly 100 per cent green energy by 2025. The change has boosted Ørsted's financial performance while reducing its carbon emissions by 86 per cent. Ørsted is on track to be carbon neutral in energy generation and operations by 2025 and is committed to halving the carbon emissions from its wholesale buying and selling of natural gas and from its supply chain by 2032. Its ambition is to achieve a net zero carbon footprint by 2040.

While the conception of the new strategy and shift to green energy was fully backed by top management, it initially faced internal and external stakeholder resistance, including from employees who thought the move was commercially risky. Then-CEO Anders Eldrup pushed ahead with conviction in spite of this, and today the results speak for themselves, with Ørsted a global benchmark on green energy and acknowledged flag bearer of the net zero brigade.

Mads Nipper, current CEO of Ørsted, says, 'We aspire to be one of the true catalysts of systemic change to a greener society by continuing to prove that there is no long-term trade-off between sustainability and financial value creation.'[31]

Primark

Primark is a fast-fashion retailer with 70,000 employees and a 2020 annual revenue of nearly $11 billion pre-pandemic. Headquartered in Dublin, Ireland, the company was founded in 1969 and today operates more than 330 stores in 11 countries.

The fashion industry has significant sustainability challenges. According to researchers at Princeton University, 'If the industry maintains its course, an increase of 50 per cent in greenhouse gas emissions is expected within a decade.'[32] To deal with such environmental and also social and economic impacts, Primark has been quietly increasing its sustainability efforts, notably since the 2013 Rana Plaza tragedy in Bangladesh.

In order to initiate a new sustainability strategy, Primark's senior leadership team participated in an intense, two-day workshop to explore their understanding of sustainability and their appetite for action. This was followed by a materiality exercise conducted by the business with the help of an experienced external consultant, Sue Garrard. The process involved the entire senior leadership team, the Primark board, and the final plans went to the board of Primark's owners, Associated British Foods.

In September 2021, the company launched an ambitious 10-year sustainability strategy, 'Primark Cares'. Its three pillars are: (1) Product: Giving clothes a longer life (with an emphasis on product durability, circularity, use of recycled fibre and clothes recycling); (2) Planet: Protecting life on the planet (reducing carbon emissions across their full value chain which they believe can be achieved without using offsets, removing waste, eliminating single-use plastic by 2027 and restoring biodiversity); and (3) People: Improving people's lives (with an emphasis on financial resilience and increasing opportunities for work and health and well-being). Primark Cares commits the company to halve its carbon impact and to pay a Living Wage throughout its supply chain by 2030. To demonstrate and communicate progress, Primark will publish Living Wage data annually and increasingly give preference to suppliers willing to support its Living Wage ambition. Primark recognizes that the infrastructure for calculating a Living Wage in many countries and collective bargaining capacity to negotiate for it has to be built up and wants to work collaboratively across the fashion industry to do this. Primark will also work with key suppliers to tackle the industry's high gender pay gap.[33] Another game-changing target is to move to regenerative agriculture practices for all the cotton it buys. Primark has already conducted pilots which show this will be better for the farmers' pockets.

The initial work on Primark's sustainability strategy was led by the Strategy Director, then handed off when a Director of Primark Cares was appointed. The appointee came from operations, knows the business inside out and has excellent internal company networks. Primark subsequently hired outsiders with specific expertise, for example, a Head of Environmental Sustainability, who joined after 10+ years at Nike. Primark also gave specific sustainability assignments to people across the business to develop their learning. In launching Primark Cares, the company also emphasized the range of external partners it works with such as Cotton Connect, the Ellen MacArthur Foundation and WRAP.

'Our ambition is to offer customers the affordable prices they know and love us for, but with products that are made in a way that is better for the planet and the people who make them', Primark Chief Executive Paul Marchant said on launching the new strategy.[34]

Summary

Sustainability strategy is critical to overall business resilience. Leading companies recognize it is no longer a choice between profits or sustainability. Rather the choice is better, long-term profits through sustainability, or inferior profits that are unsustainable in every sense of the word. Planning for enduring leadership requires sustainability to be at the heart of any company's strategy. What is crucial is that, as an integral part of strategy development, the business is planning how to measure performance, who will need to be involved in this and how it will be done. Measurement must not be an afterthought but an integral part of strategy formulation.

Action checklist

1   'Stress test' the strategy to see if it is ambitious enough to inspire and motivate and addresses the scale of global challenges.

2 Make sure it is comprehensive and credibly covers the materiality matrix priorities.

3 Check if the strategy is actionable.

4 Ensure it is internally coherent and consistent with the overall corporate strategy, and vice versa.

5 Consider if targets are bold and science- or evidence-based and how they will be measured is clear.

6 Translate the strategy into the business plans of different parts of the business and align with incentives for managers.

7 Look at how to extend the strategy through the supply chain with progressively higher standards being required and credible time horizons for engaging customers and consumers too.

8 Establish a realistic roadmap to transition from unsustainable raw materials, products, processes, behaviours and activities over time.

9 Make sure that the board and senior leadership are championing the strategy and that employees are actively engaged.

10 Create an early warning system to identify quickly where strategy implementation is lagging or where blockages are occurring, so that remedial action can be agreed.

Further resources

- SustainAbility (now part of ERM) (2015) *Sustainability Incorporated: Integrating sustainability into business*, SustainAbility (now part of ERM)
- The Corporate Citizenship Company (2016) Sustainability Strategy: Simplified, The Corporate Citizenship Company
- UN Global Compact (2021) How your company can advance each of the SDGs, www.unglobalcompact.org/sdgs/17-global-goals

Endnotes

1 EY 2018, www.ey.com/en_es/assurance/how-an-integrated-sustainability-strategy-can-help-you-stand-out (archived at https://perma.cc/B9Q5-ZZ3S)

2 Modified from an original definition by The Corporate Citizenship Company

3 Ainsbury, R and Grayson, D (2014) Business Critical: Understanding a company's current and desired stages of corporate responsibility maturity, Cranfield University School of Management

4 Deloitte Australia (June 2020) Embedding sustainability into core strategy and business operations, www2.deloitte.com/content/dam/Deloitte/au/Documents/strategy/deloitte-au-con-embedding-sustainability-into-core-strategy-and-business-operations.pdf (archived at https://perma.cc/J59N-QX7T)

5 The Corporate Citizenship Company (2016) Sustainability Strategy: Simplified, The Corporate Citizenship Company

6 www.spglobal.com/spdji/en/indices/esg/dow-jones-sustainability-world-index/#overview (archived at https://perma.cc/DCY2-EL5Y)

7 www.corporateknights.com/rankings/global-100-rankings/2021-global-100-rankings/2021-global-100-ranking/ (archived at https://perma.cc/HUC7-UF7A)

8 futurefitbusiness.org/ (archived at https://perma.cc/Y4DL-LK9T)

9 www.goodbusinesscharter.com/ (archived at https://perma.cc/NT7M-FTZH)

10 www.goodbusinesscharter.com/streamlined-version-fsb/ (archived at https://perma.cc/NT7M-FTZH)

11 bcorporation.net/ (archived at https://perma.cc/ZZN9-542L)

12 bcorporation.net/ (archived at https://perma.cc/ZZN9-542L)

13 Definition of a sustainable future from the World Business Council for Sustainable Development (WBCSD)

14 www.unglobalcompact.org/sdgs/17-global-goals (archived at https://perma.cc/JD2T-9EQ6)

15 The Grant Thornton International Business Report (IBR) is a survey of mid-market businesses. Launched in 1992, the IBR now provides insight into the views and expectations of more than 10,000 businesses across more than 30 economies, www.grantthornton.global/en/insights/articles/About-IBR/ (archived at https://perma.cc/F739-4HFY)

16 Adapted from British standard BS 65000, www.bsigroup.com/en-GB/our-services/Organizational-Resilience/ (archived at https://perma.cc/UWF2-WQFB)

17 National Preparedness Commission and Deloitte (2021) *Resilience Reimagined Handbook*, Cranfield University, National Preparedness Commission and Deloitte, nationalpreparednesscommission.uk/2021/03/resilience-reimagined-a-practical-guide-for-organisations/ (archived at https://perma.cc/X95J-HJDJ)

18 Ibid.

19 Exchange with author, 18–19 June 2021

20 sciencebasedtargets.org/ (archived at https://perma.cc/CME7-D8NP)

21 www.un.org/en/climatechange/net-zero-coalition (archived at https://perma.cc/4GUK-HPMS)

22 sustainability.aboutamazon.com/about/the-climate-pledge (archived at https://perma.cc/D9HS-8ABS)

23 blogs.microsoft.com/blog/2020/01/16/microsoft-will-be-carbon-negative-by-2030/ (archived at https://perma.cc/EEF5-SDC4)

24 Stewart E (2021) Net Zero + Nature: Our commitment to the environment, Netflix, 30 March 2021, about.netflix.com/en/news/net-zero-nature-our-climate-commitment (archived at https://perma.cc/C99X-5G66)

25 www.kering.com/en/sustainability/ (archived at https://perma.cc/3U5T-EQES)

26 corporate.target.com/corporate-responsibility/sustainability-strategy (archived at https://perma.cc/3J7D-BEWL)

27 about.ikea.com/en/sustainability (archived at https://perma.cc/96L3-LSW6)

28 www.interface.com/EU/en-GB/about/press-room/interface-mission-zero-success-en_GB (archived at https://perma.cc/TWT3-U5X3)

29 www.interface.com/US/en-US/sustainability/climate-take-back-en_US (archived at https://perma.cc/KNR3-TVVS)

30 Dunne, P (2021) From maps to a satnav world, LinkedIn, 23 September 2021, www.linkedin.com/posts/governance-publishing-and-information-services-ltd_patrick-dunne-author-of-boards-book-discusses-activity-6846722544851042304--LJ- (archived at https://perma.cc/XM4P-RFJQ)

31 This profile is based on orsted.com/en/about-us/whitepapers/green-transformation-lessons-learned (archived at https://perma.cc/GV8G-RGGJ); orsted.com/en/sustainability/our-stories/most-sustainable-energy-company (archived at https://perma.cc/N9MV-GCPE)

32 Klase, A (2021) Primark seeks to woo eco-conscious consumers with sustainability drive, *The Financial Times*, 15 September

33 Launch webinar for Primark Cares, Primark, 15 September 2021

34 Quoted in Klase, A (2021) Primark seeks to woo eco-conscious consumers with sustainability drive, *The Financial Times*, 15 September, and author's notes from launch webinar

05

Operationalizing

What is it?

Operationalizing sustainability is about putting sustainability strategy and commitments into action throughout the business. It includes detailed plans, change programmes and ongoing examination of different aspects of the business and its value chain to find ways to improve social, environmental and economic performance. It involves review and often the redesign of policies, processes, products and services and sometimes the adoption of whole new business models.

In a sense, the entire contents of this handbook are about operationalizing a company's commitment to sustainability or ESG. In this chapter, we concentrate on certain aspects of putting sustainability into effect not covered elsewhere, and the process for doing so. While the aim is to embed sustainability across the organization as quickly as possible, unless the company has a blank slate as with a purpose-led start-up, full integration takes time, and it is important to focus where effort will have the greatest impact.

Operationalizing sustainability requires systematically integrating sustainability thinking in how the organization is run. This applies from sourcing and supply chain, through product and service design and delivery, to interactions with investors, customers and consumers, through the issues associated with product end of life. Experience suggests that operationalizing sustainability goes most smoothly when the company's purpose and business case for sustainability are as widely understood and embraced as its sustainability strategy must be to allow comprehensive integration. It's also evident that companies should focus their operationalization efforts on the parts of their business where the time and resources invested will have the greatest effect.

Why it matters

Operationalizing sustainability delivers numerous benefits and also mitigates risk.

Operationalizing sustainability well generates the performance results, data and stories required for effective reporting, disclosure and communication to investors and other stakeholders, potentially boosting standing in influential ratings and rankings and improving access to capital. Organizations where sustainability is fully integrated report that leaders at all levels are better able to put sustainability strategy and commitments into action and to communicate sustainability-related information and decisions to others. Externally, fully embedding sustainability makes the company a more confident, credible and authentic advocate on the sustainable development issues where it chooses to take public positions.

Without effective operationalization and implementation, the company's purpose, sustainability strategy and commitments are rhetoric, leaving the business and its leadership open to charges of greenwashing and undermining its potential as an advocate. Failing to systematically integrate sustainability puts the trust of key stakeholders at risk and can negatively affect employee attraction and retention as well as the company's culture.

Weak operationalization also hampers the production and gathering of data needed for sustainability and ESG reporting and disclosure, limiting the company's ability to communicate effectively on sustainability performance. And all these things may lead others to overlook it when seeking to partner or collaborate on sustainability solutions and new opportunities.

For all the benefits and risks outlined above, operationalizing sustainability is particularly important for the following reasons.

- It is essential to realizing the financial and extra financial benefits promised by the business case. Without well-conceived and executed operationalization, the company may miss new, sustainability-related business opportunities. Conversely, embedding sustainability thinking supports innovation and intrapreneurship, helping keep the company ahead of regulation – and ahead of competitors in the market place.

- It elevates the business's reputation with internal and external stakeholders, from employees and investors to supply chain partners and customers, by reinforcing consistent behaviour and increasing positive impact.

- Systematically ingraining sustainability across the business better equips the company to identify and mitigate risks related to its material sustainability issues, improves planning and implementation by focusing the business's efforts where it can have the highest impact and boosts ESG performance and disclosure.

- Operationalization improves efficiency, reducing negative impacts such as water and energy use and eliminating waste, thus lowering costs. It also helps avoid costs entirely, for instance by deciding during product design not to use a material that's costly to procure and/or risky and expensive to handle.

- Overall, operationalizing sustainability makes the business more competitive and more resilient over the long term, especially in an environment where investors, regulators and others place increasing value on sustainability-related performance.

How to do it

Operationalizing sustainability is about putting sustainability strategy and commitments into action throughout the business and systematically integrating sustainability thinking in how the organization is run. While the ambition is to embed sustainability as immediately and robustly as possible, it is usually a process that unfolds gradually across a company's operations and value chain, and every business must pick the approach and pace that suit it best. Most businesses will find higher value operationalizing their sustainability strategy in certain areas and this is encouraged, for instance in the supply chain where impacts are often so large and concentrated, in finance in order to guide investment, in R&D so as to shape future products and services and in human resources given the growing role sustainability plays in talent attraction and retention.

The steps below are presented in linear fashion, and it may be beneficial to follow the order, not least because Step 1 is about equipping your people for the tasks ahead and building momentum, while Step 2 promises immediate financial impact, which can be useful in demonstrating to leadership that operationalizing sustainability can bring monetary as well as other benefits. Still, tackling them in sequential fashion is not required. In the same way that every company's sustainability strategy is unique, the precise order of steps taken to operationalize it across the business – and, critically, up and down the business's value chain – will depend on its leadership and the particular sustainability-related risks and opportunities it faces.

Step 1: Increase internal alignment

Operationalizing sustainability requires that each division and function of the business is equipped to develop and apply an appropriate sustainability action plan. For this to happen, awareness and understanding of the issues and potential solutions to address them (or ways to invent them) have to be developed across the business to support and stimulate the planning process. When this works, the plans developed in each part of the company translate the organization's overall sustainability strategy and high-level commitments into the specific actions each part of the business must take to support the embedding process.

For each team involved, from business unit and group level functions to local teams, it is key to identify the implications of the organizational strategy and goals for their part of the company, then to create plans and targets of their own that support the company's overall sustainability ambitions. Giving discrete parts of the business licence as well as accountability for developing plans to support organizational goals empowers them and creates buy-in as people come to recognize that this is about strengthening the business – their business – while reducing harmful social, environmental and economic impacts. Pilots are encouraged, as are cross-disciplinary teams, sharing best practices, training and the celebration of accomplishments along the way. This sharing of leadership and trust in others' ability to operationalize appropriately in their part of the organization is part of the cultural shift (see Chapter 6) that creating the sustainability mindset and approach operationalization needs to succeed.

Step 2: Reduce costs and eliminate waste

There is still a widespread perception that implementing a sustainability strategy will cost money. Sometimes this is true, especially in the short to medium term, when, for instance, a business may need to invest in new facilities, equipment and/or training to design, produce and sell a more sustainable product or service. But these steps are investments in the company's future, and, as indicated in Chapter 3, embedding sustainability lets a company save money and make money, especially over the medium to long term.

Commonly cited sustainability-related financial benefits include cost savings from switching to renewable energy, reducing energy consumption and eliminating waste (which means less material drawn through the supply chain and thus lower procurement and shipping costs as well as less material wasted during manufacturing, less packaging and lower landfill charges because there is less trash). According to the UK's Federation of Small Businesses, 'almost a third of small firms highlight the cost of energy as a barrier to the growth and success of their business. Finding energy efficiency savings is the single best way of reducing these costs over the long-term.'[1]

Step 3: Review the product and service portfolio

Another way to operationalize sustainability is to comprehensively and regularly assess products and services to optimize their sustainability performance. When doing this, it is essential to emphasize the products and related supply chains where the company has the most influence, for instance where there is vertical integration, and to focus change efforts there.

For businesses making and selling physical products, such an assessment might produce a 'stoplight segmentation' where each product is rated red, amber / yellow or green. 'Red' products may use unsustainable raw materials, might cause harmful (even if legal) side effects during manufacturing or might result in unacceptable damage in their use phase. 'Amber' products have notable negative impacts but ones that can be addressed in an acceptable manner and reasonable timeframe, for instance limited worker rights issues in the supply chain that can be remedied in partnership with suppliers or an end-of-life issue that can be addressed by changing product materials to ensure recyclability. Finally, 'green' products are already sustainable. They set the standard for amber ones (and products yet to be developed) to reach, albeit there may be room and reason to make them even better in the future.

Stoplight segmentation can be done for services too. For instance, a financial institution could review the investment advice it gives clients through this lens, or a food service business could look at the sustainability impacts of the menu choices it presents.

Businesses can also look for potential new business opportunities that might be realized with the introduction of new, sustainably designed products and services. In this realm, some major financial organizations have operationalized sustainability by introducing more ESG-focused financial products. Goldman Sachs, for example, is targeting $750 billion to help clients accelerate the transition to a low-carbon economy,[2] while Citi has committed $1 trillion for financing sustainability efforts between 2021 and 2030,[3] and nearly every investment organization, from local credit unions to pension funds, is increasing the number and nature of ESG-screened products it makes available to clients and customers.

Step 4: Consider sustainability in competitive benchmarking, risk identification, research and development, and innovation processes

Materiality (see Chapter 2) identifies a business's priority sustainability issues. These provide critical input to business case and strategy development. In a business environment increasingly concerned with sustainability-related performance, they must also play a central role in benchmarking competitors, enterprise risk management, research and development (R&D) and innovation. As with the product portfolio in Step 3, the business should focus effort on the priority issues the company is best positioned to influence.

A company's greatest social, environmental and economic impacts are now core to any assessment of its performance relative to its major competitors and help forecast its likely future market success. Many if not all top materiality issues will overlap the main issues on the corporate risk register, where their presence will influence the allocation of resources to address the threats – and the opportunities – represented. And, as mentioned in our discussion of leadership development (see Chapter 7), sustainability performance relies heavily on innovation and vice versa, making it essential for companies to create environments that support R&D as well as fostering innovation and intrapreneurship, in order to enhance and maintain their position in the market.

Step 5: Partner with suppliers

For many businesses, an essential part of operationalizing sustainability entails working with suppliers to ensure they have or adopt sustainability commitments and practices aligned with the business's own. It is also critical for companies to support suppliers' efforts to attain them. While it is natural to begin this with Tier 1 suppliers (companies with which you conduct business directly), it increasingly extends to the entire supply chain. Working together, companies and suppliers are far more powerful change agents than when they advocate shifts in practice alone, plus there is the fact that some issues require supplier engagement, notably the enormous challenge of addressing Scope 3 carbon emissions.

Many larger organizations put ESG-related provisions into tendering requirements. As globalization and the outsourcing of manufacturing to low-wage economies around the world accelerated in the 1990s, there were a number of high-profile cases where global brands were accused of tolerating sweatshop conditions and other poor environmental and social standards in their supply chains. This led to increasingly sophisticated auditing and collaboration among major purchasers to streamline the requirements imposed on suppliers.

There are now many ways to monitor and assess supply chain performance. Sedex, for example, has become one of the world's leading ethical trade membership organizations, working with tens of thousands of businesses across dozens of industries and well over 100 countries to improve working conditions in global supply chains. Sedex's tools and services aim to help businesses operate responsibly and sustainably, protect workers and source ethically[4] by facilitating access to information that lets companies meet the requirements of organizations such as the Ethical Trading Initiative and industry coalitions like the Sustainable Apparel Coalition.

Some large companies today host supplier sustainability-information exchanges and incentivize their suppliers to improve ESG performance through gold, silver, bronze or equivalent categorizations, with higher-ranked suppliers qualifying for less onerous audits and inspections. Closer collaboration with suppliers becomes even more crucial as businesses adopt more ambitious commitments, and especially so when they seek to change their business model and go circular (see Step 6).

Given estimates that as much as 90 per cent of a business's sustainability impact – and therefore opportunity for improvement – lies in the supply chain,[5] setting high procurement standards and having means to enforce them to ensure responsible sourcing of materials and sustainable operation of the suppliers is essential to operationalizing sustainability.

Finally, keep in mind how much innovation emerges from or is at least dependent on suppliers. It makes sense for companies to recognize that they are not the source of all breakthrough thinking and to do everything they can to foster, recognize and reward supplier innovation, for instance by minimizing supply chain volatility with clear, reliable contracts and payments and by aligning standards with other buyers to minimize operational complexity.

Step 6: Rethink business models

A powerful approach for operationalizing sustainability is to reconsider fundamental business models. One of the biggest shifts underway involves the switch from linear or take-make-waste modes of operating to circular economy models where raw materials and components are reused in perpetuity. This is often referred to as 'circular', or as 'the circular economy'. A lot of the credit for the popularization of circularity goes to the Ellen MacArthur Foundation, which defines the circular economy as:

> A systemic approach to economic development designed to benefit businesses, society, and the environment. In contrast to the 'take-make-waste' linear model, a circular economy is regenerative by design and aims to gradually decouple growth from the consumption of finite resources.[6]

The Foundation describes itself as the leading global network for circularity, and it 'brings together business, innovators, universities and thought leaders to build and scale a circular economy'.[7] The Foundation provides up-to-date and very practical guidance for businesses wanting to go circular.

While circularity is one of the most significant business model reinvention approaches to consider, others include a broader commitment to a regenerative economy. We predicted in our previous book,

All In: The Future of Business Leadership, that regenerative business models would become dominant sometime this decade (or need to, if the major sustainability challenges are to be addressed). One component of this is moving from business models based on product sales to ones based on services. The think tank and consultancy Volans has identified some 80 new sustainability business models, which we reference in the *Further Resources* section of this chapter.

Full operationalization

The operationalization of sustainability is most powerful when it focuses first on the sustainability issues where the company has most influence. When it is fully realized, operationalizing sustainability means getting to the point where a company's sustainability strategy and commitments are seamlessly integrated across the organization, appropriately influencing every decision and action it takes.

Operationalization is most effective in a business with a strong, positive culture, engaged and empowered employees, a commitment to continuous learning and effective knowledge management systems that facilitate rapid collation and dissemination of good practice across all dimensions of sustainability. Operationalization also happens faster in a business that is transparent, open and accountable, ethical and responsible, and where there is a strong focus on innovation.

GETTING EXTERNAL HELP

External consultants can help a business on any part of its sustainability journey, but they may be especially useful bringing their expertise and experience to bear on operationalization challenges.

There are now specialists with experience in every part of operationalizing sustainability whose support can increase efficiency, accelerate progress and increase impact. For example, consultants might help:

- Define the purpose of the business.
- Identify the organization's most material sustainability / ESG impacts.

- Produce a business case for action on sustainability.
- Support strategy development.
- Implement culture and other change-management programmes.
- Train current and future business leaders on sustainability.
- Assess board competencies and effectiveness.
- Guide reporting and disclosure efforts and help with sustainability-related communications.
- Fully operationalize sustainability by putting sustainability strategy and commitments into action in every part of the business and systematically integrating sustainability thinking in how the organization is run to make it more competitive and more resilient over the long term.

Here are some things to consider in deciding when hiring a consultant might be right for your organization.

First, do you really need external support? Is there untapped expertise in the company that can be accessed? This can be found by looking for:

- Employees who are involved in different aspects of sustainability outside of work.
- Members of the company's employee resource groups whose expertise can be brought to bear.
- Employees who are involved (either on their own time / resources or with company sponsorship) in an MBA or other management development programme where they have assignments to complete that could be applied to help address the company's most material sustainability issues.
- An existing internal talent development / high-flyers programme that could focus more on sustainability issues.

Wherever possible, the goal should be to build and use internal capacity instead of hiring a consultant, but there are times when buying in external expertise and experience is the right choice. Considering the following questions can help guide your decision.

How do you find a sustainability consultant suitable for your business?

The short answer is: Just as you would when choosing other professional advisers such as lawyers, accountants, digital media consultants and so on:

- Seek recommendations from other businesses you know and trust.
- Ask around at your Chamber of Commerce or small business club – word of mouth is often best!
- If your trade association has an in-house sustainability expert, ask them for recommendations.
- Consult members of the sustainability teams inside your clients and partners.
- Investigate university resources, particularly the undergraduate and graduate student teams associated with bodies focused on the intersection of sustainability and business, such as the Center for Responsible Business in the Haas School of Business at the University of California, Berkeley,[8] the Erb Institute at the University of Michigan,[9] The Hoffmann Global Institute for Business and Society at INSEAD, France,[10] and the Sustainability Group at Cranfield School of Management in the UK.[11]

How do you assess a sustainability consultant's knowledge and skills?

To assess expertise and experience, consider the following:

- Have they worked successfully with businesses like yours, for instance, businesses of a similar size, in the same business sector and/or geography, at a parallel stage of business development and/or with the same nature of ownership – as well as on assignments addressing needs similar to yours?
- Has the consultant worked for a wide range of clients, including some with whom they have worked over an extended period of time?
- Can you talk to some of their previous clients?
- Do they have relevant academic, technical and professional training and qualifications? There are institutes for sustainability professionals starting to emerge in some parts of the world, such as The Institute of Corporate Responsibility & Sustainability (ICRS) in the UK and the International Society of Sustainability Professionals (ISSP) in North

America. Is the potential consultant a member of one of these? Are they accredited in any way?

- Is there evidence of the consultant's commitment to lifelong learning and continuous improvement?

- What is the breadth, depth and length of their expertise?

- Is the approach of the consultant to do the work directly or to help their client to work things out for themselves, thereby building confidence and capacity inside the client organization? Which approach do you want in the circumstance for which you are hiring?

Ultimately, there is a question of chemistry. Does the potential consultant mesh well with your culture? Do they model the kinds of behaviours expected inside your organization? As much as past experience and depth of knowledge, fit is an essential decision factor and will have an enormous impact on the success of the engagement.

In practice

Toyota

Toyota is one of the largest automobile manufacturers and retailers globally, with more than 71,000 employees and FY2021 annual net revenue of $256.7 billion.[12] Headquartered in Aichi, Japan, Toyota was founded in 1937 and today operates in over 170 countries.[13]

While Toyota has been working towards corporate sustainability since 1963 with the establishment of its Environment Committee, awareness of its efforts skyrocketed in 1997 when the company launched the world's first mass market hybrid, the Prius. Today Toyota understands its original philosophy, the Five Main Principles of Toyota, to be aligned with the United Nations Sustainable Development Goals (SDGs). With this in mind, Toyota has developed various initiatives, policies and roadmaps aligned with the SDGs to inform the company's operational strategy.[14]

As outlined in its 2020 Sustainability Report, Toyota has developed a clear path to operationalize sustainability in a manner consistent with the SDGs. Toyota's 'Environmental Challenge 2050' defines corporate goals across diverse topics including achieving zero carbon emissions at global plants, minimizing water usage and implementing water discharge management systems.

To achieve these goals by 2050, Toyota has laid out a clear path forward that includes tracking annual goals, developing its Environmental Action Plan – 2025 Targets and creating its 2030 Milestone framework. In addition, 2020 saw Toyota achieve 100 per cent renewable electricity at all R&D centres within Japan as well as the introduction of new technologies to promote energy savings. Further, Toyota has assessed the impact of the wastewater created at all its manufacturing plants and has achieved a 5 per cent reduction in water usage per vehicle, exceeding its internal targets.[15]

As Toyota continues to enhance and align its operational approach to corporate responsibility, the business has developed a corporate governance structure to support these efforts. Several boards and teams work among this structure to report, audit, cooperate and supervise. Such a structure allows for a system of checks and balances to ensure appropriate and accurate steps are taken towards progress.[16] With clear goals and a strong governance approach, Toyota understands and exemplifies the ways in which the automotive sector can leverage and improve operations to promote sustainability.

Toyota's President, Akio Toyoda, talking about the creation of a sustainable society in the company's 2020 Sustainability Report, stated that 'Toyota cannot do this alone and achieving it will depend on cohesively leveraging mobility and infrastructure. We would like to collaborate with like-minded partners to create a blueprint for an eco-friendly society that is not reliant on fossil fuels.' The company president went on to say that the current generation 'is responsible for bequeathing this beautiful home for future generations, as a place where they can live safely… It is with this shared aspiration of the current generation that I wish to make ever greater efforts.'[17]

Pandora

Pandora, the Danish-headquartered, global jewellery business, started in a small jeweller's shop in Copenhagen in 1982. Today it employs 26,000 people, and its products are sold in 100 countries across the world, including the USA, which is its largest market. Turnover in 2021 was DKK19 billion (over $3 billion), with 100 million pieces of jewellery sold.

According to the current CEO Alexander Lacik, sustainability was part of the company's ethos and DNA from the outset, but implicitly, with no formal targets, governance and so on. Lacik joined the company in 2019 with a mandate from the board to turn the business around. He decided that, in parallel with the turnaround strategy, there would be a much more focused commitment around sustainability, deliberately concentrating on just three core ambitions where Pandora could have significant, positive impact.

These three ambitions are to become a low-carbon business, to commit to circular innovation and to excel at diversity and inclusion. On climate and carbon, Pandora has achieved 100 per cent renewable energy in its Thailand manufacturing bases and will announce science-based targets with the Science Based Targets initiative (SBTi) for its entire value chain soon. Pandora also aims to be carbon neutral in its own operations by 2025. Regarding its circularity commitment, Pandora has committed to circular innovation including the use of lab-created diamonds and to use only recycled gold and silver in its jewellery by 2025. With regards to diversity and inclusion, Pandora has committed to gender parity in hiring and promotion, aiming to have one third of leadership positions held by women by 2025 and to achieve parity at VP level and above by 2030. The company has also committed to spend 30 per cent of its advertising budget with women- and ethnic minority-owned agencies. Pandora recognizes that to achieve these aspirations it will have to engage, inspire and help educate business partners as well as its own employees.

To guide efforts and help avoid any accusations of greenwashing, Pandora has developed a responsible marketing code and related governance including training and ongoing guidance. Pandora is operationalizing its sustainability commitments, like other major change programmes in the business, with a strong focus on what really matters to the company. Evidence of its systematic integration of sustainability is provided by its annual sustainability report, which is validated by accountants EY, and by regular vetting by external groups such as SBTi, the Jewellery Council and Human Rights Watch.

CEO Alexander Lacik advises that if other businesses want to embed sustainability, and particularly to engage their grassroots, they should make sure that their sustainability commitment is 'simple, comprehensible and tangible'. Erik Schmidt, CHRO (Chief Human Resources Officer), adds that it is important to learn from others but not to do a 'cut and paste', saying 'sustainability has to be authentic and rooted in your own business'.[18]

Summary

Operationalizing sustainability makes a company's commitment real, credible and meaningful to employees and other stakeholders. It lets them see and feel the sustainability ambition and strategy come to life while literally making the company more sustainable and improving its competitiveness and long-term resilience. Operationalization requires focus and often involves significant change management including product and service redesign and the development of new business models.

Businesses need to consider where they can find early wins, for instance from cost savings related to reducing energy use and waste elimination and how long it will take for all parts of the business to develop action plans to deliver the transformation required by the sustainability strategy and systematically integrate sustainability thinking in how the organization is run. It involves not just the business, but also its suppliers and ultimately its whole value chain, thus touching every aspect of the company and its impacts.

Action checklist

1 Increase internal alignment by requiring each part of the business to review its operations in light of the sustainability strategy.

2 Identify 'early wins' for the commitment to sustainability, in the form of cost savings and the elimination of waste.

3 Review opportunities to make the company's product or service portfolio more sustainable.

4 Incorporate sustainability in competitive benchmarking, risk identification, research and development, and innovation processes.

5 Partner with suppliers to ensure their efforts are aligned with those of the business.

6 Consider where and how new business models would enable faster and more substantial progress on sustainability ambitions.

7 Use external consultants to supplement in-house skills and capacity in order to operationalize sustainability better and faster than is possible alone.

Further resources

- Long, J, Lacy, P and Spindler, W (2020) *Circular Economy Handbook: Realizing the circular advantage*, Palgrave Macmillan

- The Ellen MacArthur Foundation website has useful resources: www.ellenmacarthurfoundation.org

- Volans (2016) Breakthrough Business Models Report 2016, volans.com/wp-content/uploads/2016/09/Volans_Breakthrough-Business-Models_Report_Sep2016.pdf

- WBCSD (2021) Vision 2050: Time to transform, www.wbcsd.org/Overview/About-us/Vision-2050-Time-to-Transform

- Weetman, C (2020) *A Circular Economy Handbook: How to build a more resilient, competitive and sustainable business*, Kogan Page

Endnotes

1 UK Department of Energy & Climate Change (2015) SME guide to energy efficiency, GOV.UK, 26 March, www.gov.uk/government/publications/sme-guide-to-energy-efficiency (archived at https://perma.cc/X7QW-AWQJ)

  2 Goldman Sachs (2021) Sustainable finance, www.goldmansachs.com/
  our-commitments/sustainability/sustainable-finance/ (archived at https://perma.
  cc/A2Q8-KX3C)

  3 Skyler, E (2021) Citi Commits $1 trillion to sustainable finance by 2030 [blog],
  Citi Group, 15 April, blog.citigroup.com/2021/04/citi-commits-1-trillion-to-
  sustainable-finance-by-2030/ (archived at https://perma.cc/UUE5-L455)

  4 Sedex (2021) About us, www.sedex.com/about-us/ (archived at https://perma.
  cc/67WH-WRCQ)

  5 Bové, A and Swartz, S (2016) Starting at the source: Sustainability in supply
  chains, McKinsey Sustainability, 11 November, www.mckinsey.com/business-
  functions/sustainability/our-insights/starting-at-the-source-sustainability-
  in-supply-chains (archived at https://perma.cc/FY2V-TDC4)

  6 Ellen MacArthur Foundation (2017) The circular economy in detail, https://
  archive.ellenmacarthurfoundation.org/explore/the-circular-economy-in-detail
  (archived at https://perma.cc/PBG7-J9TJ)

  7 Ellen MacArthur Foundation (2021) Network, ellenmacarthurfoundation.org/
  network/overview (archived at https://perma.cc/7LRS-BE3U)

  8 Haas School of Business University of California (2021) Center for
  Responsible Business, haas.berkeley.edu/responsible-business/ (archived at
  https://perma.cc/AHT6-6JXH)

  9 ERB Institute University of Michigan (2021) ERB Institute, erb.umich.edu/
  (archived at https://perma.cc/Q5ML-C8TZ)

  10 www.insead.edu/centres/the-hoffmann-global-institute-for-business-and-society
  (archived at https://perma.cc/3YT7-GVUA)

  11 www.cranfield.ac.uk/som/expertise/sustainability (archived at https://perma.cc/
  XM35-LHYD)

  12 Toyota (2021) TMC announces financial results for fiscal year ended March
  31, 2021, Toyota Newsroom, 12 May, pressroom.toyota.com/tmc-announces-
  financial-results-for-fiscal-year-ended-march-31-2021/ (archived at https://
  perma.cc/GXK5-QJUD)

  13 Toyota (2021) Overview: Company information, company profile, global.
  toyota/en/company/profile/overview/ (archived at https://perma.cc/7AL8-
  FPU6)

  14 Toyota (2021) Sustainability, global.toyota/en/sustainability/ (archived at
  https://perma.cc/NZB9-6ZJ6)

  15 Toyota (2020) Environmental Report 2020, global.toyota/pages/global_toyota/
  sustainability/report/er/er20_en.pdf#page=11 (archived at https://perma.cc/
  RGG2-648E)

  16 Toyota (2021) Governance, global.toyota/en/sustainability/esg/governance/
  (archived at https://perma.cc/T96K-YRA3)

17 Toyota (2020) Environmental Report 2020, global.toyota/pages/global_toyota/ sustainability/report/er/er20_en.pdf#page=11 (archived at https://perma.cc/ RGG2-648E)

18 Lacik, A (2021) Webinar with Alexander Lacik and other members of the Pandora Executive Team, Russell Reynolds Associates, 9 September; Pandora (2021) About, pandoragroup.com/about (archived at https://perma.cc/ Q4XJ-EJV5)

06

Culture

What is it?

The culture of an organization describes its prevailing mindset and behaviours. It is sometimes referred to as the 'DNA of the business', forming the principles by which it operates and shaping 'the way people behave when no one is watching'. One British retailer describes culture as 'what it feels like to work here'.

We all remember positively when we have experienced excellent service from organizations where nothing seems to be too much trouble; where staff go the extra mile to solve problems and delight customers; and where products and services are exceptional. Conversely, we've all experienced organizations where the staff are careless and unhelpful; where service is slow, unreliable or poor; or where products or services are poor quality and/or poorly delivered. These outcomes depend crucially on culture.

Many elements contribute to organizational culture. As an official UK report on corporate governance observed: 'Culture can be defined as a combination of the values, attitudes, and behaviours manifested by a company in its operations and relationships with its stakeholders.'[1]

A useful way of thinking about organizational culture is the Cultural Web, which was developed by Gerry Johnson and Kevan Scholes in 1992. The Web has six interrelated elements, which are:

- **Stories:** The past events and people talked about inside and outside the company.

- **Rituals and routines**: The daily behaviour and actions of people that signal acceptable behaviour. This determines what is expected to happen in given situations and what is valued by management.

- **Symbols**: The visual representations of the company including logos, how plush the offices are and the formal or informal dress codes.

- **Organizational structure**: This includes both the structure defined by the organization chart and the unwritten lines of power and influence that indicate whose contributions are most valued.

- **Control systems**: The ways that the organization is controlled. These include financial systems, quality systems and rewards (including the way they are measured and distributed within the organization).

- **Power structures**: The pockets of real power in the company. These may involve one or two key senior executives, a whole group of executives or even a department. The key is that these people have the greatest amount of influence on decisions, operations and strategic direction.[2]

In large organizations, the culture in one business unit or region may be very different from another. A lot depends on leadership and the 'tone from the top', i.e. the example from the board and senior management, the 'tone from above' and the behaviours and example set by supervisors and front-line managers. One effect of this is that culture and performance can shift dramatically with the change of key leaders, meaning organizations have to manage culture especially carefully during leadership transitions.

A culture that supports sustainability

A sustainable culture is one where sustainability is baked into what a business does, why and how it does it and with whom. Our earlier book, *All In: The Future of Business Leadership*, suggested that there are four important dimensions of a positive and sustainable culture:

- Engaging and empowering.
- Responsible and ethical.

- Transparent and accountable.
- Open and innovative.[3]

ENGAGING AND EMPOWERING

A positive culture successfully blends top-down direction (clear purpose, business case and strategy as well as the strong leadership required to deliver these) with bottom-up effort (initiative taking by individual employees to make things happen so that employees can contribute effectively to the organization's success). This requires effective induction, ongoing training and continuing professional development and a focus on employee well-being.

Although it was implicit for us in what we understood by an 'engaging and empowering' culture, we would now explicitly emphasize that this includes diversity, equity and inclusion (DE&I). This is particularly so in the wake of the surging movement to end systemic racism and discrimination following the murder of George Floyd in 2020, which built on the momentum previously established by the #BlackLivesMatter, #MeToo and disability rights movements. DE&I reflects a business's cultural norms and values. It means creating an environment where all people feel fully respected and recognized. This also supports becoming more innovative due to the creativity inherent in a diverse workforce, which is enhanced by recognizing and valuing all people's knowledge and experiences.

RESPONSIBLE AND ETHICAL

This means a business taking responsibility for its material, social, environmental and economic impacts and having effective governance and oversight of its sustainability commitments. It involves a culture where employees, suppliers and business partners know what is expected of them in terms of behaving responsibly, where they are equipped with ethical decision-making frameworks to help navigate grey areas and where these things are reinforced through regular training and education. This is helped by having a code of ethics or statement of business principles and making sure that the code is regularly reviewed and updated, preferably using external benchmarking as well as internal consultations.

TRANSPARENT AND ACCOUNTABLE

Another dimension of a strong sustainability culture is transparency and accountability. This means providing evidence of performance and information on impacts so as to build trust and using 'the disinfectant of publicity' to reinforce good behaviour (see Chapter 8). A transparent and accountable culture requires intensive two-way communications about purpose, business case, strategy, operations, leadership and performance. It also relies on communications from the leadership to the wider organization and from the organization back to leaders (see Chapter 11). Without such communications, employees and other stakeholders won't know the organization's needs and opportunities and be able to communicate what they are seeing and experiencing to senior management, leaving organizational leaders without a comprehensive view of what is happening on the frontline and in terms of the organization's external impacts.[4]

Accountability especially is also about being humble as well as courageous enough to show vulnerability and admit that the organization does not have all the answers. This means showing a willingness to partner with others to solve problems that the organization is facing.

OPEN AND INNOVATIVE

Given the spread and extent of change that every business now faces, a sustainable culture will emphasize innovation and creating the conditions in which innovation occurs naturally and frequently. Embedding sustainability cannot just be incremental improvement, it needs fundamental 10× change including new business models, which demands extensive innovation. According to the 2019 Deloitte Millennial Survey, Millennials, who are already emerging as leaders across industries and who will comprise 75 per cent of the global workforce by 2025, want to work for organizations that foster innovative thinking, develop their skills and make a positive contribution to society.[5]

Sustainably successful organizations, therefore, need an open culture that is receptive to new ideas as opposed to a 'not invented here' mentality. They need to create a situation where internal and external stakeholders want to propose and champion innovations for them. So

FIGURE 6.1 The Sustainable Culture Compass: Reinforces purpose and values

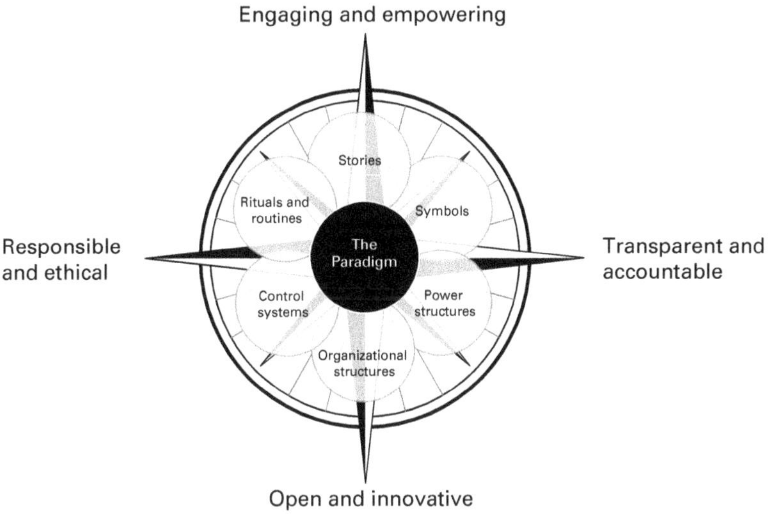

sustainable cultures are not rigid. On the contrary, they are flexible, agile and continuously improving. Leaders in particular need to have not just an innovative mindset, but also one that can envisage what the company's sustainability practices will look like a decade or more ahead as well as the ability to conceive more sustainable business models.

This can all be summarized in the Sustainable Culture Compass, which incorporates the Cultural Web and the four dimensions of sustainable culture previously outlined (see Figure 6.1).

Why it matters

There are multiple reasons sustainable culture matters, but here are some that particularly stand out.

- Absent a clearly defined and managed culture designed to support more sustainable outcomes, one will emerge organically, and it may not be what is desired. As Sir Anthony Salz, the corporate lawyer and experienced board member and chair, wrote in his independent review of the culture of Barclays in 2013: 'Culture exists regardless. If left to its own devices, it shapes itself, with the inherent risk that behaviours will not be those desired… Employees will work out for themselves what is valued by the leaders to whom they report.'[6]

- A healthy culture is critical to effective and successful organizations. Remember: 'Culture eats strategy for breakfast – but culture gets its appetite from purpose.'[7] Unhealthy cultures lead to poor performance and bad reputations. In contrast, engaged and empowered employees lead to satisfied customers, repeat business, word-of-mouth referrals and sustainable profits over time. As the Wates Report on corporate governance from the UK noted: 'A healthy culture is critical to the company's competitive advantage, and vital to the creation and protection of long-term value.'[8]

- Irresponsible or unethical behaviours harm trust and a company's reputation with customers especially, and they can undercut a business's licence to operate, at times threatening the very existence of the organization.

- Regulators and investors are putting more pressure on company boards and senior management teams to define and manage culture proactively as part of improving ESG performance. On the regulatory side, the UK Corporate Governance Code, for example, now requires that boards assess and monitor culture, asking that boards 'create a culture which aligns company values with strategy and to assess how they preserve value over the long-term'.[9] Recent revisions to Japan's Corporate Governance Code and the Dutch Corporate Governance Code also emphasize the importance of culture definition, measurement and oversight. In an example of investor focus, State Street Global Advisors, the world's third-largest asset manager, has asked boards to review their company cultures and explain their alignment with the strategy of the business.

- There is pressure from employees and potential employees for organizations to be great places to work, where employees can be 100 per cent human and bring their whole selves to work. Younger employees in particular are more critical and challenging of cultures that tolerate bullying, harassment, sexism, racism, disablism, ageism, homophobia, etc. Conversely, they are looking for engaging and empowering employers. A culture that celebrates individual and team success and offers a sense of accomplishment turns employees into advocates. The more employees feel they are part of a community, the more likely they are to be attracted to the organization and to stay. A workplace culture focused on people has profound appeal, improving engagement, making people feel more connected and providing a common purpose.

• The four dimensions of a sustainable culture are interlinked and mutually reinforcing. Take away any one dimension and, over time, the culture will likely become unsustainable. Rigid, hierarchical organizations are unlikely to inspire a modern workforce to risk taking the initiative to develop sustainability ideas and projects – especially if a lack of transparency or openness means that employees and external stakeholders don't know what the business is hoping to achieve or what help the business needs to innovate for sustainability. Similarly, if a business seems unethical or irresponsible, it will be far less likely to engage employees and other stakeholders

How to do it

We have identified five foundational steps to building a sustainable culture.

Step 1: Understand the current culture

The starting point is to understand the current culture. This will require some sort of culture audit / assessment using the general tools and techniques for communications (see Chapter 11). Some specific tools to use for a culture audit / assessment include employee engagement surveys, specific cultural audit questionnaires, focus groups, exit interviews, analysis of publications / websites, what former employees are saying online on sites like Glassdoor, net promoter scores (which reflect the percentage of employees likely to recommend their employer as a good place to work) and external stakeholder surveys. Typically, a culture audit might also examine whether the organization's values are clear, well communicated and properly embedded, how whistleblowing issues are closed out and examine any patterns of adverse internal audit findings. There may be some 'red flags' (warning signs) too – such as low levels of speak up; open, unresolved investigations; open, overdue audit issues; and low participation levels in employee surveys.

It may also include monitoring regulatory violations, looking at the number of serious accidents and health and safety incidents and examining the culture of the board and senior executive team. Typically, establishing today's culture will also involve asking employees and other stakeholders what they like about the existing culture and want to preserve, what they don't like and want to see abandoned and which different or additional cultural traits they want to see encouraged. The outcome of the culture audit should be an assessment of whether there is already a strong sustainability culture that needs to be nurtured and grown further; some good elements to keep/strengthen but with some degree of change; or one where a wholesale change of culture is required.

Step 2: Define the desired future culture

The next step is to identify what parts of the existing culture employees, management and board want to retain, what they believe the organization needs to leave behind and what additional desired behaviours and new ways of operating to encourage. Part of this is ensuring that the culture and the commitments in the business's sustainability strategy are suitably aligned and thus able to support one another. Organizations that do this well proactively engage with their workforce to co-design the target state. This marginalizes and isolates resistance and encourages people who are not signed up for the journey to move on. It massively empowers and energizes the positive agents for change.

Culture change can be planned and incremental or abrupt and dramatic due to factors such as scandal, economic turnaround, merger or acquisition. In most cases, we don't think sustainability can be achieved just with modest, incremental changes. Changing an organization's culture is difficult due to the interlocking nature of the Culture Web and the way that dimensions of sustainable culture fit together and reinforce each other, and it takes time.

A business needs to consider the Sustainable Culture Compass pictured in Figure 6.1:

- Do the points of the compass accurately describe the dimensions of the desired culture for the organization?
- Are there any modifications to make?
- Are there additional elements?

Having done this, the next step is to map actual versus desired culture and to develop an action plan to move from actual to desired. The board have to take a very active lead on this and be seen to be leading by example.

Step 3: Map actual versus desired culture and agree an action plan to achieve this new culture

Having audited the current culture (Step 1) and defined the desired future (Step 2), the organization will know how much they overlap and how much work there is to be done to align them. The challenge is how best to do this. New target behaviours need to be defined and communicated and continuously reinforced. This will require a concerted action plan. The action plan required needs the active support and involvement of the board and top management, should build on organizational heritage when possible and will likely need to include examining and adjusting the following activities:

- Recruitment criteria: hiring people with values aligned to the organization's purpose and ambition.
- Induction: ensuring employees are inducted in the company's purpose, values, code of ethics or business principles and commitments to sustainability.

- Training and continuous professional development: reviewing the sustainability leadership and management development programmes, both those run internally and those commissioned from external providers (see Chapter 7).

- Speaking up: expanding the scope of whistleblowing arrangements into a broader speak-up mechanism that encourages employees to call out whenever things don't seem right.

- Decision-making: designing values-based decision-making frameworks, since there will be new challenges not answered by current policy and procedure.

- Regular communications: making sure leaders at all levels talk about the purpose, sustainability commitments and strategy of the business as well as expected behaviours (see Chapter 11).

- Collaboration: opportunities to engage in problem-solving together with management and role modelling desired behaviours, especially as they relate to sustainability outcomes.

- Reward and recognition systems: making sure that compensation, bonuses and promotion systems all reinforce rather than undermine the embedding of sustainability.

It is sensible, at least initially, to focus on a few critical shifts in behaviour. Businesses should integrate formal and informal interventions. Formal interventions include performance management frameworks, internal communications and rewards, while informal interventions include cross-organizational working, manager communications and behaviour modelling by senior leaders.[10]

The action plan will need to address each dimension of sustainability culture.

ENGAGING AND EMPOWERING

Writers such as Daniel Pink[11] and Simon Sinek[12] have identified the importance of people having mastery, autonomy and purpose in their work. As Pink writes: 'It's about autonomy, the desire to steer your own ship; it's about mastery: the ability to be able to steer that ship well; and it's about purpose, knowing that your journey has some wider, broader meaning.'

Employees need to feel they are trusted and to understand that they have permission – indeed are encouraged – to go the extra mile to satisfy customers and to take the initiative to solve problems. The ideal is that employees feel that trying honestly is better than not trying at all and that it is OK to fail as long as they did their best and learn from the failure. This is down to both management styles and organizational processes.

One process is to do reviews after significant projects and programmes. These reviews are not designed to assign blame but to learn what worked, what didn't and what might be better solutions for the future. Developing a discipline of regular reviews for learning and continuous improvement is far better than an occasional post-mortem. One practical way of building engagement beyond feeling that there is a positive purpose is to give employees a stake in the success of the business through profit-sharing schemes and/or employee share options programmes – particularly if these can be linked both to financial and sustainability performance over the longer term.

On diversity, equity and inclusion, the business will want to increase the percentage of women, different ethnicities and disabled employees at different levels of the organization and address any pay gaps. This will probably involve a mix of board and senior management commit-ment, DE&I champions, mentoring, changes to recruitment practices and the establishment of employee networks or resource groups (groups of workers who join together based on shared identities or life experiences, e.g. for female employees, disabled employees, work-ing carers or LGBTQ+ employees.) Employee networks can play a vital role in helping identify and eliminate barriers to inclusion and forging allyship.[13] Inclusion is really important as a driver in unlock-ing discretionary effort. If colleagues can't be their true selves at work and be valued for that, they are unlikely to go out of their way to help their employer.

RESPONSIBLE AND ETHICAL

The company's materiality process (see Chapter 2) should identify the most significant impacts that the business has responsibility for, then a comprehensive sustainability strategy should clarify how the business proposes to discharge those responsibilities. Some practical initiatives that a business can take to bring responsibility to life include, for example, creating a responsible corporate tax strategy to pay all taxes they legally and morally owe in different jurisdictions. Other tangible steps to consider include non-discriminatory executive compensation schemes and ensuring that the organization is paying the living wage and eradicating in-work poverty.

The Institute of Business Ethics (IBE) recommends that organizations develop a framework to build an ethical culture (see Figure 6.2). This normally involves:

- An ethics risk assessment, to understand the issues that are most relevant for the organization.

- Developing and regularly updating a code of ethics (2021 IBE research found that less than half of the FTSE100 in the UK had an up-to-date code).

- Ongoing training and communications to ensure understanding of what is expected, which is often best done by discussing practical applications of the code and telling stories about how the code is being used in the organization.

- Mechanisms to support high ethical standards – for example, speak-up programmes to encourage employees to raise concerns at an early stage.

- Reporting mechanisms for allegations of misconduct.

- An assurance process to monitor the effectiveness of the programme and the extent to which the organization lives up to its values.

- Benchmarking.

TRANSPARENT AND ACCOUNTABLE

Transparent and accountable organizations are committed to and good at reporting and disclosure (see Chapter 8). Some businesses

FIGURE 6.2   Ethics framework

operate on the basis of 'open books' whereby employees are able to see for themselves the financial performance of the business and its forward financial health. Transparent and accountable organizations are effective communicators (see Chapter 11) and engage stakeholders more in the running of the business (see also Chapter 11).

OPEN AND INNOVATIVE

An organization that is responsible and ethical is more likely to be able to engage and empower employees because they will have more alignment and trust. This will especially be the case if the organization is also transparent so that employees have an accurate understanding of what is going on and have a better sense of future prospects. These employees will be more motivated and also better informed and able to contribute ideas and come up with innovative solutions to sustainability challenges that the business faces. Some companies use online, in-company platforms to share sustainability problems they are grappling with and then encourage employees to help find solutions.

Some companies have had success with employee-initiated innovation by encouraging social intrapreneurs and others who will help the business disrupt and innovate its way to a more sustainable future. 'A Social Intrapreneur is an entrepreneurial employee who develops a profitable new product, service or business model that creates value for society and for her company. Social intrapreneurs help their employers meet their sustainability commitments and create value for customers and communities in ways that are built to last.'[14] This may be the result of deliberate programmes by a company to nurture intrapreneurial activity, through competitions in the style of *Dragon's Den* or *Sharks' Tank*, dedicated Innovation Funds, internal or external training programmes and mentoring. Again, this can be reinforced through incentive schemes to reinforce desired behaviours. (See Chapter 7 for more discussion about how to develop intrapreneurs.)

It is also important to repurpose and – if necessary – retool R&D departments and product and service development teams and require them to apply a sustainability stage gate to determine whether to progress a particular idea, viz: 'Will this innovation produce more sustainability benefits than what is currently available or do so at less cost?' Some businesses use such sustainability stage gates as critical Go / No Go decision points. A recent Nike CEO reputedly switched from asking designers presenting each season's new trainers only 'How will this improve customer's performance?' to also asking 'How does this improve sustainability?'

Step 4: Implement action plan

Achieving an effective culture change programme goes beyond implementing a set of steps. To get it right, it is crucial to understand the key drivers of the organization's culture. For example, many technology companies' culture is driven by engineering and process; consumer product companies are driven by product and brand marketing leaders; start-ups are driven by their founders. Understanding the organization's culture will help guide what to prioritize when implementing an action plan.

Similarly, while we have presented potential elements of an action plan to build a more sustainable culture in four dimensions, it makes sense to implement them in ways that reinforce several things at once. For example, an experiential learning programme to encourage and nurture intrapreneurs could develop future leaders, engage and empower employees, build collaboration skills, produce needed innovation and demonstrate the company's openness to partnerships for sustainability.

Organizations will need to think about what changes to monthly, quarterly and half-yearly reporting formats and contents are required. It is important to determine which KPIs (key performance indicators) are needed and which should be particularly monitored and publicized by managers. As implementation progresses, boards and executive teams will be looking for evidence that the culture change is being reflected in, for example, exit interviews and other staff feedback.

In implementing the action plan to create a sustainable culture, organizations will need to consider carefully the signals sent to the organization by what leaders pay attention to, how leaders react to critical incidents and how resources are allocated.[15] They should also think about whether and how leaders at all levels exhibit desired behaviours and take into account practical considerations such as the design of physical space and buildings and how the organization projects itself both in its premises and through online media etc.

Step 5: Regularly review culture and adjust as appropriate

Organizations need to regularly repeat the culture audit described in Step 1 and use the results to refine the culture as needed and to ensure that there is alignment between actual and desired culture.

Many businesses establish a culture dashboard (with as many real-time indicators as possible) and/or use some culture measurement tool such as the Organizational Culture Inventory (OCI). The OCI consists of 10 themes and 120 questions, described as 'styles' that are used to describe two key concepts: a concern for people and an emphasis on tasks. This might include, for example, checking that managers are appraising, rewarding and promoting their employees based on what the employee has achieved and how they achieved their results.

One practical metric the board could ask for is: 'How many employees have had some or all of their bonuses withheld, even if they exceeded their targets, if they achieved their targets in ways inconsistent with the values of the business?' Organizations need to be alert to the risk of cultural 'drift' and the development of local microcultures. It is important not to become complacent and assume because the culture feels good that it no longer needs attention. The important point overall is that leaders need to remember that maintaining desired culture is a constant task and one which requires dedication, humility and empathy.

In practice

IKEA

IKEA is a home furnishing retailer with 217,000 employees and 2020 annual revenue of more than $46 billion. The company was founded in Småland, Sweden, in 1943. It is now headquartered in Delft, Netherlands.

The IKEA brand comprises many companies and people across the world. Its vision is 'to create a better everyday life for the many people'. The IKEA business model goes beyond retail, including product development, design, supply, manufacture and sales. The retail business is organized in a franchise system with 12 franchisees in 54 markets. The largest franchisee is Ingka Group, which comprises 383 IKEA stores across 30+ countries as well as 45 shopping centres in Europe, Russia and China. In 2020, 706 million people visited stores and there were over 3.6 billion visits to the website.

There are eight IKEA Key Values: togetherness; caring for people and planet; cost consciousness; simplicity; renew and improve; different with a meaning; give and take responsibility; and lead by example. These values are central to how IKEA attracts, recruits and onboards new staff. The company has a digital toolbox of resources and interview guides for hiring managers and is rolling out training on values-based recruitment to help managers assess candidates on values, competence and diversity and to identify candidates best suited to thrive in the IKEA culture. New employees learn about the values and culture during onboarding.

Ingka Group has pledged to increase ethnic, racial and national diversity at all levels of leadership by 2024. Half of managers are women, and the ambition is to have a 50:50 gender balance across all levels and positions, including boards and committees, by the end of 2022. The company is also focusing on integrating refugees. All of these elements drive a more inclusive culture.

Regular staff surveys help IKEA assess how co-workers feel about their jobs, teams and Ingka Group. In total, 85 per cent of co-workers believe Ingka Group is a great place to work and sustainability is a key driver of this. In fact, sustainability is the third reason why people choose to work and stay at IKEA. The surveys have found areas for improvement too, such as internal communications, planning and resources to help co-workers manage their workload and development pathways and training feedback.

In FY20, the company launched 'Hej!', an app designed to help employees keep up with Ingka news, access training and stay in touch via their mobiles. With Hej!, co-workers can read and reply to emails, view team documents, use their work applications, visit Yammer channels, access their MyLearning training portal and view their schedule, all in one place. An annual One IKEA Bonus programme ensures employees share in the success of the business.

The IKEA values and corporate culture support significant sustainability ambitions, including some of the most ambitious 2030 sustainability goals in the corporate world, including:

- Healthy and sustainable living: Inspire and enable more than 1 billion people to live a better everyday life within the boundaries of the planet.
- Circular and climate positive: Become circular and climate positive, and regenerate resources while growing the IKEA business.
- Fair and equal: Create a positive social impact for everyone across the IKEA value chain.

These bold sustainability commitments depend on innovation in sustainability, a willingness to partner and advocate for sustainable outcomes and a culture that embraces sustainability.

According to Pia Heidenmark Cook, the recently retired Chief Sustainability Officer at Ingka:

> Delivering on set sustainability goals is fundamentally about innovation, communication and leadership and the thread across these are people. With a clear north star and purpose of why you need to change – which fundamentally is guided by the values and culture of the company – you have a good chance of succeeding with your sustainability transformation.[16]

Suzano

The merger between Suzano Papel e Celulose and Fibria created Suzano S.A. in 2018, the world's largest eucalyptus pulp producer. With 11 business units, 35,000 employees, annual revenues of $7 billion (2020–21) 1.3 million hectares of planted trees and 900,000 hectares of preserved forests, Suzano provides bioproducts for clients worldwide.

Despite the legacy of the two original companies, Suzano created a new strategic pathway for the company. The foundational piece of the new company was the **Culture Drivers,** collaboratively developed with the contribution of employees from a diverse range of functions across the enterprise. Suzano's Culture Drivers were built on three foundational beliefs: Who we are: People who inspire and transform; What we do: We create and share value; How we do it: It is only good for us if it is good for the world. This 'tone from the top' was widely and frequently promoted by senior management throughout the business.

Without explicitly mentioning sustainability, the Drivers are greatly influenced by the concept of sustainable development and have made it easier to integrate sustainability thinking in the new company's corporate culture. This was reinforced, when it came to the development of the sustainability strategy, by talking face-to-face with more than 160 external stakeholders directly, as well as a wider survey of external stakeholders which was carried out by an independent consultancy. This was replicated internally with workshops in all Suzano's main sites, involving more than 700 employees. These workshops engaged employees on what sustainability is, what it means to Suzano and what the company should do about it. The objective is to empower all employees to take the initiative on sustainability. So, for example, it was staff working in the Treasury function that championed a sustainability-linked bond issued in September 2020. Suzano obtained the lowest rate of capital cost ever in Brazil and were the first company in the Americas to issue such a bond. Similarly, the Paper Business Unit has taken the initiative and partnered with the corporate sustainability team to design and run sustainability training for staff. There is also discussion now about how to reflect more sustainability in the first review of Suzano's Code of Ethics. There is already mandatory, online training for all employees on the Code. Investor relations, even in the predecessor companies to Suzano, were sustainability fluent and well used to providing extensive information and disclosure about sustainability performance. This has intensified in Suzano.

Sustainable culture is also reinforced by the three pillars of the company's strategic vision launched in early 2020. These pillars can be paraphrased in English as: (1) being the most efficient, profitable and sustainable company in the sector worldwide, from the forest to the client; (2) being a transformational agent in the expansion into new markets for biomass; and (3) becoming a global leader in innovative and sustainable solutions for the bioeconomy and environmental services, based on planted trees. Furthermore, through internal surveys, Suzano has identified 70–80 influencers across the company and has worked with these influencers / champions to develop and promote elevator pitches on Suzano (pitches designed (a) for a very short elevator journey and (b) for a longer one). Sustainability features heavily in the pitches.

This virtuous cycle of a strong sustainability culture began to move at an accelerated pace. On the one hand, leadership became more vocal in defence of issues such as biodiversity, conservation in the Amazon and even the reformation of capitalism. On the other hand, recent surveys with employees indicate high levels of confidence that Suzano acts in the best interests of society. Externally, the company is beginning to be recognized by experts for its leadership in sustainability, as revealed by its first-time appearance in the GlobeScan SustainAbility Leaders Survey 2021.

Cristiano Resende de Olivereira, Suzano's Executive Manager of Sustainability, commented: 'Any success we have had in driving stronger and more recognized sustainability performance began with our culture and values – these have guided and reinforced our commitments and make us a better company.'[17]

Summary

Purpose, strategy and leadership are all essential to a sustainable business, but they are not sufficient without a healthy, sustainable culture. All organizations have a culture. The issue is whether it is one that has emerged organically in the absence of any conscious identi-fication of the desired culture or one that is the result of mature consideration, planning and encouragement – and, more crucially, whether the outcome is a culture of sustainability. Ultimately this is the responsibility of the board and senior management of a business. There is a growing expectation that senior leaders will define the desired culture for their organization and also regularly check on the culture's health. Furthermore, as the organizational culture specialist Annie Auerbach wrote in *The Financial Times*:

> The shift to flexible work caused by the pandemic has brought a radical reimagining of how we work… The world of work has experienced such a huge shift in the past 18 months, it would be a lost opportunity to sleepwalk back to the old ways without proper thought about the future.[18]

Establishing and maintaining a desired culture for sustainability in more hybrid workplaces and ways of working is going to be more crucial than ever and even more challenging.

Action checklist

1 The leadership of the business needs to define the desired culture of the business, the values by which the business should be run and the behaviours expected of employees. The values must be visible, well communicated and part of the everyday language of the organization, and the specific words need to have meaning and resonance.

2 The business should regularly check whether the actual culture matches the desired culture.

3 There needs to be consistency of 'tone from the top' and 'tone from above'. Leaders should be walking their talk in terms of expected values and behaviours.

4 The business ought to be recruiting new employees with an emphasis on a sustainability mindset.

5 The organization needs to be proactive in promoting diversity, equity and inclusion, in order to benefit from a wider range of experiences and perspectives.

6 Incentives, rewards, recognition and promotion should be reviewed to ensure they reinforce the desired culture.

7 The business needs to stimulate a regular pipeline of sustainability-focused innovation, including employee-led intrapreneurism.

8 The organization should be regularly reviewing and updating its code of ethics and how it goes about communicating and socializing this code.

9 The organization may want to consider if it aspires to rank on external employee satisfaction benchmarks such as *Great Places to Work* and, if so, what it will need to do to achieve this.

10 Consideration should be given to the introduction of some form of culture dashboard or equivalent to maintain an accurate understanding of the actual culture.

Further resources

- See the Barrett Values Centre website: www.valuescentre.com/
  - The Barrett Analytics include a Culture Assessment, a Cultural Evolution Report, a Small Group Assessment, and a Merger Compatibility Assessment[19]
- See the Institute of Business Ethics website: www.ibe.org.uk
  - Business Ethics Toolkit (aimed especially at smaller firms)
  - Trends and Innovations in Effective Ethics Training Good Practice Guide (2021)
- Coyle, D (2018) *The Culture Code: The secrets of highly successful groups*, Cornerstone Digital

Endnotes

1 The Wates report for the UK's Financial Reporting Council (FRC). See Wates, J (2018) Corporate Governance Principles For Large Private Companies, Financial Reporting Council (FRC)

2 Johnson, G, Whittington, R and Scholes K (2012) *Fundamentals of Strategy*, Pearson Education

3 Grayson, D, Coulter, C and Lee, M (2018) *All In: The future of business leadership*, Routledge

4 There is an old management theory known as Yoshida's 'iceberg of ignorance' – the idea that 'only four per cent of a company's problems are known to top managers'

5 Deloitte Millennial Survey (2019), www2.deloitte.com/content/dam/Deloitte/global/Documents/About-Deloitte/deloitte-2019-millennial-survey.pdf (archived at https://perma.cc/JJ96-NL5C)

6 Salz, A (2013) *The Salz Review: An independent review of Barclays business practices*, Barclays

7 'Culture eats strategy for breakfast' is widely but perhaps incorrectly attributed to Peter Drucker (the second half of the quotation is John O'Brien's)

8 Wates, J (2018) *Corporate Governance Principles For Large Private Companies*, Financial Reporting Council (FRC)

 9 Financial Reporting Council (2018) The UK Corporate Governance Code, Financial Reporting Council

10 Katzenbach, J R, Steff, E N I and Kronley C (2012) Culture change that sticks: Start with what is already working, *Harvard Business Review*, July/August, pp. 110–117

11 Pink, D (2010) *The Surprising Truth about What Motivates Us*, Canongate Books

12 Sinek, S (2010) *Start With Why: How great leaders inspire everyone to take action*, Penguin

13 Purple Space, which is a network of Disabled Employees' Networks, shares good practice in creating and maintaining vibrant disability networks; Employers for Carers run by the charity Carers UK provides good practice guidance for networks of working carers

14 Yunus Social Business (2020) Business as unusual: How social intrapreneurs can turn companies into a force for good, www.yunussb.com/business-as-unusual (archived at https://perma.cc/G6JW-7F4H)

15 Schein, E H (2010) *Organisational Culture and Leadership*, 4th edition, Jossey Bass

16 Corporate website: www.inter.ikea.com/en/performance/fy20-year-in-review (archived at https://perma.cc/8YYC-3PTG); corporate website: en-global-jobs.about.ikea.com/lifeatikea (archived at https://perma.cc/D43E-SKG5); corporate website: www.ikea.com/gb/en/this-is-ikea/about-us/the-ikea-sustainability-strategy-making-a-real-difference-pubb5534570 (archived at https://perma.cc/JUP7-T4WK); IKEA Sustainability Report (updated in 2020): www.ikea.com/gb/en/files/pdf/6c/5b/6c5b7acd/people-and-planet-positive-ikea-sustainability-strategy.pdf (archived at https://perma.cc/F6J9-BRRS)

17 Profile based on Suzano sustainability report and interview with authors, 22 September 2021

18 Auerbach, A (2021) What do we mean when we talk about workplace culture?, *The Financial Times*, 16 July

19 Barrett Values Centre: www.valuescentre.com/tools-assessments/#orgtools (archived at https://perma.cc/4GMJ-GKZG)

07

Leadership

What is it?

Sustainability leadership requires business leaders at all levels, from the board and senior management through front-line supervisors, to manage with ESG goals in mind.

Sustainability leadership means taking into account the needs and expectations of internal and external stakeholders, from employees, consumers and shareholders, to regulators and even future generations. It looks beyond immediate, short-term gains to see the role the organization plays in a larger context and in line with its purpose.

Sustainability leadership demands setting strategies and delivering results that meet the triple bottom line of social, environmental and economic performance. This requires all organizational leaders to possess the mindset, skillset, values and character required to deliver the corporate purpose, develop the business case and drive the firm's strategy in ways that deliver more sustainable outcomes. Developing sustainability leadership requires unique types of training and engagement.

Why it matters

There are several reasons why developing sustainability leadership matters.

- At the firm level, sustainability leadership is integral to the success of the organization's purpose, business case, strategy and culture, as well as ensuring it develops the business model, skills and resources required to continue into the indefinite future.

- It is increasingly hard for business leaders today to lead employees successfully without demonstrating understanding of sustainability, championing its value and making it part of how they run their organizations. Leaders committed to ESG are expected to be advocates and to inspire others to embrace and apply its tenets.

- Leaders must be equipped to make the choices and uphold the behaviours that ensure their organization's commitment to sustainability is authentic.

- Leaders need to ensure their business is sustainable and able to meet societal expectations in a profitable manner. This is impossible without the right sustainability leadership competencies and mindset. Leaders who 'get' sustainability are likely to be more successful in enabling their organizations to exploit commercial opportunities arising from it. Implementing the SDGs, for example, is calculated to represent a $12 trillion business opportunity.[1] As Unilever's Chief Human Resources Officer, Leena Nair, observes: 'When you build better leaders, you build better businesses. When you build better businesses, you build a better world.'[2]

How to do it

Step 1: Define the mindsets and leadership competencies required

The good news is that your business does not need to start from scratch. There are numerous existing sustainability leadership frameworks that can be adopted wholesale or adapted to meet the circumstances of your organization. These include models developed by leadership and sustainability experts,[3] leadership training providers,[4] sustainability coalitions,[5] executive search firms[6] and individual companies.[7] Examining these will accelerate identification of the mindsets and competencies that your organization needs.

Common to many of the models and frameworks are:

- Personal purpose, integrity, authenticity, ethics, values and empathy.
- Understanding of long-term macro trends and their inter-relationships as well as systems thinking.
- Commercial awareness to identify sustainability-related risks and opportunities and the ability to apply that awareness in making the business case for sustainability for your company.
- Vision for how the organization might contribute to a sustainable economy.
- Passion for high performance, business acumen and results orientation.
- The sustainability literacy required to engage subject-matter experts and develop successful business strategies.
- Good communication skills and the ability to engage stakeholders, work collaboratively and inspire others to act. Leading collaboratively to solve complex challenges can be countercultural in some organizations that still operate in hierarchies and silos.
- The ability to drive agility, innovation and adaptability.
- A coaching style of leadership – which is arguably even more important in a post-COVID-19 workplace.

As much as the items listed above matter individually, the interplay and reinforcement between them is particularly important and exciting. While not a comprehensive list, these are widely identified characteristics of successful sustainability leaders.

Step 2: Audit current sustainability leadership ability and the sustainability content in existing leadership development programmes

Having defined the required sustainability leadership mindset and competencies, it is useful to conduct an audit of the current level of sustainability skill of your leadership as well as the sustainability content included in your development programmes. Do your leaders have the will and skill required for sustainability? Do your leadership development programmes include the content required to fill any gaps? It is prudent to focus particularly on 'will'; while specific technical skills can be acquired, it is harder to change mindsets.

The audit will reveal gaps requiring attention. This may involve:

- Bringing in new talent.
- Promoting suitable talent from within.
- Producing a new menu of leadership development opportunities.
- Nurturing a pipeline of future talent.

Leadership development programmes at any level of seniority can benefit from practical exercises where participants are asked to look at the details of a recent sustainability challenge that the business – or another business in the same sector – has recently confronted. Participants can be asked to discuss how they would have handled the situation and why. This can be particularly helpful if the organization has already done its own review and drawn out the lessons to be learnt and applied. Many leaders say organizations can learn more from careful analysis of failures than from previous successes, which may leave the business complacent and less open to change and improvement.

Step 3: Develop an action plan to increase sustainability leadership capacity

There are at least four levels where companies can develop sustainability leadership:

- early career high-flyers;
- middle managers;
- senior executives;
- board members.

There are many proven ways that businesses can develop the sustainability leadership skills of early career high-flyers. These include:

- Designing and running the company's own sustainability leadership modules as part of existing in-company talent development programmes and/or buying in modules from external providers.

- Encouraging high-flyers to participate in skills-based volunteering opportunities with a sustainability focus.

- Making short-term, horizon-expanding, sustainability-related secondments of young high-flyers to a government department, public agency or charity / voluntary organization.

- Helping talented young employees find a suitable appointment on the board of a charity or voluntary organization. In the UK, for example, there are a number of programmes that help talented young people acquire board skills and find suitable appointments.[8]

- Sponsoring talented young employees through a programme such as One Young World or Common Purpose.

MIDDLE MANAGERS

Heightened sustainability performance expectations for business will not go away. Yet, you still hear some operational managers asking: 'What does sustainability have to do with me?'

While middle managers can feel excluded, sustainability professionals, CEOs and senior executives sometimes express dismay at the perceived 'middle management black hole'. When it comes to sustainability, top management increasingly 'gets it' because they can see the multiple pressures now bearing down on business, while younger and/or front-line staff are often enthusiastic about making a positive difference on things like climate change or diversity, equity and inclusion. Meantime, hard-pressed middle managers often feel the competing pressure of sales targets, headcount pressures and cost-control drives – and struggle to see how to reconcile these with sustainability and being a responsible business.

Balancing these things is usually easier for operational managers inside businesses that are already established as corporate sustainability leaders, where the agenda has moved from a 'bolt on' to business operations to being core to business purpose and strategy. But sustainability performance can be a challenge for middle managers even in leadership organizations. Hence the importance of sustainability leadership development programmes for leaders at all levels and of ensuring that people-related policies and processes support sustainability (see Step 4 below).

Businesses that have embedded sustainability and linked it to corporate purpose and strategy are also more likely to have identified what they want operational managers to do about it. Companies need to incorporate sustainability into key performance indicators, management training and reward and promotion decisions. In turn, operational managers need to understand the strategy, the business case and what is expected of them – and where there are opportunities for voluntary initiatives and experimentation over and above core requirements. Applying the maxim that the best way to learn something is to teach it to others, a business can create possibilities for individuals to champion a sustainability pilot (see Taking personal initiative box).

While delivering as much training and development internally as possible, the company will also want to promote opportunities to get training on sustainability outside the business and encourage take up of what's learned via those channels.

SENIOR EXECUTIVES

Businesses may choose to design and run their own, in-house sustainability leadership development programmes for senior executives. Alternatively, they may commission programmes to be delivered by outside providers. They may also sponsor senior executives to participate in short, intensive, external executive programmes on sustainability leadership – there are now online and face-to-face programmes available from respected and well-established providers such as the Cambridge Institute for Sustainability Leadership, IMD in Lausanne, Switzerland, Harvard Business School and an increasing number of other business schools across the world. Or, typically, companies may choose a mix of all of the above programmes.

As executives move into more senior roles, it becomes even more important that they can articulate a business case and relate sustainability projects and commitments to the organization's bottom line. More senior leaders also need to develop deeper understanding of the regulatory environment in markets where they are operating, as well as a more rounded and sophisticated view of the roles their business and the private sector generally plays in society. They will also find themselves under more scrutiny to 'walk the talk'.

Early career high-flyers, middle managers and senior executives can all be encouraged to take personal initiative (see box). Most of the illustrative list can also apply to non-executive directors of the company too.

TAKING PERSONAL INITIATIVE

Even in companies without clearly defined and embedded sustainability strategies and/or existing sustainability leadership programmes, individuals have considerable scope to influence the sustainability agenda. This starts with the person's own behaviour and ways of operating. Avenues to do this include:

- Mentoring and encouraging others to take up sustainability-related training opportunities and to achieve all they can become.
- Championing talent irrespective of gender, disability, race, age or sexual orientation.
- Demonstrating that bullying and/or sexist, ageist, racist, homophobic, etc. jokes or behaviour will not be tolerated.
- Initiating recycling and/or energy-saving schemes to reduce environmental impact – and perhaps presenting results to peers and superiors as examples of ways sustainability saves money.
- Discouraging long hours by personal example.
- Being empathetic to employees' personal work–life crises, for instance relating to childcare or eldercare.

- Advocating health and wellness.

- Modelling ethical behaviour and setting a good example by talking about how they believe business should be conducted and using examples of events inside or outside the company to illustrate this.

- Talking about their own experiences of getting involved in a charity or community organization or campaign and how they benefit from it.

- Supporting and challenging suppliers and professional advisers in development and implementation of more sustainable practices.

Individuals will generally be more effective if they find and combine forces with others, perhaps through company intranets or equivalents, and by listening carefully at team meetings and company conferences, etc. Apart from reducing loneliness and self-doubt about whether one is making any impact, there are likely opportunities to support one another, for instance by facilitating action learning through communities of interest and practice or by producing and/or lobbying for innovative ideas.

Employees also have spheres of influence outside of work. This includes their own circle of family and friends, local community and leisure activities and being consumers, citizens, campaigners and co-owners of businesses (through their pension funds, life insurance and other savings). It can be powerful and satisfying to exercise this influence.

Additionally, many staff will be a member of at least one professional association. Such associations may well be looking for volunteers to develop their sector or profession's understanding of what sustainability means for them and what the professional body can be doing to raise awareness and spread good practice, creating further opportunities for impact.[9]

BOARD MEMBERS

There are a number of practical steps that companies can take to help ensure that their board members are sustainability competent. These include:

- Recruiting new, sustainability-literate non-executive directors.

- Providing sustainability training as part of ongoing individual and group professional development.

- Establishing an external sustainability advisory panel and/or youth board to advise the main board.

- Arranging inputs by internal and external experts to board meetings and board away days.

- Establishing a board sustainability committee with accountability for regular reporting back to the rest of the board.

- Circulating details of quality external conferences, meetings, roundtables, webinars, etc. that could help to upskill board members, and encouraging board directors to share insights gained from such events with one another.

(See Chapter 9 for more detail.)

DEVELOPING ETHICAL LEADERS AT ALL LEVELS

Organizations need to make clear how they want people to behave. This is often expressed through a company code of ethics and/or a statement of general business principles. Individuals need training that helps them reflect on their organization's code of ethics and how it is intended to guide or shape behaviours. Are there situations where they would personally go further than the code requires? Have they witnessed or experienced examples of ethically exemplary behaviour in their business – or ethically dubious behaviour? If the latter, what did they do about it? This is part of creating a healthy culture where employees are encouraged to challenge what might be unethical behaviour and is much broader than whistleblowing, which is typically a nuclear option when all other avenues have been exhausted.

Speaking up may be about questioning what might be wrongdoing. It may be about initiating frank conversations between colleagues around sensitive topics like the language used to discuss race, gender identity, sexuality and/or disability. As more people carry on working later in life and workplaces become more multi-generational and otherwise more diverse, the possibilities grow for misunderstandings and clashes of values and norms. Hence the importance of leaders at different levels being empathetic as well as skilled at facilitating dialogues and inquiry within teams about difficult subjects. Such dialogue is often best done through actual, work-related examples rather than abstract discussions.[10] Leading with integrity and authenticity is in many ways the foundational attribute of sustainability leadership at all levels. Leaders set the tone and heavily influence the culture of their organization.

Step 4: Review what further policies and processes need to change in order to help embed sustainability at all levels

Businesses should review on a regular basis:

- Recruitment programmes: How does the company market itself to potential employees, which managers are involved in university recruitment and what are the criteria for selecting recruits? Does the company rigorously check for character and ethical values as well as skills to increase the chances that those hired are cultural as well as executional fits? How are the business's commitments to sustainability included and explained in onboarding and induction programmes?

- Goal setting and appraisals: Is sustainability an important element in the process of setting individual targets and determining key performance indicators for individuals and teams? The mantra 'what gets measured gets managed' applies! Like anything else where a business wants to influence results, sustainability performance needs to be included in appraisals and in criteria for promotions for it to factor significantly in people's minds and actions.

- Compensation systems: Have the company's bonus schemes been sustainability proofed to ensure that incentives don't unintentionally reward development and implementation of less sustainable solutions and instead encourage sustainable innovation and operation?

- Internal communications: Are the company's commitments to sustainability and its key sustainability goals regularly and thoroughly communicated at all levels of the organization? Are employees encouraged to dissect and question the strategy and goals in order to find ways to improve them? Note communications are disproportionately important in larger organizations where there is a danger of messages being diluted as they travel through layers of management (see Chapter 11).

Step 5: Consider what additional initiatives could emphasize sustainability leadership

There are a number of additional initiatives that businesses can take to supplement and extend traditional leadership development. These include:

· Appointing a Chief Sustainability Officer or Director of Sustainability – and, resources allowing, a team to support them.

· Establishing an internal network of sustainability champions.

· Creating the kind of environment where social intrapreneurs can develop and thrive.

APPOINTING A CHIEF SUSTAINABILITY OFFICER OR DIRECTOR OF SUSTAINABILITY WITH A SPECIALIST TEAM TO SUPPORT THEM

Many organizations now have a Chief Sustainability Officer (CSO) or Director of Sustainability. The CSO role implies a level of seniority and authority in the organization and a degree of commitment, especially if the role is part of the executive team or reports directly to a member of it.

A 2021 report from the Institute of International Finance (IIF) and Deloitte argues that:

> The CSO is emerging as the organisation's 'sense-maker in chief'. Understanding and predicting changes in the external sustainability environment is essential to the role. So is navigating, influencing, and cutting through organisational complexities to allow the organisation to deliver on its ESG commitments for commercial gain.[11]

The IIF–Deloitte report found three core responsibilities for CSOs:

· Make sense of the external environment and bring insight back into the firm.

- Help the organization reconfigure its strategy.
- Provide thought leadership and help align teams by engaging, educating and connecting.

The report also argues that CSOs

> ... need to network extremely well and to partner with those across the business with specialist skill and experience. Organisational knowledge and a thorough grounding in the business are also essential attributes... CSOs also need superlative communication skills and organisational ability. The range of stakeholders the CSO needs to influence is wider than that for almost any other role within the firm.[12]

Regardless of who leads it, or their job title, the structure of the sustainability function must ensure effective execution of strategy. The purpose and culture of the company will determine what structure will work most effectively. Many experienced CSOs recommend multiplying the skills of the specialist function by effectively distributing the team across other functional teams This is often best done through a matrixed approach, where a small central sustainability team is supplemented by subject matter experts in different functions globally that report to the CSO directly or through a dotted line.

CSOs often feel that key staff need to be embedded in other parts of the business such as logistics or marketing in order to understand and support the part of the organization they are responsible for influencing and supporting. As one CSO cited anonymously in the IIF–Deloitte report says:

> In my experience, setting up a functional team to deliver sustainability sets you up for failure. Really, you want to operate in a complete matrix. Someone in finance, reporting to the CFO, with a double reporting line to you. Same with investor relations. You also want each function and region to designate someone to report back to you. And you run that as a virtual team. Their job is to hold their function or region accountable. You then run a cross-functional council – a steering group – with your senior colleagues and hold them to account. I used to get the group to report back to the CEO and senior executive and to the Board."[13]

ESTABLISHING A NETWORK OF SUSTAINABILITY CHAMPIONS ACROSS THE BUSINESS

Establishing a network of internal sustainability champions takes time and effort. Typically, champions are employees willing to volunteer to take on extra responsibilities beyond their actual role to positively impact the business and sustainability. Champions can engage others and, in the process, become themselves even more committed. Champions help connect different teams, business units and regions across the business, often finding and propagating sustainability best practices and ideas as they do. Champions also support communication between global and local leadership and between senior management and the front line.

An effective sustainability champions' network can:

- Empower champions by providing advice, training and best practice sharing.
- Collate and organize opportunities available to the organization to improve sustainability performance and channel them to the places and people who can capitalize on them.
- Spread a sense of ownership of sustainability horizontally and vertically.
- Give moral and practical support to co-workers.
- Provide leaders with an extra source of sustainability intelligence from the front line.
- Build visibility and the profile of sustainability within the organization.
- Identify new leadership talent from among the champions.[14]

It is important to keep champions' networks engaged and fresh. Some frequently used techniques include:

- Ensuring champions feel empowered in their sustainability role by providing the necessary training, personal support, materials and leadership support.

- Changing topics on the agenda frequently enough to keep people interested and learning, e.g. by rotating environmental focus from water to carbon to waste over time.

- Aligning with external events, e.g. World Day of People with Disabilities, World Environment Day or World AIDS Day, and running concurrent events internally.

- Sending champions to participate on projects with external stakeholders, e.g. Earthwatch expeditions to help in environmental research and observation.

- Running regular meetings structured to allow champions to share what is most effective in engaging colleagues with one another.

- Providing regular communication, support and space to enable champions to communicate with other champions so they don't feel isolated.

- Ensuring line managers, senior managers and the central sustainability team give positive and public encouragement, including profiling champions to others.

- Including sustainability achievements in yearly performance reviews and factoring in salary raises and bonuses.[15]

CREATING A SUPPORTIVE ENVIRONMENT WHERE SOCIAL INTRAPRENEURS CAN PROSPER[16]

As introduced in Chapter 6, social intrapreneurs are 'innovators inside companies who are imagining new products, services, business models and practices that generate business value and positive social or environmental impact'. In fact, they are not just 'imagining' these things – they often take the initiative to put their ideas into practice.

Sometimes, social intrapreneurs begin by moonlighting for their own employer, developing ideas under the corporate radar in their own time. Some major corporate initiatives and business lines, such as Vodafone's M-Pesa (mobile money services) and the Accenture Development Partnerships (a ground-breaking consultancy within Accenture serving the international development market), started as projects championed by social intrapreneurs.

By encouraging social intrapreneurs within their organizations, business leaders can drive innovation, build leadership capacity and increase sustainability impact. And as more companies adopt sustainability strategies and develop sustainable business models, they will benefit from the ideas, passion and drive of intrapreneurs.

Businesses can wait and hope that individual employees might organically take their own initiative. We think that this approach is too slow. While it may lead to incremental changes within the existing business model, it is often not disruptive enough. Disruptive change occurs when business models are questioned, challenged, rethought and redefined. We recommend that businesses actively develop an ecosystem that supports social intrapreneurs.

This can be done in several ways:

- Acknowledging where the company is struggling and needs help to deliver on its sustainability commitments.
- Creating innovation funds and the chance for employees to bid, often through competitive pitches to senior leaders, for resources, senior leadership mentoring and support and funding for their ideas.
- Running intrapreneurship labs, bootcamps and accelerator training programmes.
- Encouraging 'dynamic duos' – two-way mentoring between younger social intrapreneurs and older, more experienced managers who can provide wise counsel and help to navigate organizational politics, give 'air cover' and help find early-stage resources – and might in turn be helped, perhaps with digital skills and sustainability awareness. Such two-way mentoring can also be an effective way of tapping the enthusiasm of older employees who want to make a positive difference.
- Sponsoring high-flyers on external programmes such as the Aspen Institute's Business and Society First Movers programme.[17]

Many more organizations could benefit from initiatives that encourage intrapreneurism and that integrate those with corporate purpose and the business's strategies for innovation, new business development and talent and leadership development. By joining up their thinking and practice in this manner, companies will create more resilient leaders and a wider and more disruptive approach to innovation that helps new business models capable of accelerating sustainability to emerge.

Some things to watch out for include the dangers of loneliness or burnout – the need to stay balanced for the long haul by maintaining a work–life balance. Mental, emotional and physical well-being are all important, as is keeping one's vision of sustainability refreshed.

Over-personalization around one charismatic leader can be avoided by emphasizing distributed leadership, encouraging a wide range of leaders in the business to champion different aspects of the sustainability commitment.

High performers and others get attracted by big, bold sustainability commitments that the business makes, but when they get into the company, if they cannot get close enough to actual work on sustainability, they may grow disillusioned and leave. This can be mitigated by making sustainability part of everybody's business, creating champions' networks and promoting social intrapreneurism.

In practice

L'Oréal

L'Oréal is the world's largest cosmetics business, with 86,000 employees and annual sales of over $35 billion. The company was founded by a chemist in 1909 and remains headquartered in Paris, France, while operating in 150 countries.

L'Oréal has had a longstanding commitment to being an ethical and responsible business with intense communications and training on the L'Oréal Code of Business Ethics, including an annual Ethics Day when any employee could pose ethical dilemmas and queries to the CEO.

In 2013, L'Oréal adopted an ambitious first sustainability programme to kick off what it intended to be a profound transformation strategy. This was because the leadership recognized early on that to embed sustainability, it was not sufficient to have a few initiatives. There has to be transformational change.

In April 2021, L'Oréal launched a new sustainability strategy 'L'Oréal For the Future, Because our Planet is Worth it', integrated with the overall 'ambition' of L'Oréal. This includes commitments to 50 per cent reduction in CO_2 emissions per product by 2030, 100 per cent renewable energy (without offsetting) in all its 26 manufacturing plants across the world by 2025, 100 per cent recycled plastic, reformulating products based on 'Green science', so that by 2030, 100 per cent of the plant-based ingredients for formulas and packaging materials will be traceable and will come from sustainable sources. There is also a radical commitment to transparency with a dedicated website (Inside our Products) describing 1,000 listed ingredients and the opportunity for consumers to pose questions to the 4,000 L'Oréal scientists working on sustainability.

The company has long invested in leadership development, from new graduate trainees up to and including the leadership development needs of the top 250 leaders of the company, including a strong emphasis on the critical stage entry to senior leadership, when individuals become L'Oréal country managers. These leadership programmes include those internally developed and run and programmes conducted in partnership with long-term collaborators such as Cranfield Executive Development.

In recent years, leadership development has included an increasing emphasis on sustainability, emphasizing stakeholder engagement and how to encourage more collaborative ways of working such as 'LeadEnable'. As well as face-to-face courses and workshops, there are blended programmes with a mix of in-person and webinars and self-directed learning.

The central sustainability function headed by Executive Vice-President and Chief Sustainability Officer Alexandra Palt has also developed and runs a number of voluntary workshops and training sessions. These are available for any employee to upskill on sustainability. Each year a group of young high-flyers from L'Oréal are sponsored by the business to participate in the One Young World programme. L'Oréal has also encouraged intrapreneurship with an annual competition with cash prizes and the possibility of presenting to senior management. The sustainability department was also instrumental in ensuring that all L'Oréal brand and country managers' bonuses became linked to outcomes on sustainability targets.[18]

As Alexandra Palt says: 'Increasingly, companies are understanding that it will not be possible to thrive in a society that is not inclusive or sustainable.'[19]

Discovery Ltd South Africa

Discovery Ltd is a financial services organization that works within the healthcare, life assurance, banking and investment markets. Discovery has 12,950 employees globally[20] and FY2020 annual revenue of $64.8 billion.[21] Based in Sandton, South Africa, Discovery was founded in 1992 and operates in 20 countries.[22]

Discovery was founded on a core purpose of making people healthier and enhancing and protecting their lives. The company has a Shared Value business model to drive sustainable development. To support this, all new employees go through a five-day induction that concentrates on purpose, values, Shared Value and sustainability and all new financial products have to pass a Shared Value test. So, for example, health insurance customers are incentivized to improve their diet and eat more nutritiously, exercise more and adopt well-being practices. Similarly, motor insurance customers are incentivized to drive more carefully with a device in their car which monitors things like braking too fast or taking corners at speed. The Discovery rationale is that safer drivers and healthier policyholders mean fewer insurance claims and more profitable business, as well as being better for the individuals concerned and for the wider society.

One of the core ways in which Discovery drives corporate sustainability leadership is with a variety of governance systems and committees. Discovery's board meets with executive management and heads of control functions annually to review strategy, risks, key performance indicators and targets for executives. To supplement these meetings, the board receives periodic reports outlining the Group's sustainability strategy and its impact on communities, the planet and other stakeholders. Further, the board performs an annual assessment of the business model and sustainable development plan to ensure alignment with the Group's core purpose and to approve and supervise strategy implementation plans.

Discovery has implemented several programmes, such as the Discovery Foundation, Discovery Fund and Corporate Social Investment (CSI) initiatives that contribute to leadership development. Discovery staff participate in skills-based employee volunteering opportunities.[23] Discovery is working closely with the township of Orange Farm, outside Johannesburg, which is one of the largest informal settlements in the country. Volunteers are working with schools to develop the leadership skills of headteachers and applying the capabilities of the company to help improve local clinics and other facilities. They have developed an Entrepreneurship Centre where streetwise entrepreneurs from the vibrant, local informal sector can access telephones, computers, Wi-fi and the internet as well as marketing, sales and finance skills from Discovery volunteers.

Discovery has put a few senior leaders through the Cambridge Institute for Sustainability Leadership programme or the Global Compact Climate Accelerator course and participants then report back to the board on their learning – which also helps to determine if more Discovery leaders should go on these programmes.

At Discovery, sustainability leadership has been infused into all levels of management, from the board, to executives, to employee committees and into the community. Discovery understands that sustainability leadership can and should exist across all levels of management.

The group's Chief Executive, Adrian Gore, had this to say about Discovery's corporate sustainability vision: 'We believe strongly that business strategy cannot be executed or even conceived of separately from an understanding of its social impact.'[24] And regarding leadership, Gore states, 'We have a choice: a problem-centric leadership approach or a vision-based leadership approach, which is an antidote to declinism.'[25]

Summary

Capable leadership is critical to the success of any endeavour. Leaders have to be able to give a realistic assessment of the current situation, offer an inspiring vision of the future, articulate a credible strategy for getting from today to tomorrow and explain where and how particular teams and business units contribute to that strategy.

Our increasingly complex world makes sustainability leadership ever more critical, while changes in the world of work resulting from the COVID-19 pandemic and associated global lockdowns have created even more opportunities and new imperatives for sustainability leadership.

Action checklist

1 Review the organization's leadership competencies to include sustainability skills.

2 Update the company's in-house and external leadership training programmes and experiential development opportunities to ensure they are future fit.

3 Create appropriate learning and development strategies targeted at different levels of the business's leadership cohort.

4 Make sure individual and organizational sustainability performance is baked into bonus systems, rewards and recognition and vet incentive schemes to ensure there are no perverse incentives.

5 Consider if the company should have a specialist sustainability function and examine how this function will work closely with other functions and different parts of the business.

6 Explore additional leadership development opportunities such as the development of a sustainability champions' network and the encouragement of intrapreneurs.

7 Make sure there is an up-to-date code of ethics with communications and training to support it and that employees are encouraged to speak up and question unethical behaviour.

8 Empower leaders at all levels, from front-line supervisors to top executives, to be able and confident to talk about the organization's commitment to sustainability.

Further resources

- Brans, M, De Pree, M and Estrade, F (2020) *The Intrapreneur's Guide to Pathfinding*, League of Intrapreneurs

- For over three decades the Cambridge Institute for Sustainability Leadership has helped build individual and organizational leadership capacity and capabilities and created industry-leading collaborations, to catalyse change and accelerate the path to a sustainable economy, www.cisl.cam.ac.uk

- Grayson D, McLaren M, Spitzeck H (2014) *Social Intrapreneurism and all that Jazz*, Greenleaf Publishing (Routledge), Oxford

- Meadows, D (2008) *Thinking in Systems: A primer*, Earthscan

- SustainAbility (2008) *The Social Intrapreneur: A field guide for corporate changemakers*, Allianz, www.allianz.com/content/dam/onemarketing/azcom/Allianz_com/migration/media/current/en/press/news/studies/downloads/thesocialintrapreneur_2008.pdf

- The Oxford Character Project is an interdisciplinary initiative at the University of Oxford, dedicated to the cultivation of character and responsible leadership, oxfordcharacter.org/about-us

- There are also regularly updated resources on the website of The League of Intrapreneurs, www.leagueofintrapreneurs.com

- United Nations Global Compact and Russell Reynolds Associates (2020) *Leadership for the Decade of Action*, United Nations Global Compact and Russell Reynolds Associates

Endnotes

1 Business and Sustainable Development Commission (2017) *Better Business, Better World*, Business and Sustainable Development Commission

2 Quoted in Hougaard, R (2021) How Unilever develops leaders to be a force for good, Forbes, June.

3 See, for example, Strandberg Consulting (2015) *Sustainability Talent Management: The new business imperative,* Strandberg Consulting

4 See, for example, Cambridge Institute for Sustainability Leadership's (CISL) Cambridge Impact Leadership Model (2017), www.cisl.cam.ac.uk/resources/cisl-frameworks/leadership-hub/cambridge-impact-leadership-model (archived at https://perma.cc/4WYD-3G9V)

5 See, for example, *Leadership Skills for a Sustainable Economy* (2010), a report by a taskforce of business leaders convened by Business in the Community in the UK; or Faruk, A and Hoffmann, A (2012) *Sustainability and Leadership Competencies for Business Leaders*, BSR.

6 See, for example, Russell Reynolds (2020) *Building a Better World Through Sustainable Leadership*, Russell Reynolds Associates

7 See, for example, Hougaard, R (2021) How Unilever develops leaders to be a force for good, Forbes, June

8 See, for example, @YoungTrustees @Young_governors @DiversityGov @CharitySoWhite and @Beyond_Suffrage

9 Adapted from Grayson, D (2008) *The CR Middle-management Black-hole*, Cranfield School of Management

10 See, for example, Stern, S (2021) It is time for candid conversations at work, *Financial Times*, 29 August

11 Institute of International Finance and Deloitte (2021) *The Future of the Chief Sustainability Officer: Sense-maker in chief*, Institute of International Finance and Deloitte

12 Institute of International Finance and Deloitte (2021) *The Future of the Chief Sustainability Officer – Sense-maker in Chief*, Institute of International Finance and Deloitte

13 Institute of International Finance and Deloitte (2021) *The Future of the Chief Sustainability Officer – Sense-maker in Chief*, Institute of International Finance and Deloitte

14 Adapted from Corporate Responsibility Champions Network (2021) A 'how to' guide, #1 in the Doughty Centre 'How to Do Corporate Responsibility' Series, Doughty Centre for Corporate Responsibility – now the Cranfield School of Management Sustainability Group, www.cranfield.ac.uk/som/expertise/sustainability (archived at https://perma.cc/P5A3-XSSW)

15 Adapted from Corporate Responsibility Champions Network (2021) A 'how to' guide, #1 in the Doughty Centre 'How to Do Corporate Responsibility' Series, Doughty Centre for Corporate Responsibility – now the Cranfield School of Management Sustainability Group: www.cranfield.ac.uk/som/expertise/sustainability (archived at https://perma.cc/P5A3-XSSW).

16 This draws on earlier blogs by David Grayson for Business Fights Poverty and ESADE

17 www.aspeninstitute.org/programs/business-and-society-program/first-movers-fellowship-program/ (archived at https://perma.cc/B9ET-4GSW)

18 Developed from L'Oréal website, What Makes a Good Leader?, Beauty Tomorrow, October 21, 2019; and Sustainability – L'Oréal Master Class, Alexandra Palt, YouTube, 16 Nov 2020, www.youtube.com/watch?v=1gh-S0S1fFM (archived at https://perma.cc/Q44Q-JGV6)

19 L'Oréal Finance (2021) L'Oréal recognized for its leadership in sustainability by the UN Global Compact, press release, 20 September

20 Discovery (n.d.) Who we are: Disrupting financial services through shared value, Discovery, www.discovery.co.za/corporate/sustainability-who-we-are (archived at https://perma.cc/9RKQ-497A)

21 WSJ Markets (2021) Discovery Ltd, WSJ.com, 23 September, www.wsj.com/market-data/quotes/ZA/DSY/financials/annual/income-statement (archived at https://perma.cc/LR97-GF79)

22 Discovery (n.d.) Who we are: Disrupting financial services through shared value, Discovery, www.discovery.co.za/corporate/sustainability-who-we-are (archived at https://perma.cc/9RKQ-497A)

23 Discovery (2020) Discovery Integrated Annual Report 2020, www.discovery.co.za/assets/discoverycoza/corporate/investor-relations/2020/integrated-annual-report-2020.pdf (archived at https://perma.cc/S9T2-2J5M)

24 Discovery (n.d.) Corporate sustainability, Discovery, www.discovery.co.za/corporate/corporate-sustainability (archived at https://perma.cc/YK3D-SUC5)

25 Gore, A (2018) Are things really bad and getting worse? The case for positive leadership, Discovery, October, www.discovery.co.za/corporate/news-adrian-gore-the-case-for-positive-leadership (archived at https://perma.cc/TMR9-VWXC)

08

Reporting

What is it?

Sustainability reporting is a way for a company to disclose both its impacts on the world and how sustainability issues impact on it. Reporting improves transparency and visibility, supports sustainability strategy development and helps satisfy regulatory requirements.[1] Furthermore, it facilitates dialogue with stakeholders based on the common language it creates.

Sustainability reporting includes the disclosure and communication of ESG goals and progress towards them, and it helps companies set targets, measure performance and manage change to make their operations more sustainable.

Sustainability reporting and ESG disclosure is increasing globally. In 2011, 20 per cent of S&P 500 companies published sustainability reports; by 2019, that number reached 90 per cent.[2] The professional services firm KPMG has produced reviews of what is now called sustainability reporting since 1993. In its 2020 edition, it found that such reporting is nearly ubiquitous among the world's largest businesses. Nearly all (96 per cent) of the world's 250 largest businesses now report. Further, across the 100 largest businesses in each of more than 50 countries (the N100), KPMG recorded that the percentage of companies reporting has increased from 12 per cent in 1993 to 80 per cent in 2020. This equates to 90 per cent in the Americas N100,

84 per cent across Asia-Pacific, 77 per cent in Europe and 59 per cent in the Middle East and Africa. KPMG concludes: 'Companies not reporting are out of step with global norms.'[3]

It is important to distinguish between sustainability reporting and sustainability reports. A report is one output of the reporting process, but businesses use the data and insights generated from that process in multiple ways, such as to respond to investor requests for disclosure, sustainability ratings and rankings such as CDP, on their own websites, in speeches and op-eds and for social media posts.

A second distinction to consider is whether companies use generally accepted standards (typically the case when 'reporting financially') or whether they use self-determined metrics, which makes comparisons of performance difficult – if not impossible – and opens up those companies to accusations of greenwashing.

Why it matters

Sustainability reporting provides value to companies in many ways.

- Sustainability reporting satisfies growing investor interest around ESG. Sustainability performance may affect the cost of capital if a company is borrowing. More and more investment products use ESG rankings and ratings to determine where to invest. As Polly Ghazi writes on Triple Pundit: 'Pressure is growing on companies to manage ESG risk and harness related opportunity from across the investment spectrum.'[4]

- Sustainability reporting helps improve transparency and visibility. A 2021 survey of company reporters across the globe found this by far the main motivation quoted by businesses.[5]

- It demonstrates company purpose in action and helps reinforce an open and transparent culture.

- It creates and organizes the data and insights needed to craft a robust sustainability strategy.

- It signals commitment to sustainability to current and prospective employees, helps build trust with external stakeholders and helps meet growing expectations for disclosure for both public and privately held companies.

- It enables continuous improvement and action. As a 2020 BSR report argues: 'High-quality sustainability reports allow for business transformation and performance improvement at companies, by enabling investment in resilient business strategies that improve company performance.'[6] Conversely, reporting can create the data required to rebut allegations about poor performance.[7]

- Increasingly, governments, multilateral organizations and other stakeholders (including financial stakeholders) are using reported information to hold companies accountable for their impacts and assess risks.

- For a private company, it may be what the owners expect, and it can be used in dialogue with them – for example, to explain how sustainability may affect future value and/or to demonstrate and communicate wise stewardship in a multi-generational family business. It may also support communications to a controlling family council or family office that looks after a family's business interests or to private equity investors who hold stakes in the enterprise.

- For state-owned enterprises (SOEs), it is often a requirement. In China, for example, there has been a spike in reports from SOEs from 2006 onwards after SASAC[8] (the body that controls the Chinese state's ownership of the 115 or so largest SOEs) started requiring sustainability reporting.

- Sustainability reporting helps businesses respond to and perform well on the ratings and rankings they value most, such as CDP, MSCI, the Dow Jones Sustainability Indices, Great Place to Work, etc. It also helps to satisfy certification requirements such as B Corp.

- It is increasingly a listing requirement for the public companies quoted on stock exchanges around the world, especially for the more than one hundred exchanges affiliated to the Sustainable Stock Exchanges Initiative.[9]

- In a growing number of jurisdictions, there are growing regulatory requirements related to sustainability / ESG performance disclosure applying to both public and private companies. The forthcoming European Corporate Sustainability Reporting Directive makes reporting a market entry requirement for over 55,000 companies.

How to do it

Sustainability reporting is a cornerstone of sustainable business and involves a number of critical steps.

Step 1: Clarify some basic reporting questions

At the outset, it is important to clarify the following:

- Why the business is undertaking sustainability reporting (see the previous Why it matters section).

- The intended audiences for reporting and disclosure and uses of the results – for example, to enable investor relations teams to brief institutional investors on sustainability or ESG performance, to communicate to employees and customers and/or to respond to key ratings and rankings.

- The legal and regulatory requirements reporting must comply with, such as in the UK, where businesses with a turnover of £36 million or more must report annually on the steps that they have taken to ensure that slavery and human trafficking are not taking place in their own business or in their supply chains.[10] Also, at the time of writing, the European Union is negotiating a proposed Corporate Sustainability Reporting Directive (CSRD), which will include the launch of European Corporate Sustainability Reporting Standards.

The directive will likely be passed by the end of June 2022, and it is expected to require companies to start reporting in line with its standards in 2024. It is estimated that the CSRD will cover 55,000 companies, a great leap from the 11,000 captured under the current EU Non-Financial Reporting Directive.

- Whether the company will seek to have some or all of its sustainability reporting externally assured. The KPMG Survey of Sustainability Reporting 2020 found that assurance of sustainability has become a majority practice among the largest companies, with 71 per cent of the Global 250 using external assurance in 2020 as compared to 46 per cent in 2011.[11] Under the EU's proposed CSRD, third-party assurance of the data will be mandatory.[12]

Step 2:   Study and choose preferred options from among the major reporting guidelines and frameworks

It is not essential to use one of the established sustainability reporting guidelines or frameworks, but it is good practice to do so and it has become increasingly expected, especially for larger, more global businesses. Understanding and choosing among reporting tools can be somewhat overwhelming for first-time reporters, as the number and type of them is proliferating. Some of the key frameworks are outlined and explained below.

The Global Reporting Initiative (GRI) and the Sustainability Accounting Standards Board (SASB) are the default starting points for many organizations and the most commonly used, often in combination as they serve different purposes and audiences.

- GRI: The Global Reporting Initiative began in 1997 and published the first version of what was then the GRI Guidelines in 2000, providing the first global framework for sustainability reporting. In 2016, GRI transitioned from providing guidelines to setting the first global standards for sustainability reporting, the GRI Standards. The Standards continue to be updated and expanded and now include 34 specific Topic Standards. GRI is without question one of the most widely used and influential reporting frameworks. According to the 2020 KPMG survey of sustainability reporting, GRI remains the dominant framework for large companies, with over 7 in 10 (73 per cent) of the G250 reporting using GRI.

- SASB: The Sustainability Accounting Standards Board is a non-profit organization founded in the USA in 2011 to develop sustainability accounting standards to inform investors. SASB's unique focus is to surface the ESG issues that materially impact the financial performance of the typical company in each of 77 industries. As of June 2021, SASB comes under the auspices of the Value Reporting Foundation.

Beyond GRI and SASB, there are more specialist reporting guidelines that are worth assessing:

- CDP started life in 2000 as the Carbon Disclosure Foundation, and its remit has extended to encompass forests and water as well as carbon.

- The Task Force on Climate-Related Financial Disclosures (TCFD) aims to create 'more effective climate-related disclosures that could promote more informed investment, credit, and insurance underwriting decisions and, in turn, enable stakeholders to understand better the concentrations of carbon-related assets in the financial sector and the financial system's exposures to climate-related risks'.[13] TCFD is growing in importance as climate becomes an existential challenge for the world and as TCFD is taken up more widely by investors, governments and other stakeholders. Investors tend to recommend it, while governments are using it to shape climate disclosure regulation like that which the UK has in place, and which more than 100 other countries are presently developing / considering.

Companies embarking on sustainability reporting need to make the best choices regarding guidelines and frameworks for themselves and tailor their approach over time. Increasingly, these choices are influenced by growing demand from investors for more and better ESG performance disclosure, as well as calls from a range of stakeholders to build stronger accountability for sustainable performance of business. Significantly, in his 2020 annual letter to CEOs, Larry Fink of BlackRock wrote:

> Important progress improving disclosure has already been made –
> and many companies already do an exemplary job of integrating and
> reporting on sustainability – but we need to achieve more widespread
> and standardized adoption. While no framework is perfect, BlackRock
> believes that the Sustainability Accounting Standards Board (SASB)
> provides a clear set of standards for reporting sustainability information
> across a wide range of issues, from labor practices to data privacy to
> business ethics. For evaluating and reporting climate-related risks, as
> well as the related governance issues that are essential to managing
> them, the TCFD provides a valuable framework…
>
> BlackRock has been engaging with companies for several years on their
> progress towards TCFD- and SASB-aligned reporting. This year, we
> are asking the companies that we invest in on behalf of our clients to:
> (1) publish a disclosure in line with industry-specific SASB guidelines
> by year end, if you have not already done so or disclose a similar set
> of data in a way that is relevant to your particular business; and (2)
> disclose climate-related risks in line with the TCFD's recommendations,
> if you have not already done so. This should include your plan for
> operating under a scenario where the Paris Agreement's goal of limiting
> global warming to less than two degrees is fully realized, as expressed
> by the TCFD guidelines.
>
> We will use these disclosures and our engagements to ascertain whether
> companies are properly managing and overseeing these risks within
> their business and adequately planning for the future. **In the absence
> of robust disclosures, investors, including BlackRock, will increasingly
> conclude that companies are not adequately managing risk.** [Emphasis
> added][14]

Fink and other investors are looking from their perspective as investors as to what financial data they need. Crucially – as Peter Paul van de Wijs, Chief External Affairs Officer of the GRI, told us – 'The international debate has now reached the point where it is accepted that there will be two pillars to reporting – financial reporting (strengthened with value reporting) and impact reporting.' Van de Wijs elaborates:

1 There is inadequate publicly available information about how non-financial issues, and sustainability issues in particular, impact companies, and about how companies themselves impact society and the environment. In particular:

   a. Reported non-financial information is not sufficiently comparable or reliable.

   b. Companies do not report all non-financial information that users think is necessary, and many report information that users do not think is relevant.

   c. Quite a few companies from which investors and other users want non-financial information do not report such information. Around the globe there are major differences in the adoption level of non-financial reporting practices.

   d. It is hard for investors and other users to find non-financial information even when it is reported.

2 Companies incur unnecessary and avoidable costs related to reporting non-financial information. Companies face uncertainty and complexity when deciding what non-financial information to report, and how and where to report such information. In the case of some financial sector companies, this complexity may also arise from different disclosure requirements contained in different pieces of legislation around the world. In addition, companies are under pressure to respond to additional demands for non-financial information from sustainability rating agencies, data providers and civil society. Efforts such as mandating sustainability reporting for all companies on the European Market (the new CSRD), and the steps the IFRS is taking, go a long way towards addressing these issues.[15]

We recognize that the landscape of sustainability standards setters and ratings can appear complicated. This is why many businesses employ external consultants to help at least with their first one or two sustainability reports. There are specialist firms that can help to write and/or design sustainability reports as well as advising which frameworks to use. The reality, though, is that there are only two global reporting standards (GRI and SASB). It is best to start with one of those.

Step 3: Collect the data

The overall foundation of a business's sustainability reporting should be based on the outcomes of its materiality assessment (see Chapter 2) and its sustainability strategy and commitments (see Chapter 4). Organizations undertaking sustainability reporting must develop data management systems to track (and have auditable for assurance) all the information required to support disclosure. The objective should be to collect the data in such a way that it can be used for multiple purposes such as meeting legal requirements, providing evidence for sustainability ratings and rankings or to give evidence of the sustainability / ESG policies, practices and performance required for supplier tender lists and to meet procurement inquiries.

This requires engagement with key functions to identify relevant metrics and data and have them report on these, aggregation of the data across the enterprise, a detailed review of all metrics and a circle back to internal stakeholders to improve reporting over time.

As sustainability reporting has become more sophisticated, companies need to build on their existing internal management software to collect the data, some of which will already feed into their management reports and some of which will already be needed for regulatory reporting purposes.

There is an expectation that artificial intelligence, Big Data, machine learning and other new technologies will help to propel more innovation in the organization and wider availability of the raw material required to support sustainability reporting. As Jeanne Boillet from professional services firm EY observes: 'KPIs involving trust, culture, ESG risks, and ESG reporting can be measured using AI. But there is a learning curve, and organizations risk getting left behind if they do not understand what AI can do and have the people with the expertise to use it effectively.'[16] There is certainly more pressure to improve the quality and comparability of sustainability data.

Step 4: Report and make full use of data

Once you have your data and a disclosure strategy employing the preferred sustainability reporting guidelines and frameworks for your organization, you will be able to decide communication channels for each target audience. This is why it is important to understand stakeholders' ESG data information needs. For example, a business needs to consider how sustainability performance data will be used to support meetings with investors. It also helps if a business can publicize who in the company is responsible for each aspect of its sustainability strategy and its key targets / themes and give stakeholders a way to contact them.

Consideration is also needed as to how sustainability reporting will relate to the business's traditional annual report and accounts. For some companies, this is solved by developing and issuing an integrated report (see box, Integrated reporting). Where integrated reporting is not done, it is crucial to ensure consistency of messaging

---

INTEGRATED REPORTING

The concept of integrated reporting has been gaining support in business and the accounting profession. According to Deloitte, 'Integrated Reporting brings together material information about an organization's strategy, governance, performance and prospects in a way that reflects the commercial, social and environmental context within which it operates. It leads to a clear and concise articulation of [a business's] value creation story which is useful and relevant to all stakeholders.' The idea is that, rather than a business producing only its traditional Annual Report and

Accounts, which tend to be backward looking and compliance driven, and then a separate sustainability report, it would produce an *integrated* report, which could encourage longer-term perspectives both for the business and for investors. According to the 2020 KPMG Survey of Sustainability Reporting, the percentage of the world's largest businesses producing an integrated report continued to rise between 2017 and 2020, when the N100 rose from 14 per cent to 16 per cent and the G250 from 14 per cent to 22 per cent. The KPMG survey shows that Japan is the leader in voluntary adoption of integrated reporting by the largest companies (7 per cent). South Africa has more (94 per cent) integrated reporters, but this is because the country mandates integrated reporting on a 'comply or explain why not' basis and because it is a JSE (Johannesburg Stock Exchange) listing requirement. The International Integrated Reporting Council developed the Integrated Reporting <IR> Framework in 2013.[17] The IIRC has now come together with SASB to form the Value Reporting Foundation.

and data between specialist sustainability reporting and traditional corporate reporting as well as across platforms (report, website, social media, speeches, etc.) and to different stakeholders.

Step 5: Learn from process and innovate further

We don't underestimate the degree of work required nor the increasing complexity of sustainability reporting. As Thomas Singer of The Conference Board has observed:

> Companies face a daunting challenge… being mindful of the expectations for increased and standardized ESG disclosure, while at the same time focusing their sustainability efforts on the issues that are most material to their business and telling their story authentically and effectively to multiple constituencies.[18]

However, the majority of the disclosures are already captured within corporations as part of management systems and regulatory reporting requirements. Aligning them and compiling these disclosures to meet sustainability reporting is the challenge.

Part of the problem is that whereas companies typically have whole departments dedicated to financial reporting (and do not question that commitment), sustainability reporting is often done by one or two people and, even then, perhaps only as a percentage of their role.

In a 2021 survey of company reporters by Swedish-headquartered consultancy Worldfavour, respondents were asked to state their main challenges in producing a sustainability report. The top five quoted were:

- collecting data (57 per cent);
- poor data quality (46 per cent);
- managing data and gaining insights (41 per cent);
- lack of time (36 per cent);
- process too time consuming (34 per cent).

This makes learning from other sustainability reporters to improve the reporting process essential – ditto using the outputs from reporting to help the business improve core sustainability performance to ensure the company gets value from its investment. It helps if reporting becomes an integrated part of business processes.

Step 6: Be prepared for more reporting requirements

As the academic and sustainability activist Prof Robert Eccles wrote in a Forbes op-ed in January 2021: 'The world is no longer debating the need for global mandated standards for sustainability reporting. The debate is now about what exactly is meant by this term, what role the relevant organizations should play, and what is the best path for developing these standards as quickly as possible.'[19] As a result, as Carmine Di Sibio, Global Chairman and Chief Executive Officer, EY and Ruchi Bhowmik, Global Vice-Chair, Public Policy, EY, argue on a WEF blog in June 2021: 'The business world is soon likely to see some of the most significant innovations in corporate accounting and reporting in decades.'[20] This will likely include the EU's Corporate Sustainability Reporting Directive, which will impact beyond the borders of the EU. Crucially, the CSRD proposal applies double

FIGURE 8.1 A fusion of traditional financial reporting and extra financial reporting

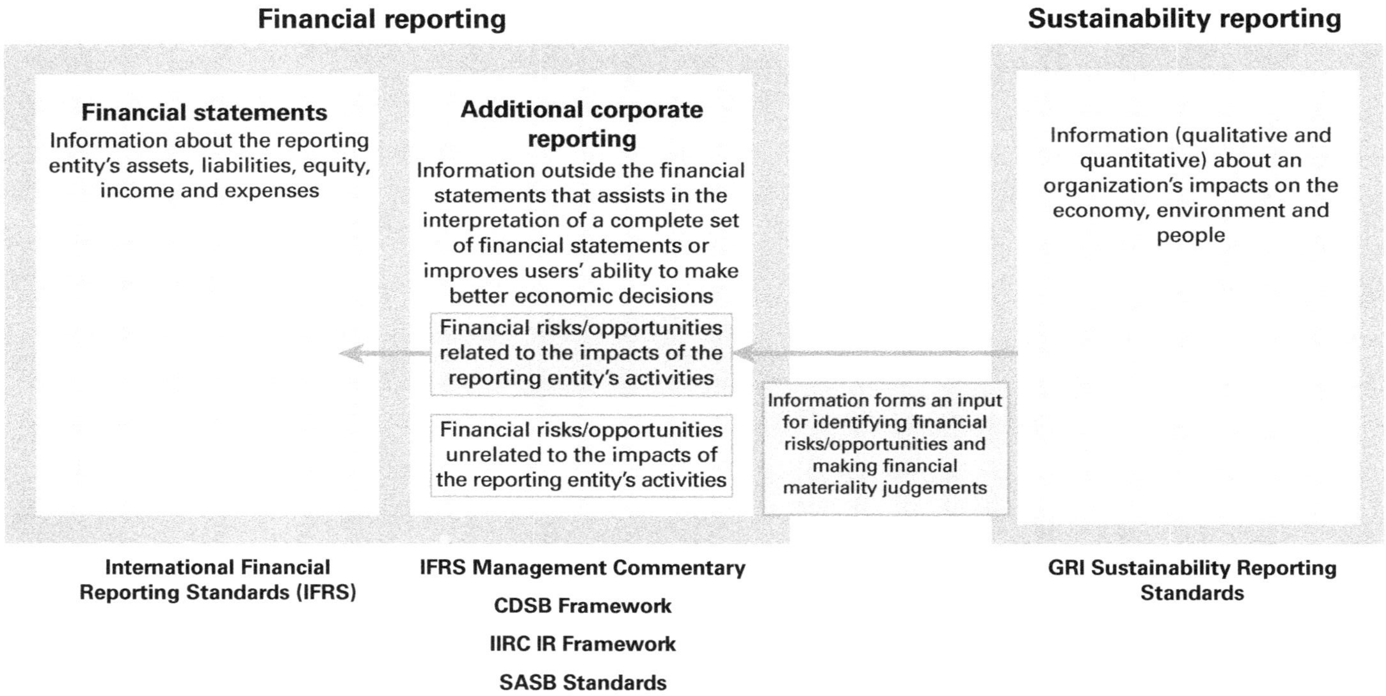
Financial reporting
Sustainability reporting
Financial statements
Information about the reporting entity's assets, liabilities, equity, income and expenses
Additional corporate reporting
Information outside the financial statements that assists in the interpretation of a complete set of financial statements or improves users' ability to make better economic decisions
Financial risks/opportunities related to the impacts of the reporting entity's activities
Financial risks/opportunities unrelated to the impacts of the reporting entity's activities
Information forms an input for identifying financial risks/opportunities and making financial materiality judgements
Information (qualitative and quantitative) about an organization's impacts on the economy, environment and people
International Financial Reporting Standards (IFRS)
IFRS Management Commentary
CDSB Framework
IIRC IR Framework
SASB Standards
GRI Sustainability Reporting Standards

Reproduced with kind permission of GRI

materiality (see Chapter 2). As a BSR blogger observes: 'For businesses that have historically assessed only risks to their business rather than their impacts on the world, the CSRD implies a fundamental shift in measurement and reporting.'[21]

The Value Reporting Foundation – as already explained – is the result of the merger of the IIRC and SASB. It is part of wider moves to simplify and improve the guidelines and frameworks for sustainability reporting. The CDP, CDSB, GRI, IIRC and SASB have published a first attempt to create a common vision of the future of sustainability reporting: Statement of Intent to Work Together Towards Comprehensive Corporate Reporting (September 2020).

There are two further developments to watch. the IFRS Foundation is a not-for-profit, public interest organization established to develop a single set of high-quality, understandable, enforceable and globally accepted accounting standards and to promote and facilitate adoption of the standards. The IFRS Foundation has a standard-setting body, the International Accounting Standards Board. The IFRS Foundation will become more involved in sustainability / ESG reporting. This is particularly so because the Big Four global accounting firms – Deloitte, EY, KPMG and PwC – have developed a set of ESG reporting metrics around four pillars of the principles of governance, planet, people and prosperity in collaboration with the World (ISSB) Economic Forum. At COP26 Climate Conference the creation of an 'International Sustainability Standards Board' alongside the International Accounting Standards Board, under IFRS auspices was announced. The goal is to develop standards focused on the impacts of sustainability issues on a company's financial health and value creation, with a focus on addressing the needs of the investors. The Climate Disclosure Standards and the Value Reporting Foundation are also to be consolidated in ISSB.

Secondly, the EU, GRI and potentially the IFRS are all considering developing biodiversity standards, perhaps influenced by the TNFD (the Taskforce on Nature-Related Financial Disclosures), which began work in June 2021 as a 'new market-led global initiative to provide financial institutions and corporates with a complete picture of their environmental risks and opportunities'. The objective is 'to support a shift in global financial flows away from nature-negative outcomes and towards nature-positive outcomes'. The TNFD framework will be tested and refined in 2022 before its launch and dissemination in 2023. TNFD's intention is to build on the success of the TCFD.

In practice

Stora Enso[22]

Stora Enso is a pulp and paper industry company with close to 23,000 employees and a 2020 annual revenue of slightly more than $10 billion. With roots going back as far as the 1300s, the company is headquartered in Helsinki, Finland, and sells goods in more than 50 countries globally.

The company utilizes its expertise in renewable materials to create value in packaging, biomaterials, wooden construction and paper sales. It develops and produces solutions based on wood and biomass for a range of industries and applications worldwide, leading in the bioeconomy and supporting its customers in meeting demand for renewable eco-friendly products. Stora Enso's purpose, 'Do good for people and the planet. Replace non-renewable materials with renewable products', underpins its belief that everything that can be made with fossil-based materials today can be made from a tree tomorrow.

Stora Enso's 2019 Annual Report is highlighted by WBCSD in its *Reporting Matters 2020: Maintaining ambition amidst disruption* compendium as a great example of conciseness and alignment with outcomes of materiality assessment. The report is praised for being drafted in a manner that helps avoid information overload while improving coherence and shining a spotlight on the issues that are the most important to the organization and its stakeholders. The report also provides a concise overview of Stora Enso's KPIs, corporate targets and progress on each materiality topic and makes this page separately downloadable online. The 2020 Annual Report continues this legacy, putting on the cover that sustainability is one of the five core aspects around which disclosure revolves.

Stora Enso's sustainability reporting webpage is reader-friendly, avoiding information overload and listing clear categories for stakeholders to pick among in order to get to the disclosure they are seeking. In addition to reporting in accordance with the GRI guidelines, Stora Enso has aligned its disclosure to the SASB guidelines and the TCFD framework, helping keep it abreast of the needs of its stakeholders.

Stora Enso's Executive Vice President of Sustainability, Annette Stube, commented: 'You can regard annual reporting as a compliance exercise, but it is actually much more value-adding if it is approached as storytelling – telling the story of the company – while standing firmly on the sound accounting principles, e.g. reporting on what is material to the company and its impacts – both the positive and the negative.'[23]

CEMEX[24]

CEMEX is a vertically integrated heavy building materials company with more than 41,000 employees and 2020 annual revenue of $13 billion. The company, headquartered in San Pedro Garza García, Mexico, was founded in 1906 and now operates in more than 50 countries worldwide.

CEMEX has four core businesses: cement, ready-mix concrete, aggregates and urbanization solutions. The company's mission is 'To create sustainable value by providing innovative products and solutions to satisfy the construction needs of its customers around the world.'

CEMEX has invested heavily in ESG disclosure and performance, and its inclusion in leading ESG indices is a testament to its commitment towards continuous improvement of its reporting and communications. In addition to aligning its reporting with the GRI guidelines, the company also reports in line with the SASB Construction Material industry-specific requirements and the TCFD guidelines. CEMEX's efforts have been recognized by inclusion in CDP's Climate Change Leaders of the Industry, DJSI's MILA Pacific Alliance Index, FTSE4Good, the MSCI ESG Leaders Index, Vigeo Eiris and the Mexican Stock Exchange Sustainability Index.

A significant milestone in CEMEX's reporting journey came in 2008 when the company assembled a group of independent, external experts to advise on its sustainability disclosure efforts. CEMEX's Sustainable Development Reporting Advisory Panel provides feedback on its sustainability reporting to ensure continuous improvement. The panel members, who work in various fields related to sustainability, represent the company's key stakeholder groups and the regions where it operates. Members are asked to be on the panel for two years so that they will have time to gain a deeper understanding of CEMEX and be able to comment on the progress. This advisory panel has helped enhance and distinguish CEMEX's sustainability reporting.

CEMEX's 2019 Integrated Report is featured by WBCSD in *Reporting Matters 2020: Maintaining ambition amidst disruption* as a strong example of a well-balanced report. The report is praised for being transparent about the organization's present and future risks, successes, failures, challenges and opportunities.

According to CEMEX's 2019 report, 'Targeting our stakeholders' needs, since 2008 we have advanced our commitment to sustainability reporting by following the GRI standards and creating our materiality assessment.'[25]

Summary

We can do no better here than quote guidance from the New York Stock Exchange (NYSE) on sustainability reporting, which states that sustainability reporting needs to be 'accurate, balanced, comparable and contextualized'. The NYSE goes on to say:

> ESG reporting and disclosure is an opportunity for companies to tell their own ESG story. High-quality ESG reporting builds trust with shareholders and key stakeholders and demonstrates that a company understands how ESG issues affect its ability to create long-term value. Reporting should be an output, not an end in itself. It should reflect what your company is doing to manage your ESG risks and

opportunities. ESG disclosure is most compelling when your company explains:

- Why you have focused on the issues that you have (stakeholder engagement, materiality)
- What your company is doing about those issues (strategy, measurement, targets)
- What oversight your company has in place to make sure you stay on track (governance).

The NYSE also wisely notes that, 'The best report is not the longest one, but the one that demonstrates focus and understanding of the issues.'[26]

Action checklist

1 Be clear about legal and listing requirements as well as stakeholder expectations for sustainability reporting.

2 Ensure that there is a rigorous process for accurate and timely data collection and consider using a data-collection platform or software system.

3 Choose the sustainability reporting guidelines and frameworks that will meet the needs of your business and the expectations of its key stakeholders including investors.

4 Develop a compelling narrative that is accurate, clear, concise and comparable over time, provides sufficient context and gives a balanced, honest account of both successes and failures in the implementation of the company's sustainability strategy.

5 Make key information and insights available through a variety of media and formats to optimize engagement with different stakeholders.

6 Treat the sustainability reporting process as a fundamental component of embedding sustainability into the business and as a powerful driver of continuous improvement.

Further resources

Websites of GRI, SASB, TCFD, TNFD, various ratings, IIRC, WBA, WBCSD and other reporting analysis such as:

- *A Practical Guide to Sustainability Reporting Using GRI and SASB Standards*, produced by GRI and SASB, with support from PwC, The Impact Management Project and ClimateWorks Foundation

- BSR (2020) Five steps to good sustainability reporting: A practical guide for companies, BSR, November, www.bsr.org/en/our-insights/report-view/five-steps-to-good-sustainability-reporting

- EY (2021) The Future of Sustainability Reporting Standards – EY2021, assets.ey.com/content/dam/ey-sites/ey-com/en_gl/topics/sustainability/ey-the-future-of-sustainability-reporting-standards-june-2021.pdf

- For examples of sustainability reports, there are portals such as sustainability-reports: www.sustainability-reports.com

- GRI/UNGC (n.d.) Integrating the SDGs into corporate reporting: A practical guide integrating SDGs into sustainability reporting, www.globalreporting.org/public-policy-partnerships/sustainable-development/integrating-sdgs-into-sustainability-reporting/

- KPMG IMPACT (2020) The Time Has Come: The KPMG survey of sustainability reporting, December, home.kpmg/xx/en/home/insights/2020/11/the-time-has-come-survey-of-sustainability-reporting.html

- The Climate Disclosure Standards Board (CDSB) is an international consortium of business and environmental NGOs. They are committed to advancing and aligning the global mainstream corporate reporting model to equate natural capital with financial capital. CDSB does this by offering companies a framework for reporting environmental information with the same rigour as financial information

- The UN Global Compact website has a section with reports from signatory companies: www.unglobalcompact.org

Endnotes

1 Authors' composite definition developed from definitions of Boston College Centre for Corporate Citizenship, Intertek and Worldfavour

2 Ghazi, P (2020) Sustainability reporting by the largest US companies hits new highs, Triple Pundit, 27 July, www.triplepundit.com/story/2020/sustainability-reporting-new-highs/121006 (archived at https://perma.cc/Y3T8-847X)

3 For key trends in global sustainability reporting see: KPMG IMPACT (2020) The time has come: The KPMG survey of sustainability reporting 2020, December, home.kpmg/xx/en/home/insights/2020/11/the-time-has-come-survey-of-sustainability-reporting.html (archived at https://perma.cc/YD6L-45KF)

4 Ghazi, P (2020) Sustainability reporting by the largest US companies hits new highs, Triple Pundit, 27 July, www.triplepundit.com/story/2020/sustainability-reporting-new-highs/121006 (archived at https://perma.cc/4MT9-N39G)

5 Worldfavor (2021) Worldfavor Report 2021 – Navigating the landscape of sustainability reporting, blog.worldfavor.com/news/navigating-the-landscape-of-sustainability-reporting (archived at https://perma.cc/7REF-XYNV)

6 BSR (2020) Five steps to good sustainability reporting: A practical guide for companies, November, www.bsr.org/en/our-insights/report-view/five-steps-to-good-sustainability-reporting (archived at https://perma.cc/YD8L-TC5Y)

7 Swartz, J (2010) How I did it: Timberland's CEO on standing up to 65,000 angry activists, *HBR Magazine*, September, hbr.org/2010/09/how-i-did-it-timberlands-ceo-on-standing-up-to-65000-angry-activists (archived at https://perma.cc/5AC3-URCW) This is a fascinating *Harvard Business Review* article by the then CEO of Timberland about what happened when the campaigning NGO Greenpeace organized a campaign alleging Timberland complicity in the destruction of Amazonian rainforest to make way for grazing lands for cattle from which Timberland sourced leather for its boots, belts etc. As Jeff Schwartz explains in the article, when the campaign began, Timberland simply didn't know about where it sourced its leather from.

8 The State-Owned Assets Supervision and Administration Commission of the State Council (SASAC), en.sasac.gov.cn/ (archived at https://perma.cc/2QKW-DSRY)

9 sseinitiative.org/ (archived at https://perma.cc/R86Z-NAN8)

10 Section 54 of the 2015 Modern Slavery Act.

11 KPMG IMPACT (2020) The time has come: The KPMG survey of sustainability reporting 2020, December, home.kpmg/xx/en/home/insights/2020/11/the-time-has-come-survey-of-sustainability-reporting.html (archived at https://perma.cc/8T4C-JESA)

12 Bancilhon, C (2021) What business needs to know about the EU corporate sustainability reporting directive, BSR [blog], 6 July, www.bsr.org/en/our-insights/blog-view/what-business-needs-to-know-about-the-eu-corporate-sustainability-reporting (archived at https://perma.cc/2L75-ZJG4)

13 www.fsb-tcfd.org/about/ (archived at https://perma.cc/5X5G-4UQY)

14 Larry Fink letter to CEOs 2020, 14 January, BlackRock

15 Exchange with authors September 2021

16 Boillet, J (2020) How AI will enable a better understanding of long-term value, EY [blog], 25 September, www.ey.com/en_fi/assurance/how-ai-will-enable-a-better-understanding-of-long-term-value (archived at https://perma.cc/6SC5-2CML)

17 www.integratedreporting.org/news/iirc-publishes-revisions-to-international-framework-to-enable-enhanced-reporting/ (archived at https://perma.cc/FGL2-8VPU)

18 Stringer, Thomas (n.d.) The Conference Board quoted in Green Biz, www.greenbiz.com/article/4-things-you-should-know-about-sustainability-reporting-practices (archived at https://perma.cc/XJH6-YHHA)

19 Eccles, R (2021) 2020: The year the narrative changed for sustainability reporting, Forbes, 6 January

20 Di Sibio, C and Bhowmik, R (2021) Sustainability reporting: Five ways companies should prepare, WEF [blog], 21 June, www.weforum.org/agenda/2021/06/sustainability-reporting-five-ways-companies-should-prepare/ (archived at https://perma.cc/5J8C-3CXS)

21 Bancilhon, C (2021) What business needs to know about the EU corporate sustainability reporting directive, BSR [blog], 6 July, www.bsr.org/en/our-insights/blog-view/what-business-needs-to-know-about-the-eu-corporate-sustainability-reporting (archived at https://perma.cc/9NMM-HX8L)

22 This profile has been sourced from Stora Enso Annual Report 2020, www.storaenso.com/en/about-stora-enso (archived at https://perma.cc/6UDF-AE5U); www.storaenso.com/en/sustainability/sustainability-reporting (archived at https://perma.cc/6RCT-8ULY); docs.wbcsd.org/2020/10/WBCSD_Reporting_Matters_2020.pdf (archived at https://perma.cc/4JQZ-YEQV)

23 Exchange with authors September 2021

24 Profile sourced from Cemex Integrated Report 2020, www.cemex.com/sustainability/overview (archived at https://perma.cc/A4CC-AP3Y); www.cemex.com/sustainability/reports/external-advisory-panel (archived at https://perma.cc/CM3M-4Q27); docs.wbcsd.org/2020/10/WBCSD_Reporting_Matters_2020.pdf (archived at https://perma.cc/C7UB-S9BZ)

25 www.cemex.com/documents/20143/49694544/IntegratedReport2019.pdf (archived at https://perma.cc/QB8F-WG79)

26 www.nyse.com/esg-guidance (archived at https://perma.cc/7L93-9G9Q)

09

Governance

What is it?

Good corporate governance means that the board is responsible for approving strategy, monitoring progress against strategy, providing independent challenge and counsel to the executive team, setting senior management compensation and ensuring robust succession planning for the board itself as regards the appointment and, where necessary, removal of the CEO. Ultimately, the board is accountable for the long-term success of the company. The board also is responsible for determining the nature and extent of the risks it is willing to take to achieve the firm's strategic objectives, and it is the ultimate custodian of corporate purpose, values and culture.

We define sustainability or ESG governance as: The formal processes established by the board of a company to ensure oversight of the company's responsibilities for its social, environmental and economic impacts and to guarantee that a company's specific sustainability commitments are met. A sustainability / ESG-competent board will be one 'where board members are proficient in sustainability, with the right governance, and confident asking management the right questions'.[1]

A commitment to good sustainability governance extends traditional board roles in several ways, including:

- Ensuring the purpose of the business is authentic, clear, compelling, inspiring and practical (see Chapter 1).

- Supporting sustainability strategy development and then approving and reviewing it as well as overseeing performance on the company's material ESG issues and its purpose. As sustainability strategy becomes more central to overall corporate strategy this is ever more key to the work of board directors (see Chapter 4).

- Articulating what corporate sustainability specifically means for the business and how improving the ESG performance of the business will enhance long-term value creation and increase resilience (see Chapters 3 and 4).

- Clarifying that the board has a holistic and comprehensive philosophy of corporate responsibility and sustainability, meaning a view that encompasses both risk mitigation and opportunity maximization.

- Defining the desired culture of the business ensuring that culture encourages the embedding of sustainability throughout the organization (see Chapter 6).

- Checking on the operationalization and implementation of agreed strategy, regularly examining the most material sustainability risks to strategy and ensuring effective risk mitigation (see Chapter 5).

- Considering whether risks related to the company's environmental, social and economic impacts are part of the company's corporate risk register, ensuring internal audit sees poor management of material sustainability / ESG issues as a potential risk to be monitored and tracking these impacts and issues during board discussions of corporate risk.

- Taking sustainability / ESG performance into account when setting CEO and senior management team remuneration and bonuses.

- Ensuring that sustainability considerations are taken fully into account when debating proposed mergers and acquisitions and joint ventures to identify any financial, reputational and other costs / risks that could surface if any involved party has a poor sustainability track record.

- Signalling to the enterprise, shareholders and other stakeholders that sustainability is a priority, and it is being led from the very top.

Why it matters

There are many reasons why getting the role of the board right is a critical part of a successful sustainable business:

- Unless boards own and act on the commitment to embed sustainability, progress will be limited at best because boards are not pressing management for high performance on sustainability.
- Board engagement on sustainability signals this is a priority and galvanizes the rest of the organization.
- Unless vision, purpose and strategy are aligned with sustainability objectives and vice versa, the organization may be working to competing goals. If the activities of the company diverge from its stated purpose or public commitments, then stakeholders in particular customers will notice, possibly putting the business's reputation in jeopardy. Inconsistency also risks accusations of purpose washing or greenwashing
- Effective boards hold management to account for the development and implementation of appropriate sustainability goals. When boards fail to do this, institutional investors and other shareholders may seek to change the composition of the board. This happened to Exxon Mobil in May 2021 when shareholders demanding a more robust Exxon response to the climate emergency voted in three new non-executive directors not recommended by the company.
- For companies based in the European Union, the EU is currently preparing a proposal for a European Directive on Sustainable Corporate Governance.[2] It is likely that the proposed new EU directive will cover board oversight of ESG issues, the role of boards in oversight of corporate sustainability strategy, sustainability-related incentives and long-term perspective and an EU-wide legal framework for supply chain due diligence.

How to do it[3]

Step 1: Define board approach to governance and to sustainability

First, the board needs an open conversation about whether it sees its governance role as primarily one of holding management to account? This is the board as 'cop, monitor, auditor'. Or does the board have a more expansive view of the role it can play? This is the board nurturing as well as holding management to account. In this view, the board are coaches **and** cops, mentors **and** monitors, stewards **and** auditors.

Similarly, a board needs to clarify its views on sustainability. Is it just about risk mitigation? About the business reducing its negative social, environmental and economic impacts? For many companies and boards, this is the default mindset, but it does not live up to our governance definition above. There has been an accelerating shift in thinking from the idea of corporate sustainability as being primarily about risk mitigation, recognizing true integration means addressing both risk mitigation and opportunity maximization.

Companies are at different stages of corporate sustainability maturity. Some perhaps are still in denial that sustainability is even material. Some have a compliance mindset, believing the company should follow legal requirements and meet industry standards but no more. Others emphasize risk mitigation, recognizing that sustainability pressures and stakeholder expectations demand a more proactive approach. And then there are those seeking to maximize opportunity related to sustainability / ESG performance. Best practice today means addressing both risk mitigation and opportunity maximization. A small number of businesses go even further, recognizing that to future proof their business, it is not enough to change themselves – they also need to help change their sector and other businesses through leadership and knowledge sharing. This is what various maturity models refer to as the champion or leadership stage.

Step 2: (If necessary) shift the board's mindset

Depending on a business's current stage of maturity, there are different board engagement techniques that a chair, lead independent director, CEO or Chief Sustainability Officer might employ to shift a board's collective mindset. Some boards use future scenarios or provocations from external speakers such as futurists or critical campaigning voices. Some engage a youth board or take their board out into the field to get some very different perspectives on the world. Some rely on CPD (Continuing Professional Development) for existing directors and recruiting new ones who are already more sustainability literate and competent. Whatever the techniques, the goal is to develop a board sustainability mindset, which can be defined as (adapted from Grayson and Kakabadse 2013, see Figure 9.1):

A collectively held view that long-term value creation requires the company to embrace the risks and opportunities of sustainable development; and that the board are simultaneously mentors **and** monitors, stewards **and** auditors of the management in their commitment to corporate responsibility and sustainability.

FIGURE 9.1   Board mindset for corporate sustainability matrix

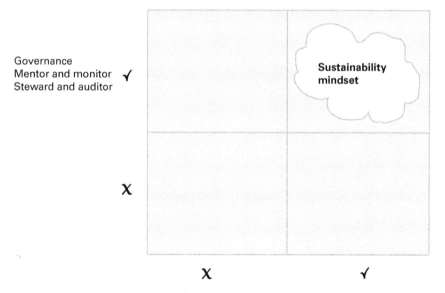

Achieving a sustainability mindset cannot be legislated. It can only occur by conducting sustained and open dialogue among the board and senior management team until there is consensus about the centrality of sustainability for long-term business survival and success. A 2018 report from the INSEAD Business School and Mazars, Leadership in Corporate Sustainability, European Report 2018 – Mazars, INSEAD, Board Agenda, makes clear that a significant minority (almost 20 per cent) of company boards still don't consider sustainability a boardroom issue. For those that do, the next step is to choose the most appropriate structure for dealing with sustainability.

Step 3: Choose the most appropriate governance model for the business

There are several different models for board overview and governance of sustainability.[4] These include:

- Formal sustainability or similarly titled board committees where all the committee members are board members (which may include some executives if they are also board members). This model sends a clear signal internally and externally that sustainability is taken seriously. It also creates the option of using a report from the Sustainability Committee as a part of the annual report. One caution is that this model can reinforce a silo mentality. The 2018 INSEAD / Mazars report on European company practices suggested that just under a fifth had a dedicated committee of this type.

- A mixed committee including at least one board member and senior executives who are not board members. This can help ensure an effective link between strategy and implementation, but, if mishandled, risks blurring boundaries between the roles of NEDs and executives.

- Sustainability-related issues can also be defined as 'matters reserved to the board'. In this model, there usually exists an explicit statement that sustainability / ESG issues are matters to be addressed by the board without delegation to a board committee. If the board is experienced, properly trained in sustainability and consciously considers sustainability as a fundamental part of every decision, this model can deliver a holistic approach. On the other hand, for inexperienced boards, it can become a 'cop out'. Another potential problem related to this approach is that it can be hugely time-consuming for the full board to do this properly, and most boards don't have such extra time available on the main board agenda for the detailed discussions required.

- Public designation of a lead board member (usually a non-executive director) as the lead director for sustainability. A variation on this is where several board members are each given lead responsibility for a particular aspect of sustainability such as climate change or health and well-being. This model ensures there is a sustainability / ESG focal point on the board, but its effectiveness depends crucially on the designated board members' expertise, capacity and credibility. The INSEAD / Mazars report suggested that around 5 per cent of companies had a lead board member without a separate committee.

- Explicit extension of the remit of an existing committee of the board such as Audit and Risk, where all the members of the selected committee are board members (which may include executives if they are also board members). This approach can aid joined-up strategy and implementation, but it risks committee overload. Sustainability may struggle for attention within a well-established, annual committee work schedule. Another disadvantage is that it reduces the impact of sustainability on the overall board agenda, as, for instance, if made part of the audit committee's remit, sustainability will form part of any audit committee report to shareholders rather than being individually highlighted. Furthermore, it may lead to an overly 'risk' focus and reinforce a compliance and risk-mitigation approach by the organization.

- Below-board committees that include only non-board members, except perhaps the CEO who might chair the committee in their executive capacity and report on its decisions and actions to the board. This model can optimize operational effectiveness, but it creates a risk of divorcing the board from sustainability / ESG issues. Arguably this is akin to no effective board oversight.

In practice, these models are not mutually exclusive, and some companies employ more than one of these models simultaneously. This may involve a specific board committee as well as regular, full board discussions, extending the remit of existing committees (most often one of the Audit and Risk or Nominations and Remuneration Committees) and a more operational committee below the board.

There is no right or wrong model. It is what works best for an individual company. In weighing up the pros and cons of different models, it is worth considering the volume of work to be undertaken, the skills of existing non-executive directors and the current board mindset. The general view of many experienced non-executive directors seems to be that in the current climate and average stage of maturity, a dedicated board committee which can do much of the 'heavy lifting' is preferable, adds gravitas and focus – and this is our default recommendation. Crucially, however, where there is an explicit board sustainability committee, The Corporate Governance Centre at INSEAD notes in a recent paper that 'for sustainability committees to be effective and impactful, their work must be taken back to the board and efficaciously communicated, to ensure recommendations are understood and have the support of all board members'.[5] We agree: it is fundamental that the entire board owns the company's commitment to sustainability and that this is understood internally and externally. Similarly, the Terms of Reference (charter) for a board sustainability committee needs to clearly delineate areas of responsibility in order to minimize overlap with other board committees.

It is also important that the board as a whole and any specialist committee focuses on the most material impacts of the business, where the business can make the greatest difference. Hence the importance of boards regularly discussing materiality.

Step 4: Ensuring sustainability expertise on the board

It is standard board practice to maintain and regularly update a board skills matrix. This typically has a section on generic skills that all board members are expected to have to do their job. There is then usually a second section on specific skills that at least one member of the board is expected to have. The board skills matrix must include basic awareness of sustainability / ESG issues and their implications for business as generic skills and require more specialist understanding of the most material sustainability / ESG issues as specific skills. Interestingly, according to the Sustainability Board Report 2020, family businesses have double the proportion of non-executive directors with sustainability experience serving on board sustainability committees (34 per cent) versus the Forbes Global 2000 (17 per cent).[6]

It is also good practice for boards to conduct regular reviews of overall board effectiveness and appraisals of the performance of individual directors, including the chair. These existing processes can be stretched and upgraded to incorporate sustainability aspects, including the degree to which individual directors understand sustainability and use it as a lens for making decisions.

A report from the international business school INSEAD postulates five archetypes of NEDs regarding sustainability and suggests some strategies to overcome objections that each archetype might raise (see Figure 9.2).

Something like the INSEAD archetypes and their segmentation could be used to assess existing board members' skill / will on sustainability, and the table might help guide decisions on engagement strategies for individual NEDs.

Board reviews should explore how well the board manages oversight of the company's sustainability performance. This can include adding specific questions to annual board appraisals designed to elicit insights into board effectiveness relating to oversight and governance of corporate sustainability. These reviews may identify individual / collective training and continuous professional development needs. Such needs can be handled internally or externally, but it is critical that they are addressed. Options include traditional learning programmes as well as more experiential approaches that involve getting out of the boardroom – for example, to visit areas hard hit by climate change impacts. Some external organizations offer customized board training programmes around sustainability, such as Earth on Board (www.earthonboard.org/) and Competent Boards (competentboards.com/),

FIGURE 9.2 INSEAD: Sustainability archetypes of non-executive directors

Board sustainability archetypes and how to respond

Archetype	Belief	How to spot	Typical comments	How to respond
'The Deniers'	Sustainability is a fad that will go away.	More typically in hiding today — evident through absence of discussion of sustainability or its relegation to end of agenda. Absence of discussion of sustainability or its relagation to end of agenda.	'I don't see how these issues are our problem, let governments and NGOs take care of them.' In private: 'climate change is a hoax'.	Careful timing. Focus on risk exposure. One-on-one initially. Patience and perseverance.
'The Hardheaded'	We'll act if it makes business sense, otherwise it's not our problem.	Often found in less sustainable industries. Focus is on strategic reasoning coupled with healthy skepticism. Supports sustainability only to the extent it pays or is clearly demanded by stakeholders (e.g, ensures license to operate).	'Sustainability in the short-term means value destruction.' 'The end user isn't as demanding as you think - there are a few who care, but not the masses.' 'I don't see the business benefit.'	No grand speeches, introduce sustainability as good management. Stay close to existing practice and look initially for low hanging fruit. Incorporate within existing board committees (especially as strategic risk factor). Aspire to be 'best in class'.
'The Superficial'	Look at us, we're beautiful.	Speak of importance of sustainability but may only be a superficial acceptance and understanding of the real issues. Failure to walk the talk. May become manifest in greenwashing.	'Sustainability affects society and business, so we need to be seen to do out bit.' 'We'd like to adopt the recyclable plastic but we need industry-wide agreements first.'	Play to their good intenstions. Make positive suggestions closely aligned with the business. Create board sustainability committee to focus on turning good intentions into good actions.
'The Complacent'	We have good practices in place already.	Not always so easy to spot. Can point to sustainability achievements as an early adopter of sustainability practices, but they may be some years back.	'We have been doing our fair share for a very long time.' 'We reduce CO_2 and have many social and community engagements... what else can we do?'	Acknowledge past successes while pointing to shortcomings of current practices. Emphasis on best practice and more strategic approach. Include sustainability expertise in board/CEO recruitment criteria.
'The True Believers'	Sustainability is fundamental to good governance and long-term value creation.	Rare but increasing in number. Passion and rigor. Strong commitment to Sustainability as innate to the business. While undertaking careful analysis and decision-making.	'Sustainability is not a box-ticking exercise. It's about business purpose.' 'The challenges facing the planet and society are immense and business must change fundamentally.'	Sustain sustainability, by keeping it in the DNA and on the agenda. Act consistently and always with a view to the long-term. Seek out uncomfortable realities and business opponents. Keep asking questions.

Reproduced with permission. Excerpt from 'Turning Board Sustainability Aspirations into Action' authored by N. Craig Smith and Ron Soonieus – INSEAD Working Paper No. 2020/08/ATL[7]

which prove good options for some companies. Finally, sustainability should also be included in board onboarding and orientation.

An easy win is to make sure that the board makes full use of the expertise of directors who also serve on the boards of other companies considered to be sustainability leaders or the boards of sustainability coalitions. Longer term, companies can contribute to future board talent pools by encouraging high-flying employees to serve on NGO and public sector boards to build board experience at an earlier stage of their careers. This can be particularly valuable if the NGOs concerned are involved with sustainable development and/or ESG issues.

While some leading search firms report that relatively few mandates for new board members mention sustainability, when recruiting new non-executive directors directly or giving mandates to search firms or headhunters, Nominations Committees and board chairs should include sustainability knowledge and experience as essential, sought-after competencies. Unless boards have sustainability-savvy members, they will increasingly struggle in the 2020s and beyond.

A minority – at least of large, publicly quoted companies – now supplement core board sustainability expertise with the appointment of an external sustainability advisory panel to advise the CEO and the board on sustainability / ESG matters. Frequently, such panels become powerful outside–inside advocates for faster progress on sustainability commitments. Frequency of meetings of such expert panels varies, but two to four each year seems common, sometimes supplemented with ad-hoc meetings with board directors and/or the CEO and members of senior management, for instance to look at future trends and strategy.

Companies without an external sustainability advisory panel may wish to consider establishing one and, if so, to consider what format would be most appropriate. If such a panel already exists, the company should pause regularly to consider whether it remains the best structure and whether the board and senior management make effective use of what its members offer.

Step 5: Ensure board is truly diverse

On both the main board and on any internal sustainability and/or external sustainability advisory panels, it is important to ensure diversity in all its forms. Historically, attention has focused on gender and (more recently) the ethnic diversity of boards and advisory panels. Organizations need to consider other dimensions of diversity including age and critical areas of insight and expertise such as digital. As Bob Wigley, chair of UK Finance, experienced NED and author of *Born Digital: The story of a distracted generation*, observes: 'The digital wallets of Gen Z drive future demand and boards need to reflect this in their approach to governance and how they present it.'[8]

Businesses need real diversity and inclusion in the boardroom. As an Institute of Business Ethics 2021 checklist on diversity for boards concluded:

> Too many companies have been approaching the different elements
> of diversity sequentially, and with a compliance mindset, rather than
> embracing the opportunity to broaden thinking and blend very different
> life experiences around the boardroom table. That approach is not
> sustainable. Pressure is growing for real change and companies that do
> not get ahead of the curve in addressing all dimensions of diversity may
> find themselves at a significant disadvantage.[9]

This is an urgent challenge for boards across the world and particularly for board chairs, Nominations Committees and the recruitment mandates they give to headhunters (search firms). This will undoubtedly involve looking beyond the conventional sources for new NEDs and recruiting talented individuals from non-business sectors as well. In the longer term, the solution will be ensuring there is a more diverse talent pipeline coming through the executive ranks of business and that these talented individuals are encouraged to acquire board experience early on through serving on corporate youth boards, public sector boards and NGO boards, as well as through mentoring programmes and formal training.

It is then up to boards to satisfy themselves that the CEO and senior management team are truly diverse too and able to grasp the business-critical nature of sustainability for the future success of the business.

Step 6: Ensure the rest of the board's structures and processes reinforce the commitment to sustainability

Whatever governance structure is favoured, a commitment to sustainability creates an added dimension for boards: embedding sustainability / ESG within overall strategy; overseeing relevant initiatives; and approving related public commitments. This impacts the remit and work of the board as a whole and of existing board committees.

The board needs to consider carefully any significant potential fracture points where things might go wrong – for example, in relations between the board and the executive or senior management team or, in a large, international company, in relations between the executive team and divisional leads, country heads and the heads of strategic business units. According to the governance expert Professor Andrew Kakabadse, fracture points are especially relevant around intangibles such as the localization of ethical codes, stakeholder engagement or other core elements of sustainability.[10] This may mean, for example, the board holding meetings in locations where there have been sustainability challenges or significant successes, so members of the board can see for themselves what is happening.

- Audit and Risk Committee: how will regular work to keep the corporate risk register up to date adapt to the need for a more comprehensive definition of material future risks to the company that embraces sustainability / ESG impacts and issues? How is the overall work programme of the internal audit function agreed where there is a specialist sustainability committee as well as an Audit and Risk Committee? It is important on the one hand to avoid unnecessary duplication. On the other hand, it is also critical to ensure there is no falling between the stools, with each committee thinking the other committee will deal with a particular sustainability crisis.

- Remuneration (or Compensation) Committee: how will the performance of senior executives on sustainability be appraised, what key performance indicators will be used and how will this long-term performance be reflected in executive compensation including bonuses?

- Nominations Committee: how will understanding of how sustainability affects the future of the business be reflected in the generic and specific skills matrix, in the criteria for appointment of new board members and in the mandate to search firms who help identify and recruit those people?

- Strategy / Business Development Committee (where it exists): how does commitment to sustainability change overall corporate strategy and the relative attractiveness of different business opportunities? The board might consider asking management to present sustainability business case documents, adding sustainability to financial considerations to inform board decisions.

The veteran sustainability expert Coro Strandberg identifies some of the top sustainability issues that boards should address.

- **Climate change** is a systemic risk for all organizations, and all boards must address climate change as a macro disruptor of the economy and their organizations.

- **Income inequality**, covering both CEO and workforce compensation. This links to how organizations manage their human capital and whether workers are valued and recognized as an asset, not just a cost.

- **Ethical practices**, such as the ethical implications of emerging digital technologies and organizational diversity and inclusion.

- **Stakeholder governance** is an essential board practice; boards need to be much closer to the organization's stakeholders to understand their issues and expectations – having diverse stakeholders on the board can address this.[11]

Step 7: How the board can keep S.C.O.R.E. on sustainability

Experts in the Said Business School in Oxford have developed a S.C.O.R.E. framework for embedding organizational purpose. S.C.O.R.E. stands for: simplify, connect, own, reward and exemplify. We believe it can be useful for boards as they embed a sustainability mindset and we have adapted it for this.

- Simplify: sustainability can quickly become very complicated and jargon laden. Boards can insist on a ruthless focus on materiality.
- Connect: it is easy for sustainability to be siloed in a specific function. Boards can ensure that all parts of the business are taking into account material ESG risks and opportunities.
- Own: boards can set their stamp on sustainability by ensuring appropriate societal purpose, strategy and culture.
- Reward: as previously emphasized, sustainability gets real for many when compensation and bonuses depend on it. Hence the crucial role of board remuneration and compensation committees.
- Exemplify: the board's own behaviours send important signals to the organization. There is a world of difference between boards that treat sustainability as an occasional AOB (any other business) item versus ones where directors are constantly interrogating proposals for their impact on the sustainability performance of the business and for the achievement of sustainability goals.

Like every other aspect of embedding sustainability in a business, nothing presented here is a once-and-for-all exercise. Effective governance of sustainability needs to be kept under regular examination.

In practice

Tata Group[12]

The Tata Group, with over 750,000 employees, is a global conglomerate, headquartered in India, which includes companies in steel, auto manufacturing, power generation and distribution, IT, hotels and consumer goods. It owns global brands such as Jaguar Land Rover and Tetley. The group operates in more than 100 countries, with a mission 'To improve the quality of life of the communities we serve globally, through long-term stakeholder value creation based on Leadership with Trust.' As of September 2021, the market capitalization of the Group was in excess of $300 billion. From the original start-up in 1868, Tata has been a values-led business and a pioneer in corporate responsibility and now sustainability. Since 2014, the Tata Sustainability Group (TSG) has been a central hub supporting Tata companies to embed sustainability in their business strategies, thereby demonstrating responsibility to the planet and its people.

The Tata Group defines sustainability governance as 'ensuring ethical and transparent business conduct, addressing sustainability risks and opportunities and aligning with robust disclosure requirements under the aegis of the board'. While there are 29 publicly listed Tata enterprises and each operates independently with its own board of directors, the Group believes that sustainability is a strategic imperative and should be firmly on the agenda of Tata boards. TSG advises on this, including:

- Board oversight: Globally, board oversight of sustainability is often considered as a proxy for good governance. Shareholders and other stakeholders are looking to board ownership of the sustainability agenda as an indication that risks and opportunities are adequately dealt with at the highest level.[13] While sustainability issues are the responsibility of the full board, given their packed agendas boards may oftentimes find it challenging to give them adequate attention. Tata companies are encouraged to have full board oversight of sustainability and, where possible, have a dedicated board committee for sustainability, which reports back to the full board. Eleven Tata companies have dedicated sustainability committees with their own charter. Five companies have separate board committees for HSE and CSR, which between them cover a majority of the sustainability issues. TSG also advises companies on the charter for Sustainability Committees of the Board.

- Board sensitization on sustainability: Given the fast-evolving sustainability landscape, keeping boards up to date on the latest developments is critical. Tata companies adopt several measures for this, which include board immersion programmes with global leadership institutes such as CISL (Cambridge Institute for Sustainability Leadership), 'Advisory Councils' comprising experts on specific sustainability topics to advise the board and a 30-minute e-module curated by TSG especially for Tata boards. The module equips boards with knowledge on corporate sustainability and provides an insight into the Tata group level, as well as company level, material issues. It also provides a strategic checklist to help the board engage with management and ensure that the organization has a robust sustainability strategy in place. The board module has already been rolled out by large companies such as Tata Steel (for its own board and for the boards of all its subsidiary companies), Tata Power and Tata Motors. TSG continues to work with companies on board sensitization and periodic updates to the e-module.

- Sustainability disclosures: Sustainability disclosures are a critical aspect of governance, and TSG is working with Tata companies to ensure robust disclosures. Twelve of the largest Tata companies report on both Integrated Reporting and CDP. Tata companies are also preparing for TCFD disclosures, with Tata Steel leading the way (Tata Steel was a part of the Global Taskforce for climate-related financial disclosures). To support Tata companies to enhance their sustainability disclosures, TSG periodically curates capability building workshops focused on reporting frameworks for Tata companies and has also developed guidance documents, one on Integrated Reporting and another on TCFD reporting.

As Siddharth Sharma, Group Chief Sustainability Officer, Tata Sons, summed it up:

Aspects of corporate governance such as ethical and transparent business conduct have been cornerstones of the Tata philosophy since inception. A quick look at the Tata Code of Conduct, which was first formalized by Mr. Ratan Tata and governs the conduct of our companies, will make it evident that sustainability considerations like ethical business conduct, fair treatment of workforce and value chain partners, focus on communities and the environment are all embedded deeply in the Tata ethos.[14]

Swire Pacific[15]

Swire Pacific Limited is a conglomerate active in the property, aviation, beverage, marine services, trading and investment industries with more than 85,000 employees and 2020 annual revenue of more than US$10 billion. This Hong Kong-headquartered organization is the publicly traded part of Swire Group, which was founded in Liverpool, England, in 1816. Swire Pacific was formed in 1974 to become the main holding company for Swire's Hong Kong-based assets and has been active throughout the Asia Pacific region since. The company has a long history in Hong Kong and mainland China, where the name Swire has been established through prominent brands such as Swire Properties, Swire Coca-Cola and Cathay Pacific, among others.

Sustainable development has always been a core principle for the company. The Swire Pacific Board, led by its chair, is ultimately accountable for sustainability matters. A group-level strategy 'SwireTHRIVE' facilitates best practice sharing and consistent implementation of sustainability, also helping achieve effective governance. SwireTHRIVE addresses five areas: climate, waste, water, people and communities (see Figure 9.3).

The board is kept informed of sustainability risks and performance by a Group Risk Management Committee (GRMC), which reports to the board via the Audit Committee. The GRMC oversees committees and working groups that deal with specific areas of risk and these include representatives from the operating companies.

The Sustainable Development Office (SDO), the Group Risk Management and Diversity & Inclusion departments and the Group Head of Philanthropy are jointly responsible for implementation of SwireTHRIVE. The SDO, led by the Group Head of Sustainability, advises senior management of key developments and emerging risks related to sustainable development and is responsible for setting Group environmental policies and targets, ESG policies and internal and external reporting on ESG matters.

In a step to ensure 360-degree accountability, the management of risks and the implementation of sustainability policies are subject to scrutiny by the internal audit department with support from specialist external consultants where necessary.

According to Mark Watson, Group Head of Sustainability at Swire:

> When it comes to driving sustainability inside an organisation, the importance of an effective governance structure cannot be overstated. Whilst no one size fits all, our approach highlights the strong working relationship between our Board, senior decision makers, technical experts and functional departments. Swire Pacific's sustainability model is based on empowering its operating companies to drive sustainability efforts within their own sectors of expertise, but supported at the centre with an overarching structure that provides general direction, sets expectations and offers technical expertise to our teams at the coal face of our business.[16]

Summary

Heightened expectations on business and global challenges such as the climate emergency and hyper global inequality require a step change in business commitment to and performance on sustainability and ESG. Boards have a crucial role to play here in setting the company's ambition for sustainability, establishing the right tone at the top of the organization and modelling desired behaviours and ensuring that purpose, strategy and culture are all aligned in a manner that supports embedding sustainability. Boards need to check that they have the right mechanisms for handling sustainability and they have, collectively and individually, a mindset for sustainability. They need

FIGURE 9.3 Governance at Swire

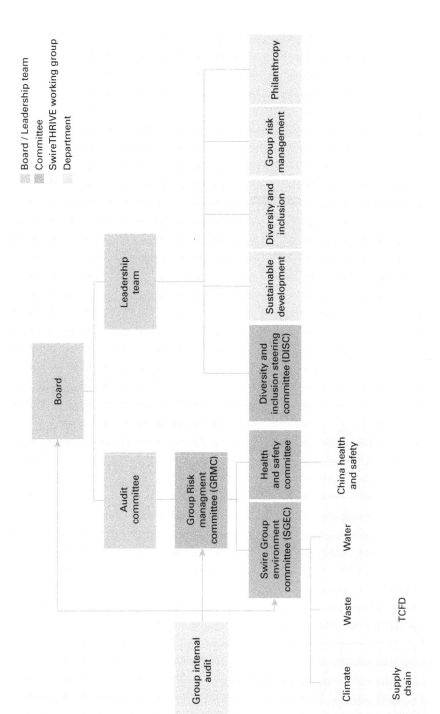

Board / Leadership team
Committee
SwireTHRIVE working group
Department

Board

Audit committee

Group internal audit

Leadership team

Group Risk managment committee (GRMC)

Swire Group environment committee (SGEC)

Health and safety committee

Diversity and inclusion steering committee (DISC)

Sustainable development

Diversity and inclusion

Group risk management

Philanthropy

Climate

Waste

Water

China health and safety

Supply chain

TCFD

SOURCE Reproduced with permission by Swire Group, Sustainability Governance Structure to ensure they have genuine diversity of perspectives and experiences and that they are regularly evaluating their own performance.

Action checklist

1 Assess whether the board has a sustainability mindset and, if not, identify how to help create this.

2 Periodically evaluate whether the current model for board oversight and governance is fit for purpose in sustainability / ESG terms, the board is giving sufficient time to it and whether existing board committees are effectively incorporating sustainability within their remit.

3 Review the board skills matrix and whether this reflects the company's commitment to sustainability; ensure that executive search firms appointed to identify potential new board members are including a mindset for sustainability within their brief.

4 Ensure that sustainability is effectively incorporated into induction and continuous professional development for board members as well as in the annual appraisals of the board.

5 Commit to ensuring the board has access to truly diverse perspectives and experiences and is actively thinking ahead in terms of succession planning.

6 Consider if a sustainability advisory panel to advise the board and senior management team would be useful and acceptable.

7 Be explicit on corporate websites and in annual reports about the terms of reference and membership of the sustainability committees in the same way that companies typically publish the membership of audit and risk, remuneration and nominations committees.

Further resources

- Competent Boards (2020) *Future Boardroom Competencies – the great reset – do we need new competencies in the boardroom and C-suite?*, Competent Boards

- Dunne, P (2021) *Boards: A practical perspective*, 2nd edition, Governance Publishing & Information Services Ltd
- High Meadows Institute and Tapestry Networks (2020) *Corporate Governance for the 21st Century*, High Meadows Institute and Tapestry Networks
- Institute of Business Ethics (2021) *The Ethics of Diversity Board Briefing*, Institute of Business Ethics
- Mazars, INSEAD and Board Agenda (2018) Leadership in Corporate Sustainability, European Report 2018, Mazars, INSEAD and Board Agenda, www.insead.edu/sites/default/files/assets/dept/centres/icgc/docs/leadership-in-corporate-sustainability-european-report-2018.pdf
- Reynolds, R (2021) *The Board's Role in Sustainable Leadership*, Russell Reynolds
- Smith, N C, INSEAD and Soonieus, R C (2019) *What's Stopping Boards from Turning Sustainability Aspirations into Action?*, INSEAD The Corporate Governance Centre

Endnotes

1 Cambridge Institute for Sustainability Leadership (n.d.) Board education: Making better decisions for long-term performance, www.cisl.cam.ac.uk/education/executive-education/board (archived at https://perma.cc/WL7S-L5YS)
2 The European Directive on Sustainable Corporate Governance aims to introduce new rules on incorporating sustainability in long-term business strategies. It is complementary to the proposal for a Corporate Sustainability Reporting Directive, which amends the existing EU reporting requirements on sustainability matters
3 The How to do it section draws extensively on Grayson, D and Kakabadse, A (2013) *Towards a Sustainability Mindset: How boards organise oversight and governance of corporate responsibility*, Doughty Centre for Corporate Responsibility, Cranfield School of Management and Business in the Community

4 This list of different board approaches was originally published in Grayson, D and Kakabadse, A (2013) *Towards a Sustainability Mindset: How boards organise oversight and governance of corporate responsibility*, Doughty Centre for Corporate Responsibility, Cranfield School of Management and Business in the Community, and in an accompanying article for *The Ethical Corporation* magazine: Grayson, D (2013) Sustainable business leadership – take it from the top, *The Ethical Corporation*.

5 Smith, C and Soonieus, R C (2019) *What's Stopping Boards from Turning Sustainability Aspirations into Action?*, INSEAD The Corporate Governance Centre

6 The Sustainability Board Report, 2021, www.boardreport.org (archived at https://perma.cc/Q5WU-4GDD)

7 papers.ssrn.com/sol3/papers.cfm?abstract_id=3536342 (archived at https://perma.cc/3UNP-74QY)

8 Interview with authors, August 2021

9 IBE publish a board briefing on the Ethics of Diversity, IBE News Release, 14 April 2021

10 Author interview, July 2021

11 Standberg, C (n.d.) ESG Governance: A new expectations of boards, Governance Professionals of Canada, corostrandberg.com/wp-content/uploads/2019/11/esg-governance-new-expectation-of-boards.pdf (archived at https://perma.cc/6VSK-UPB4)

12 www.tatasustainability.com/AboutUs/TataSustainabilityGroup#Knowledge (archived at https://perma.cc/6SQE-QRJ6); www.tatasustainability.com/Home/Governance (archived at https://perma.cc/38G7-QSJK)

13 UN Global Compact (2015) Corporate sustainability: An important agenda for board of directors, October, www.unglobalcompact.org/docs/issues_doc/Corporate_Governance/Global-Compact-board-programme-intro.pdf (archived at https://perma.cc/4MQD-YBY9)

14 Email exchange with authors, September 2021

15 Source(s): Swire Pacific Sustainable Development Report 2020, www.swire.com/ourjourney/tablet/en/index.php (archived at https://perma.cc/BP2T-Z2W7)

16 Exchange with authors, September 2021

PART THREE

Taking it to the world

10

Engagement

What is it?

Stakeholder engagement is the systematic identification, analysis, planning and implementation of actions designed to allow a company to interact effectively with stakeholders.[1] Stakeholders are anyone who is impacted by or who can have an impact on an organization. For virtually all companies, core stakeholders include employees, customers (for B2B companies) and/or consumers (for B2C companies), suppliers, investors, regulators and local communities. Companies often have their own discrete set of stakeholders that go beyond these usual suspects, for instance unions, NGOs and academics.

The purpose of stakeholder engagement is to consider the perspectives of stakeholders and respond to their inputs and concerns in a strategic manner, as well as to explain the company's strategy and points of view. It is part of a business being transparent and accountable, and it contributes to trust-building and strong relationships. We distinguish between stakeholder management (which implies a one-way process from the company to stakeholders and a focus on risk mitigation) and stakeholder engagement (which is about dialogue, interaction and a two-way process involving both risk mitigation and opportunity maximization for all involved).

Mizila Mthenjane, Executive Head of Stakeholder Affairs at Exxaro, describes stakeholder engagement as 'the act and activities of interacting and exchanging with stakeholders. It is a demanding process which does not happen organically but requires great effort and attention.'[2]

Why it matters

Stakeholder engagement is a cornerstone of strong corporate sustainability performance. BSR states:

> Stakeholder engagement is – and will remain – a core element of the sustainability toolkit. It is a fundamental component of materiality assessments, which are then used to inform sustainability strategy, reporting, and disclosure. Corporations need strategies in order to understand and respond to existing and emerging societal concerns. Without input from key stakeholder groups, any approach to sustainability will be limited by an organization's self-interest and inward focus.[3]

Stakeholder engagement is important for myriad reasons, including:

- Good stakeholder engagement provides an early warning system regarding changing stakeholder expectations, emerging ESG issues and broader societal attitudes, and it reduces the risks of a business being caught out. As such, engagement can be a powerful part of a company's anticipatory issues management.

- Stakeholder engagement supports innovation of all kinds, from product and service innovation to solutions to social and environmental challenges. Tapping into the 'wisdom of the crowd' helps guide new thinking and approaches.

- Engagement identifies stakeholder concerns and, given the right and appropriate engagement circumstances, encourages stakeholders to volunteer solutions to help a business reduce negative impacts and increase positive ones, making the business more competitive and sustainable.

- Stakeholder engagement builds trust and enhances reputation; by aligning the business with stakeholder interests, it can build support for the company and its positions also.

- Engagement is not only valuable for businesses but also for stakeholders. Done well, engagement often translates into better outcomes for a company's stakeholders.

How to do it

While many companies engage *some* of their stakeholders regularly, it is often done without sufficient intention, structure or responsiveness. Intention is important because companies need to decide who their stakeholders are and why they matter, and to determine expected mutual outcomes from the engagement. Structure is critical as it provides a framework from which companies can execute engagement in terms of who from both sides must engage, when and where. Responsiveness matters because this refers to the conscious response that acknowledges the contact from the stakeholder and indicates that the company will respond.

Step 1: Map your stakeholders

Stakeholder mapping is the process of thinking through who your most important audiences are and why.

Stakeholder groups that can impact and who are impacted by nearly every company include employees, customers and/or consumers, suppliers, investors, regulators and local communities. For most businesses, there is ongoing interaction with these stakeholder audiences as a matter of course and necessity as, for example, organizations need to understand what employees and customers think and expect in order to remain viable over the long term.

It is also important to stretch perspectives and go beyond these core groups as the long-term success of most businesses is dependent on additional stakeholders. Extended mapping exercises often include additional stakeholders such as civil society (NGOs, charities), multilateral organizations such as the UN (if you are a global company), academics, the media and trade unions.

The process goes deeper still, as it's identifying specific organizations and individuals within each stakeholder group that makes a stakeholder mapping exercise most useful. For instance, if considering governmental stakeholders, it's essential to identify which government department or ministry most directly controls policies or programmes related to your industry. Similarly, when scanning civil society organizations and media, it's important to learn which NGOs and media outlets are most closely aligned with your organization's material issues.

Business sector has an impact too. For instance, for a food company, health and wellness issues are central, which will mean mapping the stakeholders in government, civil society and any others that have influence on this topic. In contrast, for a mining company, health and safety and environmental issues will be more prominent material issues, and the company's mapping efforts need to reflect this. As emphasized here, a company's understanding of its material issues (see Chapter 2) is critical to effective stakeholder mapping and engagement.

Step 2: Develop an engagement plan

After key stakeholder audiences have been identified and mapped, it is time to develop a detailed plan for specific organizations and groups. This will help operationalize engagement with your stakeholders.

The Stakeholder Action Framework in Table 10.1 outlines a structured approach to stakeholder engagement and includes overarching strategic objectives and tactics to operationalize the engagement. It captures stakeholders by type, why each audience matters to the business, the issues that are most relevant for each audience, who specifically represents the issues from within the wider stakeholder group, the level of influence the stakeholder may have on the business, the proximity of the stakeholder to the company, internal ownership of the stakeholder relationship, which engagement tactic is most appropriate and the desired outcomes with this stakeholder audience.

This tool (or your company's custom version of it) can be used to state the desired outcome of engagement with each stakeholder group so that planning and resource allocation can align with that objective.

Step 3: Activate the engagement plan

The next step is to identify and implement specific engagement approaches suited to each stakeholder group and the outcomes you are seeking.

TABLE 10.1 Stakeholder action framework

Organizations and individuals (stakeholder representative)	Stakeholder group (investor, customer, government, NGO, etc.)	Why they matter	Key Issues	Influence (high, medium, low)	Proximity (high, medium, low)	Internal owner (accountability – function, individuals)	Engagement tactics (inform, engage, partner)	Desired outcome (impact)
Stakeholder 1								
Stakeholder 2								
Stakeholder 3								

While there are many ways to engage internal and/or external stakeholders, these methods can be grouped into three main forms: communications, feedback and dialogue.

COMMUNICATIONS

Communications primarily comprises one-way messaging from the business to key audiences, allows a company to reach many stakeholders at scale and affords the company a great deal of control. While this is not the whole picture, and often not sufficient given engagement is, at its best, about two-way dialogue and the exchange of ideas, it has a role to play as an enabler. Practically speaking, communications set the stage or provide a foundation for deeper engagement by sending a signal that an organization is trying to share information proactively and in a manner tailored to certain groups. Communication can also be used to reinforce or follow up after other types of engagement.

Communications approaches include:

- **Information sharing:** One-way communications provide information on a particular sustainability topic relevant to a given individual, group or organization. Information sharing includes reports posted on the company's website and/or shared via social media or perhaps sent directly by email or post. It may also include press releases, speeches, policy statements and even advertising. While information sharing relies heavily on stakeholders spotting and interpreting which messages are relevant to them, this largely unidirectional and sometimes passive way of engaging stakeholders can reach large audiences and can be effective in the right circumstances.

- **Webinars:** Pre-COVID, webinars were an option for engagement; at the time of writing, in the second half of 2021, they have become the dominant form of gathering for many organizations. Webinars have proliferated and have allowed companies to interact with many stakeholders by not only sharing information but also by allowing time for live Q&A by voice or electronically. Many online platforms (from Zoom to Microsoft Teams to more specialist collaboration software) provide tools that let stakeholders (and the business host) ask questions, discuss what's happening with other participants using 'chat' functions, post reactions in the form of emoticons or otherwise, or even participate in polling and other interactive exercises that can show the collective mood of a group and tap its wisdom.

• **Town halls:** Town halls can be held in person (depending on event size and the geographic dispersion of stakeholders) or online using voice, video and other tools. Town halls all have a similar spirit, gathering employees (for instance, from a particular business unit or companywide) or other stakeholders with common interests (such as civil society organizations from a community or communities where a business has physical operations) to hear business leaders share relevant information and take questions from the audience. Town halls may include presentations, speeches and/or panel discussions on particular topics or are sometimes designed to be Q&A sessions in their entirety (with the intention of letting the questions set the agenda and inform the company which issues stakeholders care most about).

FEEDBACK MECHANISMS

Feedback mechanisms go deeper and are more interactive than most communications, allowing companies to obtain a more comprehensive understanding of stakeholder concerns, expectations and suggestions.

Some common feedback mechanisms include:

• **Surveys:** Conducting a survey via a questionnaire (either online, in person or by phone) is standard and a common way for companies to engage employees, customers and sometimes other stakeholders like suppliers and community organizations. A strength of surveys as a tool is scalability: they can be expanded to cover stakeholder audiences of virtually any size, often generating hundreds or even thousands of responses. Surveys provide structured feedback that can be dissected and analysed by audience, geography and demographics. When repeated, surveys allow tracking over time, which can be invaluable to a business trying to ascertain shifting expectations or perspectives among its stakeholders. The very act of conducting a survey can be a signal that the company cares about the opinions of others. The survey process also allows a company to demonstrate responsiveness, for instance by sharing survey results with stakeholders and communicating the company's response to the information that has been gathered. Potential responses can include simply acknowledging the feedback, pointing out existing policies and commitments that relate to it and/or spelling out the actions the business will take to address what it has learned from hearing stakeholder views or concerns in this manner.

- **Interviews:** One-on-one and small group interviews offer another way of getting stakeholder feedback. These may be conducted in person, by phone or by video. This more qualitative approach means smaller numbers of stakeholders engaged compared to surveys, but the method can provide a deeper and richer way to listen to stakeholders. This more intimate approach allows for dialogue, resolution where there may be tensions or conflict, or identification of ways to partner or collaborate. As with surveys, stakeholder interviews provide an opportunity to circle back with stakeholders to demonstrate responsiveness.

- **Social media analysis:** Companies are increasingly using social media or digital listening to better understand stakeholders' interests and concerns. The variety of tools enabling this are becoming ever more accessible at the same time as they get more and more sophisticated. The advantages of social media analysis or digital listening include their ability to process vast amounts of online data and to assess stakeholder perspectives in real time. However, there is a significant challenge of lack of representativeness on social media, and the medium can amplify extreme views, so data collected in this manner has to be sifted with care.

DIALOGUES

Dialogues comprise deeper, two-way, intensive approaches to engagement. They serve especially well in some specific situations, for instance to go deep on particular issues with subject matter experts steeped in a topic or to resolve conflicts that may exist among stakeholders and/or between stakeholders and the business. Dialogues can also be used for more general information sharing and relationship building.

Dialogue options include:

- **Convenings**: Gathering stakeholders together is a powerful means of engagement that can deepen understanding, build trust, resolve conflicts, enable co-creation of solutions and more. Convenings can be large gatherings such as forums or conferences (with dozens, hundreds or even thousands of stakeholders), or they can be intimate, roundtable-style events gathering just a handful of people or up to one or two dozen individuals. The stakeholders attending may all be expert or interested in a single issue or more diverse issues. Historically, most convenings have happened in person given a core objective is to create intimacy and allow people to get to know one another during the formal programme and on its edges. However, with the concerns about the climate impacts of travel plus, of course, COVID-19, more and more convenings are moving online. Regardless of format, successful convenings require a clear agenda, strong facilitation, time to reflect and space for open conversation and discussion. For these reasons, and to provide more neutral facilitation, convenings are often designed and run for companies by external consultants.

- **Advisory boards**: Inviting a select group of senior and influential stakeholders to be a part of an external sustainability advisory board can be of great value to a business. Some companies create an independent advisory board of experts to help the company guide development and rollout of its sustainability strategy. All three of the authors have helped private sector clients develop such boards, often serving as facilitators to the process, and we have experience serving as members of such groups also. This experience has shown us how powerful an impact such stakeholder boards can have on a business's ability to craft and deliver a smart, pragmatic and ambitious sustainability strategy (see Chapter 9).

- **Workshops and innovation labs:** Companies occasionally will want to engage stakeholders to solve very specific sustainability challenges. This can be done in person or virtually. The idea here is to identify a problem and then invite diverse stakeholders with related expertise or experience to help develop potential solutions. A great deal of planning as well as expert facilitation or moderation is usually required in order to make these successful. The advantages of this format stem from engaging stakeholders very purposefully and from the degree of innovation that can result. IKEA's One Home One Planet programme is a high-profile example of this type of engagement, where stakeholders are invited to help innovate ways in which the company can be more impactful in driving forward its sustainability impacts.[4] Another specialized form of workshops and innovation labs are sustainability-focused hack-a-thons, which generally seek to develop (quickly and collectively) software-based solutions to sustainability challenges.

- **Collaboration:** Working collaboratively with other companies and organizations in partnership or coalitions can be another valuable form of stakeholder engagement. While membership does not guarantee collaboration will happen, becoming a member of BSR, the World Business Council for Sustainable Development (WBCSD) or the United Nations Global Compact (UNGC) affords companies the opportunity to join working groups on particular issues and to partner in other ways. In addition to working with other companies, such working groups often involve interactions with a broad range of non-business stakeholders. Such collective stakeholder engagement is a relatively easy way to learn, listen to and share information with a range of stakeholders from across the sustainable development community. (This is discussed further in Chapter 12.)

Step 4: Engagement and conflict resolution

Best practice for stakeholder engagement is to employ as many techniques and tools as can benefit your company and its stakeholders while being sure to tailor choices to your business's needs and culture. A combination of more passive communications approaches, feedback mechanisms such as surveys, and the deep listening and engagement characterizing dialogues, coupled with responsiveness, can make for a robust approach.

Proactive stakeholder engagement, driven by an understanding of mutual needs and expectations, is critical to the fulfilment of your sustainability strategy and to overcoming blockages to implementation.

Where there are especially challenging stakeholder relationships or acute issues, engagement can take on a dispute resolution approach. Building or rebuilding trust with stakeholders involves a process of listening, then dialogue and then shared accountability as a pathway to resolution. Developing common values and desired outcomes is key.

Often companies can't or won't meet all stakeholder demands, and it may be difficult to keep all stakeholders engaged over time, but careful, sustained effort can strengthen relationships and open up possibilities that one or both sides hadn't considered before.

In practice

CDL

City Developments Limited (CDL) is a global real estate company with over 9,300 full-time employees and 2020 annual revenue of $2.1 billion. This Singapore-headquartered company was founded in 1963 and now operates in 29 countries around the world.[5]

CDL is fuelled by a desire to be recognized by customers, employees and peers as an innovative creator of quality and sustainable spaces. The company aims to set benchmarks in innovation and sustainable development and transform the eco-landscape. CDL has developed over 47,000 homes and owns over 23 million square feet of gross floor area in residential, commercial and hospitality assets globally in addition to operating 152 hotels and 44,000 rooms worldwide.

For over two decades, the environment has been a top priority in the way CDL designs, builds and manages its properties. Guided by its ethos of 'Conserving as we Construct', the company has steadily integrated Environmental, Social and Governance (ESG) issues into its core business since 1995, continuously pushing the envelope with climate-focused strategies.[6]

Anchored on the four key pillars of its ESG strategy – Integration, Innovation, Investment and Impact – CDL's value creation model steers the company in mitigating and adapting to unprecedented climate and health threats. CDL continues to drive change by investing in R&D for green innovations and sustainable solutions, using smart green building features to reduce environmental impact and future proof its products and operations.

The company often speaks to the need for urgent and collective action along the value chain as a key to winning the race to zero, and it partners with like-minded organizations to engage with sustainability experts and the community at large through climate action exhibitions, conferences and webinars to share ideas, knowledge and build expertise.

In 2013, CDL built the first zero-energy Green Gallery in the Singapore Botanic Gardens, engaging and educating visitors through various exhibitions on global and national climate and greening subjects. In 2017, CDL designed and built the Singapore Sustainability Academy (SSA), the first ground-up and zero-energy facility in Singapore dedicated to advocacy and capacity building for climate action. An extensive partnership involving government agencies, industry partners and non-governmental organizations, the SSA has become a hallmark of CDL's community engagement efforts. Since its launch, SSA has hosted more than 450 events and trainings, reaching out to more than 18,300 attendees.[7]

Esther An, CDL's Chief Sustainability Officer, said:

> The health of our planet, people, business and economies are interconnected and interdependent. The climate emergency calls for all sectors to join the global race to zero. CDL will continue to stay the course and create impactful collaborations by addressing issues that matter most to our business, stakeholders and most importantly to our planet. With greater engagement and collaboration amongst more stakeholders, ideas will spark and actions will amplify to build a more resilient future for all.[8]

Safaricom

Safaricom is an African telecommunications company with more than 4,500 employees and FY 2020–2021 annual revenue of $2.3 billion. Headquartered in Nairobi, Kenya, the company was licensed in 1999 and launched in 2000. It operates only in Kenya, where it plays a central role in the lives of millions of customers.[9]

Safaricom is a digital innovator providing a wide range of communication services, including mobile voice, messaging, data, financial and converged services, which it delivers in line with its 'Transform Lives' vision. Safaricom provides a broad array of products and services based on voice and data telecommunications platforms to subscribers that range from individuals to businesses of all sizes and the government.

The company aspires to use its products and services to transform lives and contribute to sustainable living throughout Kenya. To demonstrate the integration of sustainability into its business decisions, the company has mapped the SDGs against the three pillars of its corporate strategy and each of its material topics. Since 2016, the company has incorporated 9 of the 17 SDGs into its performance objectives, both as a company and on the individual employee level. Its three strategy pillars rely heavily on effective stakeholder engagement.

Safaricom's business model and the geography in which it operates makes it key to listen to a wide range of stakeholders and in turn learn from them. The company employs a variety of informal and formal methods to gather and exchange information with its stakeholders.

The company has taken an expansive view of its most important stakeholder audiences and these include: customers, society (largely the Kenyan people), employees, regulators, business partners, shareholders and the media. The company further outlines the nature of the relationship it has with each of these stakeholder groups, articulating key touch points and shared interests. For instance, the main channels Safaricom uses to engage its customers are through its call centre, Interactive Voice Response (IVR) and ZURI chatbot self-service options. The company uses these avenues to gather feedback on its existing services and consumer expectations, using what it learns to design new offerings.

As part of their pledge to stakeholders, Chairman Nicholas Nganga and CEO Michael Joseph state:

> Safaricom remains committed to putting our customers first, delivering relevant products and services, and enhancing operational excellence. By running a sustainable business, we seek to contribute towards improving the quality of life of every Kenyan. We also seek to contribute to sustainable living throughout the country and are committed to managing our operations in a responsible and ethical manner.[10]

Summary

Stakeholder engagement allows a company to identify emerging sustainability issues early, respond effectively to minimize risks and innovate towards solutions, and helps drive a company's success forward. Importantly, it also helps companies better understand how key issues and expectations are evolving and helps them anticipate future risks and opportunities.

One of the most important aspects of stakeholder engagement is responding to stakeholders' expectations and concerns and building trust with them. While this takes many forms, the most powerful response is to embed engagement learning in the company's ESG strategy, policies and commitments – and in the actions taken to bring them to life and achieve them.

Action checklist

1 Identify primary and secondary stakeholders of the business as well as their respective priorities. Establish a mechanism to keep this stakeholder mapping up to date as a living, dynamic document.

2 Prioritize key stakeholders, then target and engage the most important ones first.

3 Look for existing channels of communication that the business is already using that could be used to communicate with other stakeholders too. For example, employee engagement can be a good mechanism for communicating with local communities in which the employees reside.

4 Use a broad range of engagement tools to ensure that stakeholders' insights and perspectives are effectively harvested and make sure these are taken seriously within the organization and acted upon.

5 Make this a constant part of core operations.

6 Particularly for smaller firms, it may be appropriate to find an outside organization such as a sustainability coalition that can serve as an intermediary stakeholder and enhance the capacity of the business to engage with more organizations (see Chapter 12).

Further resources

- BSR (2019) Five-step approach to stakeholder engagement, www.bsr.org/en/our-insights/report-view/stakeholder-engagement-five-step-approach-toolkit

- Freeman, R E (2009) What is stakeholder theory?, YouTube, youtu.be/bIRUaLcvPe8

- ING Bank (2021) How we engage, www.ing.com/Sustainability/The-world-around-us-1/How-we-engage.htm

- O'Neill, R (2018) *Common Threads: Designing impactful engagement*, The SustainAbility Institute by ERM

- Syngenta (2021) Stakeholder engagement, www.syngenta.com/en/sustainability/stakeholder-engagement

- Unilever describes its approach on its website. Unilever (2021) Engaging with stakeholders, www.unilever.com/planet-and-society/responsible-business/engaging-with-stakeholders/

Endnotes

1 Association for Project Management (2021) What is stakeholder engagement?, www.apm.org.uk/resources/find-a-resource/stakeholder-engagement/ (archived at https://perma.cc/L46T-T59K)

2 Mthenjane, M (2021) Interview by Chris Coulter, 22 September

3 Taylor, A and Bancilhon, C (2019) Five-step approach to stakeholder engagement, http://prod-edxapp.edx-cdn.org/assets/courseware/v1/9c75b1f4b6 68f786d32a777261529227/asset-v1:DelftX+RI102x+2T2019+type@ asset+block/BSR_Five-Step_Guide_to_Stakeholder_Engagement.pdf (archived at https://perma.cc/P6FR-TNXG)

4 INGKA (2021) One home, one planet 2021, www.ingka.com/one-home-one-planet/ (archived at https://perma.cc/2UMB-ELYX)

5 City Developments Limited (2020) Annual Report 2020, ir.cdl.com.sg/static-files/c4f2430d-1470-407a-b8ff-599e755a1eb7 (archived at https://perma.cc/D5SE-N3PG)

6 City Developments Limited (2021) Integrated Sustainability Report 2021, ir.cdl.com.sg/static-files/10dac0e1-206f-429b-a655-0d63dd39f23d (archived at https://perma.cc/H3NP-9UJ5)

7 City Developments Limited (2021) Our heritage, www.cdl.com.sg/our-heritage# (archived at https://perma.cc/V54Z-GBNZ)

8 City Developments Limited (2021) Integrated Sustainability Report 2021, https://ir.cdl.com.sg/static-files/10dac0e1-206f-429b-a655-0d63dd39f23d (archived at https://perma.cc/73WX-CQDL)

9 Safaricom (2020) 2020 Annual Report, www.safaricom.co.ke/images/ Downloads/Safaricom_AR2020_bookmarked_ONLINE_29_07_2020.pdf (archived at https://perma.cc/ZA9M-RHQA)

10 Safaricom (2021) Stakeholder engagement, www.safaricom.co.ke/ sustainabilityreport_2020/stakeholder-engagement/ (archived at https://perma. cc/6QW2-PVNC)

11

Communications

What is it?

Communicating sustainability is not only about sharing information, news or progress regarding a company's sustainability strategy or performance. It is also about building belief, recognition and momentum for its sustainability leadership, which ultimately helps build trust and supports the business case for sustainability- or ESG-related investment and effort.

Communications flow through a variety of mediums and channels, including initiative and policy announcements, press releases, speeches, advertisements, earned and paid media, websites, social media, films, reports and thought leadership. As in other aspects of corporate communications, the best sustainability communications involve storytelling and proof points and lead to two-way dialogue with stakeholders.

It is important to note here that sustainability reporting (see Chapter 8) is a critical part of overall sustainability communications. While reporting is largely about tracking sustainability performance and disclosure, broader communication is targeted at wider audiences and has more diverse objectives than reporting.

Effective sustainability communications begin with strong ESG performance. Communicating sustainability without credible performance is greenwashing and leaves a company seriously exposed to potential reputational damage. We outline our understanding of a performance-driven approach to sustainability communications below, acknowledging that it is not totally comprehensive – there are other ways companies can communicate sustainability.

Sustainability communications begin with strong ESG performance from which platforms for communication can be built including reporting, a branded sustainability strategy, big sustainability initiatives and affiliations and certifications that demonstrate a commitment to strong performance. There are many tactics that companies can employ to communicate with stakeholders and to gather feedback to be even better communicators (see Figure 11.1).

Why it matters

Communications play a key role in the success of a business's sustainability strategy. Being a leader in sustainability is important, but when a company becomes a *recognized* leader it builds value in at least three ways (see Figure 11.2): *talent equity* (for example, more motivated work force, higher employee retention and attraction); *brand equity* (for instance, increased market share, enhanced customer and supplier loyalty); and *reputation equity* (for example, higher levels of trust, more opportunities for partnerships, more influence on policy).

There are many ways that effective communications support sustainability and ESG performance, including:

- Helping employees and external stakeholders understand that the company is committed to sustainability and has a strategy for embedding it.
- Articulating what sustainability means for the business and highlighting opportunities for employees to contribute to fulfilment of the sustainability strategy.
- Informing owners or investors about the sustainability / ESG impacts and performance of the business.
- Signalling to others about your strategy and future plans, which can create opportunities for collaboration and partnership.

FIGURE 11.1 Performance-driven sustainability communications

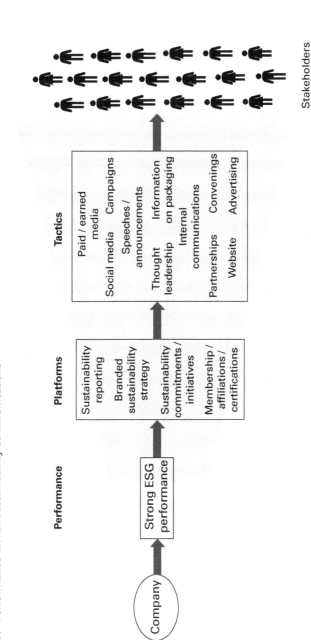

Performance

Company

Strong ESG performance

Platforms

Sustainability reporting

Branded sustainability strategy

Sustainability commitments / initiatives

Membership / affiliations / certifications

Tactics

Paid / earned media   Campaigns

Social media   Speeches / announcements

Thought leadership   Information on packaging

Internal communications

Partnerships   Convenings

Website   Advertising

Stakeholders

FIGURE 11.2   Three forms of equity from being a recognized leader

Reputation equity

Governments, NGOs, media, communities

- Higher levels of trust
- More opportunities for partnerships
- More influence on policy

Talent equity

Current and furture employees

- More motivated workforce
- Higher employee retention
- Increased talent attraction

Brand equity

Customers, suppliers, shareholders

- Increased market share
- Enhanced customer and shareholder loyalty
- Stronger supplier allegiance

- Building deeper understanding and brand trust through the value chain, from suppliers to consumers. According to GlobeScan's 2021 Healthy & Sustainable Living Research Program, 57 per cent of consumers across 24 markets (up 7 points from 2019) say they would be willing to pay more for products or brands that improve society and the environment.[1]

- Catalysing action and commitments inside and outside the firm, changing mindsets and behaviours and differentiating the business in the marketplace through narrative and storytelling.

How to do it

Sustainability-related communications help connect many different parts of this handbook, from purpose (as a guiding theme, see Chapter 1), to strategy (where many proof points and possible stories will reside, see Chapter 4), to reporting (which itself comprises multiple powerful communications elements, see Chapter 8), to engagement (which makes communications more personal, see Chapter 10), to partnering (another powerful way to communicate a company's leadership, see Chapter 12), to advocacy (an impactful form of signalling what you believe in, see Chapter 13). Good communications bring these elements together in different ways and increase their overall impact.

Here are seven steps central to effective sustainability-related communications.

Step 1: Frame the narrative

The first step for building out a powerful sustainability communications strategy is to frame the narrative of the future you are trying to create. Considering that every sustainability strategy maps a path towards a desired future state, communication is essential to set expectations and define the journey.

Ideally, your narrative is aligned with your company's purpose and speaks to your values and sustainability strategy. This narrative helps provide the contours of your messaging.

The narrative your company develops should be flexible enough to adjust along the way, given how fast-moving sustainability is and how rapidly things shift from expectations to regulations to competitive context.

Step 2: Identify sustainability stories

A company's sustainability strategy, commitments and reporting contain a range of stories – anecdotes, events and accounts that describe a company's approach and commitment to sustainability – that have the chance to resonate with stakeholders.

BBMG, a branding agency based in New York, works to identify stories for clients that sit at the intersection of what is most meaningful to consumers and stakeholders and what is most material to the business, society and the planet. Raphael Bemporad, BBMG's Founding Partner, notes: 'By prioritizing stories that are meaningful and material, you build relevance, resonance and credibility.'[2]

Asking colleagues to help identify possible stories or examples of strong sustainability performance is an excellent way for a company to engage internally. From our experience, colleagues in different functions and business units often relish the opportunity to explore their work and come up with possible stories for inclusion.

Very often there will be more stories available than you can use, so it will be important to identify which of these are most relevant to your stakeholders, which ones are most timely and topical and which best align with the company's purpose and sustainability strategy.

Step 3: Brand effectively

Companies that have been able to become recognized for their sustainability performance have often done an exceptional job of defining and branding their sustainability strategy for stakeholders. They have gone beyond a generic approach to sustainability and have created a framework for what sustainability means for their company specifically.

Examples of this type of branding include M&S's 'Plan A', Unilever's 'Sustainable Living Plan' and new 'Unilever Compass', IKEA's 'People & Planet Positive' and Anglo American's 'Sustainable Mining Plan'. These companies each created a branded platform to describe their myriad sustainability activities, which supports creation of the differentiation and stickiness so critical for effective communications.

For this type of branding to work, it has to be memorable and the commitments of the sustainability strategy itself need to be big and bold to justify the time, resources and effort to build up the brand. It then needs to be pushed consistently and compellingly over time to employees and to external stakeholders.

Step 4: Get the message right

Given the ongoing low trust in business and high levels of scepticism about corporate communications around sustainability, it is critical to ensure your messaging is carefully thought through and rigorously vetted.

Our Five Cs of sustainability communications (see Table 11.1) can help in refining your messaging and overall communications. They include being *clear*, *credible*, *complete*, *compelling* and *customized*.

TABLE 11.1 The Five Cs of sustainability communications

Focus	Rationale	Action
Clear	Is the message understandable and accessible?	Make sure the language is as simple as possible; test it with stakeholders to ensure clarity.
Credible	Is the message believable and trustworthy?	Focus on evidence of impact and performance; include proof points and, where possible, third-party endorsements or certifications.

(continued)

TABLE 11.1 (Continued)

Focus	Rationale	Action
Complete	Is the message fulsome and does it meet expectations?	Ensure communications connect different elements of the sustainability agenda with your strategy and frame it with a sense of ambition; direct people to where they can find further information.
Compelling	Does the message inspire and demonstrate leadership?	Use emotive language that connects the message to the bigger picture and gives it meaning.
Customized	Is the message targeted and does it differentiate?	Don't copy competitor language or storytelling; speak directly to your stakeholders in a way that is unique to your company.

CORPORATE SUSTAINABILITY COMMUNICATION STYLES

Research conducted by Lundquist, a communications consultancy based in Milan, Italy, identified four substantive types of sustainability communicators among European companies (plus a fifth group, 'Sleepers') by evaluating them on two axes: one for the *substance* of the communications and the other for their *distinctiveness*. These styles of communication may provide a useful sense check for how your company chooses to communicate sustainability.

1: The 'narrators'

These companies present accurate, comprehensive and information-rich content – through stories or blogs – and support this with proactive user engagement and social media. Their strategic approach to sustainability runs through all communications and is conveyed in both a rational and an emotional way.

2: The 'glitterati'

These are businesses that communicate effectively on both form and substance. They are engaging, visual and modern. However, they sometimes lack specific data supporting their communication. This superficiality and perceived inability to explore topics in depth can frustrate users.

3: The 'explainers'

These companies present plenty of data and figures and explain their strategies at great length and detail. They describe sustainability at a rational level but do not engage their stakeholders well.

4: The 'traditionalists'

Perhaps the least advanced of these four types, these are businesses that handle their sustainable development communication in a very simple way. There's no real culture of transparency nor much interaction with their stakeholders via digital. These companies tend to focus on technical and compliance disclosure, without demonstrating a distinct corporate identity.

5: The 'sleepers'

Lundquist also refers to companies that haven't disclosed enough information to pass the core evaluation.[3]

Step 5: Get tone right

A number of principles offer guidance on communicating sustainability in a tone stakeholders will accept and appreciate.

- Be honest: Given ongoing low levels of trust in business and scepticism regarding corporate performance on sustainability, being honest in sustainability communications is critical. Sometimes this can take the form of being humble and acknowledging that, despite the commitments and progress your company has made, there is more to do. There is truth to the cliché that *sustainability is a journey*; companies that claim to have got everything right do so at risk of being viewed as greenwashing. Sometimes this honesty also takes the form of courage and telling it like it is, especially by expressing the urgency of the sustainability agenda.

- Be authentic: Some of the most successful brands in communicating, such as Dove (Unilever), Natura and Patagonia, have developed their own way of transmitting their messages that brings them closer to their stakeholders. They communicate with great authenticity and humanize their stories, making them honest and open.

- Be optimistic: While we face deep environmental, social and economic challenges, good sustainability communications find ways to remain hopeful about a better future. This sense of stubborn optimism and positivity is important when engaging stakeholders, and many leading companies have taken this approach. Where pessimism and stress can shut down creativity and problem-solving, optimism can help you find new solutions and avoid burnout. Meanwhile, where fear can put people off, a shared optimistic vision can help people get together behind a bigger idea.

- Be evidence based: Companies can gain credibility with stakeholders by framing their sustainability commitments and initiatives in ways that are connected to science and which are evidence based. A 2021 GlobeScan public opinion survey across 31 markets showed that people across the world trust science and academia (+70 net trust rating) much more than any other institutions, especially global companies (+8 net trust rating).[4] Communicating your sustainability messages with reference to relevant scientific context, proof points and expert perspectives continues to be an important part of effective communications, despite the 'fake news' and anti-elitism rhetoric in public discourse.

- Be expansive: One of the most effective ways to handle sustainability-related communications, especially with more sophisticated stakeholders, is to speak about the broader sustainability agenda, rather than just the elements your company will address. This means considering how your actions, commitments and business model address broader sustainable development challenges and being able to articulate your contribution to creating a more sustainable future. For some companies, especially multinationals, the SDGs may be a good reference point. For a local company with a big footprint in a particular community, the health and well-being of that city or that region's people and environment might provide a suitable frame.

An example that showcases effective tone can be found in an excerpt of an email from Amanda Nusz, Senior Vice President, Corporate Responsibility and President of the Target Foundation at American retailer Target, introducing the company's 2021 Corporate Responsibility Report:

> We've come so far over the last year. We've set bold goals, we've pushed ourselves and we've made strong progress toward our sustainability ambitions. However, we know that there is much work to be done as we strive to deliver on our goals. And we remain committed to keeping people and the planet at the heart of what we do – co-creating an equitable and regenerative future with our team, guests and communities we serve.[5]

Step 6: Match messages, proof points and channels

An effective communication strategy requires connecting the right messages to the right stakeholders using the right messaging and channels. Making each of these choices count is fundamental to communicating well.

It is important to check regularly that the business has an appropriate spread and prioritization of channels and forms of communication to serve each stakeholder group and significant subgroups. The company also needs to make sure channels and their content align to stakeholders' expectations for the company and vice versa (see Chapter 10).

Businesses need to be precise in their selection of messages, proof points and the channels they use for discrete stakeholder audiences. The framework in Table 11.2 outlines an example of how to build an integrated messaging strategy for key stakeholder audiences.

TABLE 11.2 Sustainability messaging framework: example

Stakeholder audience	Key message	Proof point	Channel
Investors	• Value of sustainability for growth	• Higher margin for sustainable products	• ESG presentation as part of AGM
Customers	• Innovative energy-efficient product	• Better product performance	• Eco-label on package
NGOs	• Commitment to address climate change	• Corporate sustainability targets	• Partnership

Step 7: Be consistent, disciplined, proactive and repetitive

Once the business has established itself with clear sustainability commitments and performance, it can be increasingly confident with communications – reacting to external news, articulating a company point of view on sustainability matters and becoming an advocate (see Chapter 13).

It is an ongoing challenge to ensure coherence and consistency of authentic and inspirational messaging across all of a company's communications channels and formats. It is essential that non-sustainability messaging does not contradict sustainability communications. Companies need to avoid mixed messaging or anything that might bring accusations of hypocrisy, inconsistency or greenwashing.

GlobeScan conducted a review of sustainability strategy and initiative launches to explore how companies have shifted the way they communicate in this field. The results showed an evolution of approaches, which are summarized in Figure 11.3.

In many ways, the communications landscape in sustainability has changed significantly. The new paradigm for communications going forward may be an inverse of the traditional approach, as illustrated in Figure 11.4.

FIGURE 11.3 Communicating leadership: The new era

	Past – Leadership by example	Today – Catalyzing collective action
Intent	Build profile / reputation	Accelerate change and mobilize
Target	Stakeholders as 'recipients'	Stakeholders as participants and partners (a collective movement)
Focus	Our (company) strategy Full sustainability strategy	Our shared challenges Sustainability strategy and singular initiatives
Goals	Less bad; complex	Positive (reversing, improving); simple
Timing	A one-off 'launch'	A campaign approach with ongoing engagement
Story	Corporate storytelling, distinct from brand / business narrative	Bolder 'human' storytelling, tailored to the audience and integrated within brand / business story
Story 'owner'	Sustainability leader / CEO	Broader range of leaders, employees, partners, customers, etc

Reproduced with kind permission of GlobeScan (2021)

FIGURE 11.4   New sustainability communications paradigm

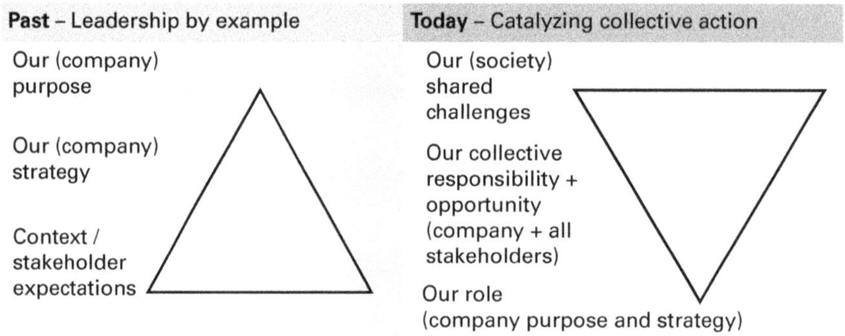

Reproduced with kind permission of GlobeScan (2021)

In practice

Patagonia

Patagonia is an outdoor apparel company with around 2,400 employees. While privately held, its annual revenue is reported by third-party sources as being around $1 billion. The business, headquartered in Ventura, California, was founded in 1973 and now has stores in more than 10 countries.[6]

While Patagonia is engaged in the manufacturing of outdoor clothing, outdoor gear and footwear, its purpose statement 'We're in business to save our home planet' suggests a higher calling. The company believes in building the best product, causing no unnecessary harm and using business to inspire and implement solutions to the environmental crisis.

Since 1985, Patagonia has pledged 1 per cent of sales to the preservation and restoration of the natural environment, awarding over $140 million in cash and in-kind donations to domestic and international grassroots environmental groups making a difference in their local communities.[7] The brand wants to be known for the transparency of its supply chain, promoting social justice for its workers and creating durable products that, where possible, are made from recycled, fair trade or organic materials and that are produced in ways that facilitate regeneration of ecosystems. Fittingly, its communications strategy is centred around these tenets.

Patagonia uses its website landing page to highlight environmental causes and to advocate purchasing used gear or 'worn wear'. Indeed, the top line navigation of the company's home page is 'Shop, Activism, Sports and *Stories*' (emphasis added). This focus on stories has been a part of Patagonia's approach to engagement with consumers from the beginning. The website is full of short stories about inspirational experiences in nature and illustrations of how the company is driving more positive social and environmental impact and standing up for causes it believes in. This carries on a tradition started by its founder, Yves Chouinard, who has written many books about the environment, sport and business.

Similarly, Patagonia's social media channels actively promote a minimal resource-use lifestyle and create awareness of environmental and social causes that customers can support or engage with themselves. Patagonia's pathbreaking 2001 'Don't Buy This Jacket' campaign wanted to address mass consumerism and deter people from apparel shopping on Black Friday.[8]

Patagonia communications are consistent and centred around its ethos of being in business to save the planet. Most of its marketing campaigns are focused on building a movement based on the values the company shares with its communities. The company believes in using its influence to bring largely hidden environmental issues onto the global agenda through its communication campaigns. For example, the 2018 'Save the Blue Heart' campaign focused on preserving the pristine beauty of the Balkan River network in Eastern Europe, featuring a full-length documentary produced by Patagonia and ultimately presenting a 120,000-strong petition to the European Bank for Reconstruction and Development.[9]

Vincent Stanley, Director of Philosophy at Patagonia, summarized the company's approach to communications in this way:

> We started as a climbing-equipment company, with a small band of customers removed from us, at most, by three degrees of separation.

So we wrote to and for our customers as friends and equals. When we learned something new about a sport, a beloved place, or an environmental threat, we shared it, as you would with a friend. We have many more customers now, but we still relate to our whole community along the same lines.[10]

Microsoft

Microsoft is a multinational software and technology company with more than 200,000 employees and 2020 annual revenue of $143 billion. Headquartered in Redmond, Washington, the corporation was founded in 1975 and today operates in 190 countries globally.[11]

The company's products include operating systems, cross-device productivity applications, server applications, business solution applications, desktop and server management tools, software development tools and video games. It also designs, manufactures and sells devices, including PCs, tablets, gaming and entertainment consoles, other intelligent devices and related accessories. Microsoft is a technology company whose mission is to empower every person and every organization on the planet to achieve more.

Microsoft continuously strives to promote sustainability in its operations, products and policies and, more importantly, helps its customers and partners to do the same. The company has been carbon neutral since 2012 and is actively trying to reduce its footprint by evolving the way it operates. In addition to designing devices with an emphasis on eco-friendly materials, the company is pushing cloud and AI services that help other businesses cut energy consumption, reduce physical footprints and design sustainable products of their own. In early 2020, the company made an ambitious commitment to become carbon negative by 2030, and it promised to remove from the environment all the carbon the company has emitted directly or by electrical consumption since it was founded in 1975, by no later than 2050.

A critical lever in sharing Microsoft's ambition with its stakeholders has been crisp and transparent communication. The fact that the message came directly from the top (CEO, CFO and President) when Microsoft launched its 2030 and 2050 ambitions for carbon, water, waste and biodiversity had significant positive impact on stakeholders, including other companies. Following a live broadcast on the internet, extensive information about the goals was published on the company's website. Coupled with informative videos, Microsoft's approach made it easier for the audience to understand the context and scale of the company's ambition.[12]

Over time, each of the four key parts of Microsoft's sustainability strategy (carbon, ecosystems, water and waste) has been profiled on the official Microsoft blog. The company's commitment to sustainability takes centre stage on its investor homepage too, sending a strong message that it is integrated into the way Microsoft conducts business. A progress report on its commitments and video content demystifying how it plans to meet its targets are featured on its sustainability microsite also.

Brad Smith, Microsoft's President, says in his foreword to the company's 2020 Environmental Sustainability Report:

> Microsoft can't solve the world's environmental challenges
> alone, but we can play a significant role in driving a broader
> societal transformation if we use our positions of influence and
> our technologies to effectively bring others along with us on our
> sustainability journey.[13]

Summary

Given how fast-moving and all-encompassing sustainability has become, it is important to be agile and opportunistic in the realm of sustainability communications. Having the right stories and communications toolkit for executives ready to go helps, as does having a close working relationship with the company's communications team, web developers and so on.

Persistent low levels of trust in business and especially in communications related to sustainability among stakeholders and particularly younger generations necessitates robust, accurate and proactive communications. Despite suspicions, stakeholders of all types are increasingly interested in what companies are doing in sustainability: 86 per cent of consumers across the world say they are interested in learning more about what companies are doing to be environmentally and socially responsible (up 15 points from five years earlier).[14]

Responding to events or to criticism of your industry or business requires confidence in your narrative and approach to sustainability communications. Having a strong communications programme in place reinforces the sustainability strategy and helps internal and external stakeholders better understand the commitments the company has in place and the integrity within which it is operationalizing sustainability (see Chapter 5). Without effective communications, much of the business case for sustainability is lost, making this a critical aspect of a company's sustainability approach.

Action checklist

1 Frame your company's narrative in a sustainable future.

2 Identify sustainability-related stories that fit with your purpose and which bring your narrative to life.

3 Brand your sustainability strategy, commitments and stories in ways that are memorable and engaging.

4 Shape your messaging and tone for each stakeholder audience and each communications channel.

5 Align stories, messages and proof points to serve diverse stakeholder information needs.

6 Be consistent, disciplined, proactive and regularly reinforcing with your sustainability communications.

Further resources

- BBMG (2021) Radically Better Future, bbmg.com/radically-better-future

- Futerra (2018) *Futerra's Honest Product Guide*, www.wearefuterra.com/wp-content/uploads/2018/11/The-Honest-Product-Guide.pdf

- Lundquist.future (2020) Europe Top 50 2019: Assessing communication for sustainability, lundquist.it/wp-content/uploads/2020/06/future-EU.pdf

- Nordic Sustainability (June 2021) Communicating sustainability: Achieving effective and truthful communication, www.youtube.com/watch?v=fBfdpH8rs7g

- For advice and insights on story-telling, see: zoearden.com

Endnotes

1 GlobeScan (2021) Healthy & Sustainable Living Research Program

2 Interview with Raphael Bemporad, Founding Partner, BBMG, 22 September 2021

3 Lundquist (2019) Europe Top 50: 2019, lundquist.it/wp-content/uploads/2020/06/future-EU.pdf (archived at https://perma.cc/6AXH-RFVY)

4 GlobeScan Radar Research Program 2021

5 Nusz, A (2021) Email to stakeholders, 13 August

6 Patagonia Works (2019) Annual Benefit Corporation Report: Fiscal year 2019, www.patagonia.com/on/demandware.static/-/Library-Sites-PatagoniaShared/default/dwf14ad70c/PDF-US/PAT_2019_BCorp_Report.pdf (archived at https://perma.cc/H9HQ-4M3R)

7 B Work (2017) Patagonia Company Profile, www.bwork.com/employer/company/877/Patagonia (archived at https://perma.cc/97S9-CEQ9)

8 Addady, M (2016) Patagonia's donating all $10 million of its Black Friday sales to charity, Fortune, 29 November, fortune.com/2016/11/29/black-friday-2016-patagonia/ (archived at https://perma.cc/CZ2G-ENYD)

9 Rogers, C (2018) Patagonia on why brands 'can't reverse into purpose' through marketing, MarketingWeek, 18 July, www.marketingweek.com/patagonia-you-cant-reverse-into-values-through-marketing/ (archived at https://perma.cc/E2MY-4285)

10 Authors' exchange with Vincent Stanley, September 2021

11 Microsoft (2020) Annual Report 2020, www.microsoft.com/investor/reports/ar20/index.html (archived at https://perma.cc/R6YQ-TBYY)

12 Microsoft (2021) Investor Relations, www.microsoft.com/en-us/Investor/ (archived at https://perma.cc/VR78-4N8Z)

13 Microsoft (2021) Corporate Social Responsibility, www.microsoft.com/en-us/corporate-responsibility/sustainability?rtc=1&activetab=pivot_1:primaryr3 (archived at https://perma.cc/5JP5-JJNP)

14 GlobeScan (2020) Healthy & Sustainable Living Research Program, globescan.com/trends/healthy-sustainable-living/ (archived at https://perma.cc/XNT4-XLD4)

12

Partnering

What is it?

Sustainability partnerships involve a business joining with one or more other businesses and/or with non-private sector actors such as NGOs, governments, multilateral organizations and academic institutions. Companies do this to advance sustainability strategy and increase positive impact in ways which they couldn't do on their own or which they can do more easily at pace and scale in collaboration with others. Such partnerships may be defined as follows:

> A collaborative relationship focused on sustainability outcomes in which all participants agree to work together to achieve a common purpose or to undertake a specific task and to share risks, resources, competencies, and benefits, with reciprocal obligations and mutual accountability for outcomes.[1]

Where the partnership involves two or more companies within the same industry, this is sometimes described as pre-competitive collaboration, which typically involves coming together to address a shared problem or pain point that doesn't impact direct business competition and which is often focused on joint social or environmental impacts.[2]

The current landscape of partnerships for sustainability

Sustainability partnerships have become much more common in recent years as global challenges become more urgent and better understood and as more businesses appreciate the potential benefits to themselves and to society from successful partnerships.

These partnerships can be on a spectrum from transactional (just delivering a service) to leveraging resources, combining assets or even working for systems change. They come in many shapes and sizes including: business and an NGO; groups of businesses together; and businesses working with governments, international development agencies and/or civil society groups (NGOs, social enterprises, universities, active citizens). See box below.

TYPES OF SUSTAINABILITY PARTNERSHIPS

- Business and an NGO

    - Partnerships between a company and an NGO around a particular project or task. They may evolve over time into a more strategic relationship like the partnership between UK-headquartered retailer Marks & Spencer and the development charity Oxfam, or the 20+ year partnership between the global drinks company Diageo and WaterAid, which over time has developed into joint advocacy for universal access to safe water, sanitation and hygiene at local, national and global levels.

- Business-to-business (B2B)

    - General corporate responsibility coalitions of businesses, both national (such as Business in the Community in the UK, and Maala: Israel Business for Social Responsibility) and international business coalitions such as BSR (formerly known as Business for Social Responsibility) and the World Business Council for Sustainable Development.[3]

    - Industry-specific coalitions such as the Responsible Business Alliance, which focuses on worker rights and well-being in the electronics supply chain, and the collaborative platform 'Drive Sustainability' (DS) facilitated by the international, generalist coalition CSR Europe. Drive Sustainability now has a common strategy and action plan for a circular and sustainable automotive value chain.[4] Similarly,

---

the generalist coalition BSR hosts a number of industry-specific collaboration initiatives for member companies. Most industry sectors now have some form of pre-competitive coalition around sustainable development as well.

○ Initiatives within existing trade associations or spun out from trade associations such as the sustainability programmes of the Consumer Goods Forum, the Plastic Waste and Food Waste coalitions, a Global Food Safety Initiative and the Collaboration for Healthier Lives Coalition.

○ The GSM (Global System for Mobile Communications), which represents 800 mobile operators and other companies in the mobile ecosystem, was the first representative industry association to produce a public report outlining the industry's contribution to the Sustainable Development Goals.

- Businesses and other parts of society

○ Multi-stakeholder initiatives between multiple businesses, NGOs and other players such as governments, development agencies and universities, for instance for improving social and environmental performance in consumer goods, electronics and apparel supply chains, like the work of the Fair Labor Association and the Ethical Trading Initiative.

○ Issue-specific coalitions of businesses and others formed to foster collaboration to address a specific sustainability issue such as the CEO Water Mandate convened by the UN Global Compact, or initiatives tackling corruption and money laundering such as Transparency International's sector-and country-based Integrity Pacts and The Maritime Anti-Corruption Network (MACN).

These various forms of sustainability partnerships can fulfil one or more different roles such as:

- Standards-setting and certification, such as the long-established Marine Stewardship Council or the more recent Better Cotton Initiative.

- Clearinghouses for sustainability-related knowledge and good practice such as the Circular 100 Network of the Ellen MacArthur Foundation for the Circular Economy.[5]

- Forums for difficult conversations and frank exploration of frontier topics where ethics of and responsibility for the impacts of new technologies, etc, can be honestly explored, such as The Artificial Intelligence Partnership.

- Brokers to match help available from partners with help needed and to facilitate collective solutions to common industry / societal problems such as the National Business Initiative (NBI), which is a voluntary coalition of South African and multinational companies working towards sustainable growth and development in South Africa.[6]

- Vehicles for collective advocacy around sustainable development and social justice, for instance those designed to nudge consumer or citizen behaviour or to influence governments to change tax, laws and policies. The We Mean Business Coalition, for instance, brings together several non-profit coalitions to accelerate an inclusive transition to a net zero economy.

There are a number of efforts that seek to catalogue partnerships for sustainability. In spring 2021, for example, the campaigning British think-tank The ReGenerate Trust mapped in excess of 300 organizations and initiatives operating in the UK and in some way promoting the idea of purpose-led business.[7] There isn't, however, a single comprehensive list of sustainability-related collaborations. Indeed, it would quickly become out of date as new coalitions emerge. One good place to start to find partnerships relevant for a business in a particular sector is to look at the websites of leading companies in the same sector to see which partnerships they are involved with or to consult a relevant trade association for advice. Additionally, throughout this *Sustainable Business Handbook* we highlight relevant partnerships for sustainability, which might serve as a jumping-off point for finding others.

Why it matters

Direct business benefits:

- It helps a business to do things it can't do on its own – for example, by filling knowledge and capacity gaps.
- It increases resilience and can contribute to long-term, enduring success.
- It can amplify and improve communications, build engagement, develop external advocates and help reach more audiences, which can help build trust, reputation and legitimacy.
- Partnerships may help facilitate the creation of new business models. It can be reassuring to be part of a pack.
- Companies are finding more opportunities to collaborate in a way that is not challenging their competitive advantage. To quote a BSR report, partnering for sustainability can be 'a business strategy that enables future competition between companies within a more sustainable market system'.[8] (See also the extract on sustainable tea.)

Wider, societal benefits:

- It can generate more impact, faster and at greater scale to support growth that is more responsible, inclusive and sustainable.
- It facilitates innovation and skills / capacity building among partner organizations and their individual employees.
- Partnering can be a 'safe space' to address systemic risks and to share risks, especially on contentious topics or 'wicked problems' that defy conventional solutions.

And at an industry or system level:

- Partnerships can shape industry strategies for sustainability with agreed standards, a common road map and shared long-term goals for achieving systemic transformation of markets.
- Partnerships can underpin effective advocacy for systemic policy changes that favour sustainability, such as in terms of taxes and subsidies or new laws and regulations.

As a report from The SustainAbility Institute by ERM (2020) notes:

> Competitors are also partnering in areas that are closer to historical trade secrets. For example, the two biggest exporters of tea in the world, Hindustan Unilever and Tata Global Beverages, came together in 2014 to drive long-term sustainable improvements in tea farming practices for smallholder farmers with help from the Sustainable Trade Initiative. Given their positions in the market, this collaboration brought every value chain partner in the tea sector to the table. Since the launch of the program, more than 55,000 tea growers have been awarded a sustainable farming certification.[9]

How to do it

Step 1: Define what the business needs partnerships to do

The development of your company's sustainability strategy (see Chapter 4) will likely have identified gaps in the business's capabilities, including:

- knowledge;
- technical solutions;
- delivery capacity;
- certification requirements;
- collective industry solutions;
- systems change.

In all these situations partnerships might be a viable response. The first step, therefore, is to identify where partnerships could help address specific business needs. BSR cites common motivations for business engagement in sustainability partnerships (see Table 12.1).

Where strategic gaps or other potential motivations are identified, a business should explore whether existing partnerships might address specific needs or opportunities or where an existing partnership's remit might be extended to fill the gaps. Even when partnering

TABLE 12.1 Commonly cited motivations for business engagement in sustainability partnerships

Strategic opportunity creation/problem resolution	• Co-investing in new market opportunities
	• Building resilient, sustainable supply chains
	• Overcoming regulatory supply chains
	• Sharing the risk of new approaches with peer organizations
Leveraging financial resources	• Accessing donor funding
	• Mobilizing and optimizing pooled resources toward a common purpose
Influencing others	• Shaping industry standards
	• Influencing policy and garnering political support
	• Encouraging behaviour change
Gaining access to partner assets	• Accessing new networks
	• Accessing technical support and complementary skills
	• Accessing new technologies
	• Accessing information and knowledge
Improving legitimacy, credibility, or visibility	• Enhancing brand value and reputation
	• Inspiring, attracting, and retaining top talent
	• Building legitimacy and support for a preferred approach

SOURCE BSR Private-Sector Collaboration for Sustainable Development (2018)[10] – reproduced with permission.

appears to offer solutions, companies need to remember that working in partnership can be challenging and time-consuming, with high transaction costs. It is important to be certain that the business can't do what it needs to do on its own or with the help of consultants or with a smaller, ad-hoc group and to enter partnership only when that is truly the best available solution.

Step 2: Identify a shortlist of relevant potential partnerships

The next step is to think about who the business could work with to solve issues identified in the strategy. Often, businesses don't think about other businesses / competitors as potential partners. For companies starting out on sustainability or beginning a more substantive approach for the first time, there will likely be at minimum several relevant potential partnerships including both industry-specific and issue-specific ones. This is not least because so many partnerships have been created in recent years. If in doubt, look at the partnerships in which leading companies in your sector are involved.

Even if a business has no prior experience of working in sustainability partnerships, it is likely that there will have been some prior involvement in a trade association, Chamber of Commerce or local small business club. Among the management team, there will be some people personally active in voluntary organizations with partnering mindset and experience to share. Depending on the business, starting with partnerships to improve sustainability performance and profitability in the supply chain could represent an early win.

More typically, at least for existing businesses, there will be a patchwork quilt of mostly ad-hoc and reactive involvements, and perhaps some where the sustainability dimension has been largely ignored to date. It can be useful to do a mapping exercise of existing memberships and involvements. A modified version of the classic Boston Consulting Group (BCG) Product Portfolio 2×2 Matrix could be used to map sustainability partnerships in terms of business effort and resources required against low / high positive impact from the partnership for the business and the sector (see Figure 12.1). Alternative axes might be effectiveness of coalition and importance of issue to the business, linking back to the materiality mapping (see Chapter 2).

A more sophisticated version of this exercise might include considering not just current impact but also the potential for greater impact in the future, with a changed strategy and better execution of it.

A small but growing number of companies including ING and Google list the sustainability partnerships they participate in on their websites.[11] Other companies like Adidas and Cargill explain their rationale for being in specific partnerships,[12] while a handful such as Nestlé publicize the criteria they use to choose which collaborations to join and remain in.[13] Similarly, Shell lists its key partnerships for sustainability on its website and explains why it partners, the key subject areas in which it does so and its approach to partnering,[14] and

FIGURE 12.1   Prioritizing sustainability partnerships

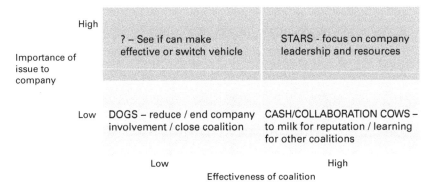

Modifying BCG portfolio 2×2 matrix to a company's collaborations

Danone lists its partnerships according to the SDGs they are intended to help address.[15]

It is good practice to track sustainability partnerships and articulate the reasons for participating in each. Reasons might relate to the business's goals, the partnership's goals and the wider benefits to society. We expect public disclosure related to partnering for sustainability to increase in company sustainability reports, websites and elsewhere.

There are other ways to identify potential partnerships relevant to your business, and each company needs methods that suit its own situation. For instance, if you are a B-Corp or an aspiring B-Corp, then the B Lab team for your country / region should be able to help you find other B-Corps keen to learn from each other, pool sustainability R&D efforts and examine possible solutions to commonly faced problems.[16]

Once partnership options are clear, they should be assessed before decisions are taken to join any. There can be a danger of an illusion of progress just by joining a partnership. A business may feel that it has acted. The action really occurs only when the business does things because of being in the partnership.

Several recent studies outline what makes a strong partnership for sustainability, including:

- Clear understanding of the system / scope of interest and boundaries of the project; partners might be collaborating here but still competing / campaigning against each other elsewhere.

- Awareness of the potential power imbalances in a partnership, particularly between large and small businesses or between larger businesses and NGOs or local governments, in terms of resources and capabilities.

- Common purpose, including joint transformation vision, goals and activities, with each participating organization also knowing why they are involved.

- Strong champions who are leaders in their own organizations and able to take decisions, allocate resources, motivate and mobilize others, secure sufficient commitment in their organizations and support long-term commitments. This is much easier where there is clear understanding of direct and indirect benefits.

- High levels of trust between partners and individuals in the partnership and between member organizations based on empathy and mutual respect (through listening and immersing in each other's worlds).

- Stable membership of organizations and individuals in the partnership.

- Fit for purpose, with effective implementation capabilities including sufficient, competent staff, funding and time.

- Good governance mechanisms to track performance and ensure rigorous oversight and accountability and clear reporting lines into the respective partner organizations.

- Effective performance tracking that integrates systems thinking, facilitates shared learning and with the flexibility to course correct and adapt when this is needed in the partnership.

- Strong track record of leveraging support from external stakeholders of the partnership.

Step 3:   Agree approach and clarify goals and resources required

Having identified potential partnerships, it is necessary to define the business objectives – for instance the desired change / impacts (the purpose) for involvement, anticipated timescales and what inputs and contributions (financial, human and corporate commitments to change) each will require, as well as the business case (the perceived benefits) for participation. It is important to consider whether the company will focus on a few initiatives or spread itself out across many and to identify any specific models that have worked well in the past and fit the organizational culture, such as peer coalitions where all participants are companies or multi-stakeholder groups with members from more than one sector. Ideally, this assessment will be guided by a vision that sets out the high-level ambition for all of a company's collaborations.

Given limited resources and the need to focus on material issues, it is important to prioritize which and how many partnerships to join. As with Step 1, this requires focusing on a company's key issues, which should be informed by materiality (see Chapter 2) and making a link to organizational strategy and purpose. This key issue focus can then be complemented by a gap analysis between capabilities and capacity, which assesses what an organization can do alone versus where it needs partners.

For many businesses, one significant partnership may be enough at the outset – not to mention as much as the organization can cope with initially. Given the danger of being too thinly stretched, a business should not try to do everything at once; a business needs to preserve sufficient resource to be effective in the partnerships in which it does engage.

Once a business gets used to working in partnerships, further opportunities for learning often open. Similarly, chances to take advantage of the partnership's knowledge may emerge, which is often a precursor to identifying further partnerships and collaborations. Research conducted some years ago for the *MIT Sloan Management Review* found that the more businesses got used to using their 'collaboration muscle', the more they reported benefits from working in sustainability partnerships. Specifically, 8 per cent of businesses involved in three or less partnerships thought collaborations were very successful, while 35 per cent said they were quite successful. By contrast, for those with experience in more than 50 partnerships, the figures were 45 per cent and 50 per cent respectively.[17] As experience in partnering has increased very substantially since the MIT Sloan study was published in 2015, we would anticipate that the difference in assessments would be even more pronounced now. Similarly, there is evidence that, with more collaboration practice, greater benefits and higher impact are better tracked and articulated today than in the past, a trend expected to continue.

While few businesses yet codify their approach to partnering for sustainability in a formal strategy, it is worth a business exploring questions such as:

- depth versus breadth;
- active or passive role in membership;
- attitude to taking a leadership role;
- company policy redlines;
- internal and external understanding of what each partnership sets out to do and internal champions for this;
- the specific challenges of working with different types of partners such as possible power imbalances arising from having very different levels of resources.

It is also worth double-checking that any public stances taken by the partnerships that a business might join are compatible with the company's own policy positions and actions.

Another preparatory question is which internal stakeholders need to be engaged, consulted or simply informed about developments in particular partnerships. Understanding this in terms of the degree of relevance of a partnership for internal stakeholders as well as their power in the business can help to overcome opposition and build internal champions for the work of particular partnerships.

Step 4: Building capabilities for partnering

The next step is to assign enough talent from the business to ensure that partnership objectives can be met. How the company shows up in collaborations contributes to the reputation of the business and how far it is trusted by partners and other stakeholders. Accordingly, the business will want to project the same degree of professionalism in collaborations as in any of its other activities. It will want to establish a reputation for playing its full part, taking its fair share of responsibility, being constructive and solutions-orientated and doing what it says it will do. It is important, therefore, that company representatives in the partnership have sufficient authority to be able to commit the business and its resources as required to meet its partnership obligations. It is also important that assigned personnel have the mindset and the skillset needed. This includes the empathy and creativity to be able to see things from the perspective of their partners, especially where the partnership involves participants from other sectors.

A collaborative mindset needs to be part of the desired organizational culture (see Chapter 6) and a defined part of leadership competencies (see Chapter 7). The NGO The Partnering Initiative has defined what it calls 'MUST-have partnering competencies' (see Figure 12.2).

Admittedly, this is a very comprehensive skillset. In practice, few business leaders or companies will start out with all these skills, which are generally developed and refined over time. Nevertheless, this MUST-have framework is a useful summary for human resources departments and learning and development teams inside companies to use in preparing staff to work in partnership. Several specific skills such as stakeholder engagement, as well as being a good communicator and an effective networker are now considered an essential part of any leader's toolkit. Perhaps the critical extra skills for successful partnering are a degree of humility and willingness to 'walk in the other person's shoes'.

FIGURE 12.2 MUST-have partnering competencies

M	U	S	T
Mindset	Understanding of other sectors	Human relationship skills	Technical partnering knowledge
• Humility to realise that others may have more appropriate knowledge / resources • Inclination to reach out to work with others • Willingness to give up autonomy of decision-making • (Measured) risk taking • Propensity for innovation • Ability to work for the benefit of the partnership as a whole	• Language • Values and culture • Interests • Motivations and drivers • Resources and capabilities • Systems and process • Capacity limitations • Legal limitations • AND understanding of your own!	• Ability to look from others' perspectives • Networking and connecting • Approaching and engaging potential partners / selling ideas • Relationship / trust building • Interest-based negotiation • Facilitation • Communication • Coaching and mentoring • Meditation / conflict resolution / troubleshooting	• Understanding the partnering lifecycle • Key principles and building blocks • Best practice approaches to setup and governance • Ability to assess critically when and when not to partner • The relationship black box of trust, equity and power • Partnership agreements • Reviewing partnerships • Developing exit strategies

Reproduced with permission: The SDG Partnership Guidebook, Darian Stibbe and Dave Prescott, The Partnering Initiative and UN DESA 2020

One major global company discovered that many of the managers that it has put in to represent the company in cross-sectoral sustainability partnerships come from a brand management or procurement backgrounds. Sometimes, these managers have found it hard to put on one side their super-competitive spirit. Consequently, they are sometimes unable to find common ground or make common cause with partners. Conversely, some managers become so absorbed in the spirit of partnerships they join that they prioritize the partnership to the expense of their own company's needs.

Over time, this company's approach has evolved significantly to ensure that clear responsibility for particularly sensitive partnerships and relationships, such as those with campaigning NGOs, is held by experienced, specialist managers, often with a public affairs background, and that managers new to representing the company in a sustainability collaboration are assigned a mentor, usually from public affairs or legal. More fundamentally, the company now hires differently, putting much more emphasis on values rather than just skills and on recruitment from other sectors to ensure a diversity of mindsets. The core training of their brand managers is also changing. Training now includes an emphasis on systems thinking as well as organizational thinking, internal stakeholder management and on how to mark out collaboration space as well as competitive space. This is a long-term shift. It takes time to get managers comfortable, enthusiastic and capable working in sustainability collaborations. Skills-based volunteering and secondment opportunities can help to build skills and confidence.

It is good practice to have main company contacts and back-ups who can step in with minimal preparation. It is important that company representatives have sufficient time for their role and that this is recognized in their key performance indicators, appraisals, rewards and recognition. Few if any significant partnerships survive long term without the commitment and sponsorship of senior executive champions in the business.

The business may also need to think about the capabilities of the other partners such as community groups and grassroots NGOs – especially in low-income countries – and how capabilities can be enhanced. This may need to be done through intermediaries where there might otherwise be potential or actual conflicts of interest.

Step 5: Make the most of partnerships

Core business functions such as finance, purchasing and logistics, marketing, innovation, new business development, legal and external affairs need to be kept abreast of developments in the company's key sustainability partnerships if these are truly to be at the heart of the business.

As partnering for sustainability becomes a more important part of business and central to the achievement of corporate strategy, it becomes more necessary to establish robust measurement, evaluation, learning and reporting (M.E.L.R.) systems to track sustainability partnerships, to ensure there is continuous learning and improvement in partnerships and to help integrate learning from the partnership back into the business. In truth, however, this remains an aspiration rather than current reality, even for companies with broad experience of partnering.

Sometimes, there may be questions raised about whether a particular partnership constitutes anti-competitive behaviour, even when the purpose of the partnership is for the public good. There should be a public interest defence where the partnership is demonstrably advancing sustainability, but there is also an onus on participating companies to be consistent in their overall approach to sustainability.[18]

There is likely going to be a degree of tension in any partnership since there are typically at least three sets of goals that won't be fully aligned even just in a dyad – namely Organization A's goals, Organization B's goals and the partnership's goals. A business needs to find the overlap of common interests and drive those forward, achieve its own objectives and support partners to achieve theirs. This is why it can be harder to measure and monitor the 'success' of a partnership. There may well be different measures for the business and the partnership, and there are often different expectations of the timelines over which benefits will be achieved. Businesses need to think about how they will measure impacts overall: success is typically about external change as well as direct benefit to the business.

Step 6: Keep partnerships under regular review and know when to exit

An effective M.E.L.R. system can help identify when it is time for the business to exit from a particular partnership and move on. This may be because, despite best efforts, the partnership is not delivering or, more positively, because there is a common agreement that the designated tasks for the partnership have been completed or that residual tasks can be handed over to another group.

One of the areas where we expect to see more focus in future is at the level of a particular industry, with corporate sustainability leaders in the sector being encouraged to help raise the sustainability standards of their sector. Almost certainly, this will involve sustainability leaders in partnering to build the capacity of existing trade associations or new, industry-specific sustainability coalitions to set and promote sustainability standards and help laggard businesses to improve their performance in order to stay competitive in the future.

In practice

Novartis

Novartis is a global pharmaceutical company that specializes in gene therapies, oncology and medicine. It was founded in 1966 and has its headquarters in Basel, Switzerland. Novartis has 106,000 employees, a 2020 revenue of $48.6 billion, and its products are sold in 155 countries around the world.

Novartis has been engaged in sustainable development for well over a decade. For the company, sustainability is closely aligned with its wider purpose to 'Reimagine Medicine' for people all around the world.

In response to the growing environmental crisis and the UN's Sustainable Development Goals, Novartis has adopted progressively more ambitious sustainability targets. It aims to be 'fully carbon, plastic and water neutral over the next decade', according to its CEO, Vas Narasimhan.

Novartis also harnesses the power of partnerships (Goal 17 of the United Nations Sustainable Development Goals) to discover and develop breakthrough treatments and deliver them to as many people as possible. Novartis launched its Code of Ethics in 2020 to strengthen integrity in decision-making and help the company achieve its ambition to be among the most trusted partners in healthcare.

A core part of Novartis's strategy is grounded in collaboration. For instance, in 2021, Novartis partnered with MedShr to support its healthcare systems and services efforts in Sub-Saharan Africa. MedShr is a platform that provides free, interactive case-based learning and disease-specific discussion groups through a smartphone app. Novartis is also collaborating with Hewlett Packard Enterprise to accelerate the use of data and digital technologies as a means to improve access to healthcare and medicines across the world. To fight against COVID-19, Novartis quickly partnered with more than one multi-stakeholder consortia, including the COVID-19 Therapeutics Accelerator coordinated by the Bill & Melinda Gates Foundation, the Wellcome Trust and Mastercard.

Novartis has also been proactive in engaging its supply chain partners to identify and develop integrated energy strategies to increase efficiency, secure renewable energy and identify credible offsets. Moving forward, the company is working to include sustainability language in every new contract with suppliers, partly in order to drive even greater cooperation and collaboration.

Joerg Reinhardt, Novartis' Chairman, articulated the company's pledge to stakeholders to work with others in pursuing positive social and environmental outcomes: 'Novartis will remain a committed partner to support private and public ventures designed to help patients, protect the environment, promote business integrity and support international efforts to address future challenges.'[19]

Reckitt

Reckitt is a UK-headquartered multinational fast-moving consumer goods company that specializes in hygiene, health and nutrition with a portfolio of well-known brands such as Dettol, Lysol, Harpic, Finish, Vanish, Durex, Enfamil, Nurofen, Strepsils, Gaviscon and more. Every day, more than 20 million Reckitt products are bought globally.

Reckitt was founded in 1840 in Hull, England, with its headquarters now being in Slough, England. Reckitt has 43,000 employees globally and a 2020 net revenue of $19.1 billion.

Reckitt's near 200-year heritage is rooted in a commitment to be an ethical and responsible business. The company's ambition by 2030 is to reach half the world with brands that help people live cleaner, healthier lives and enable a cleaner, healthier world. It also aims to engage two billion people to make a positive societal impact through its partnerships, programmes and campaigns. The company recognizes that to live up to these aspirations, it will need to invest in partnerships and collaborations.

Reckitt is actively working with partners to deliver on the UN Sustainable Development Goals (SDGs). Each of its 24 global brands has a purpose aligned with at least one of the SDGs. For example, Vanish, through its partnership with British Fashion Week, promotes cleaning and reusing clothes, while Dettol and Harpic focus on water and sanitation for health and hygiene. Another successful result is Reckitt's pilot partnership with National Geographic and WWF to build awareness of water scarcity and protect fresh-water ecosystems, especially in the Ganges and Amazon basins. Reckitt's Finish brand encourages people to skip the rinse for dishwashing; beginning in the USA, UK, Australia and Turkey, this global campaign enables millions of gallons of water to be saved every year.

Through Reckitt's partnership with the Danish Institute for Human Rights, the partners identified risks for rubber plantation workers and their communities. As a result, Reckitt works with the plantation companies to ensure that their policies on labour standards and human rights are met. Reckitt has also partnered with the Fair Rubber Association to support plantation workers and farmers in Malaysia and Thailand, paying a premium that enables stronger livelihoods and enhanced standards of living. The programme also supports supply of the natural latex that Reckitt uses in its global condom brand, Durex.

Finally, Reckitt works with many of its customers through partnerships including the Ellen MacArthur Foundation on plastics, AIM-Progress on labour standards and human rights and the Consumer Goods Forum.

As Miguel Veiga-Pestana, Reckitt's Head of Corporate Affairs and Chief Sustainability Officer, says:

> Reckitt exists to protect, heal and nurture in the relentless pursuit of a cleaner, healthier world. We believe that access to the highest-quality hygiene, wellness and nourishment is a right, not a privilege. We draw on our collective energy to meet our ambitions of purpose-led brands, a healthier planet and a fairer society. Partnerships are at the heart of our approach. We know we can only succeed by working with others, in our value chain and beyond. Partnerships are key to unlocking our ambition to build impact for society, engage 2 billion people and enable a cleaner healthier world.[20]

Summary

As a business grows more confident in the value of partnerships and more adept at partnering, it may choose to take more prominent leadership positions and/or expand its portfolio of active sustainability partnerships. The complexity of global challenges facing businesses means that, despite what may be high transaction costs, partnerships with other businesses and with other parts of society will become increasingly important and common.

Action checklist

1 Identify the gaps / needs that the business has that partnerships can help address.

2 Clarify if there are any existing partnerships in which the business is involved that could fill any of these gaps / needs.

3 If not, explore if there are other, established partnerships that would meet the needs and which the business could join.

4 Explore if there is an ambition / cultural fit with current members of these existing partnerships.

5 If there remain significant gaps / needs to be met, explore whether other businesses have similar needs as well as the hunger and commitment required to establish a new partnership.

6 Consider the partnering mindset and skillset your company's representatives will need.

7 Identify relevant people to represent the business in particular partnerships and assess any training gaps they may have for partnering as well as how these gaps can be filled.

8 Regularly review the performance of different partnerships in which the business is involved.

9 Establish a proportionate and robust measurement, evaluation, learning and reporting system to keep track of involvement in sustainability partnerships and to ensure the business can continue to learn and to optimize involvement in partnerships.

Further resources

The website of The Partnering Initiative (founded in 2003) has many guides and resources, such as:

- BSR / Rockefeller Foundation (2018) *How Businesses Must Lead to Achieve Sustainable Development*, BSR / Rockefeller Foundation

- Grayson, D and Nelson, J (2013) *Corporate Responsibility Coalitions: The past, present & future of alliances for sustainable capitalism*, Stanford University Press and Greenleaf Publishing
- Nelson, J (2017) *Partnerships for Sustainable Development: Collective action by business, governments and civil society to achieve scale and transform markets*, Business and Sustainable Development Commission
- Stibbe, D and Prescott, D (2020) *The SDG Partnership Guidebook*, The Partnering Initiative and UN DESA
- The CR Initiative in the Kennedy School of Government, Harvard, has a rich back catalogue of reports and case studies on collaboration
- The SustainAbility Institute by ERM (2020) *Leveraging the Power of Collaborations*, The SustainAbility Institute by ERM
- Watson, R, Wilson, H N and Macdonald, E K (2020) Business-nonprofit engagement in sustainability-oriented innovation: What works for whom and why?, *Journal of Business Research*, Vol. **119**, 87–98
- World Resources Institute (2020) A Time For Transformative Partnerships: How multistakeholder partnership can accelerate the UN sustainable development goals, World Resources Institute

Endnotes

1 Nelson, J (2002) Building Partnerships: Cooperation between the United Nations system and the private sector, United Nations, Department of Public Information, quoted in Nelson, J (2017) *Partnerships for Sustainable Development: Collective action by business, governments and civil society to achieve scale and transform markets*, Business and Sustainable Development Commission

2 Resonance Global, www.resonanceglobal.com/ (archived at https://perma.cc/V2UZ-CV3J)

3 To be clear, we don't think it is sufficient for a business to be a member of a coalition; they have to be collaborating through the coalition for it to be partnering

4   www.csreurope.org/newsbundle-articles/new-common-strategy-for-sustainable-automotive-value-chains (archived at https://perma.cc/NDD8-AS3E)

5   www.ellenmacarthurfoundation.org/explore (archived at https://perma.cc/GR7R-E9NF)

6   Since its inception in 1995, the NBI has made a distinct impact in, among others, the spheres of housing delivery, crime prevention, local economic development, public sector capacity building, further education and training, schooling, public, private partnerships, energy efficiency and climate change, www.nbi.org.za/ (archived at https://perma.cc/W8YH-ZVYH)

7   www.re-generate.org/ecosystem-map (archived at https://perma.cc/M7R4-VVEK)

8   www.bsr.org/en/our-insights/report-view/private-sector-collaboration-for-sustainable-development (archived at https://perma.cc/5PJV-DGAF)

9   The SustainAbility Institute by ERM (2020) Leveraging the Power of Collaborations, www.sustainability.com/globalassets/sustainability.com/thinking/pdfs/report-leveraging-the-power-of-collaborations.pdf (archived at https://perma.cc/5PJV-DGAF)

10 www.bsr.org/en/our-insights/report-view/private-sector-collaboration-for-sustainable-development (archived at https://perma.cc/5PJV-DGAF)

11 ING, www.ing.com/Sustainability/The-world-around-us-1/Memberships.htm (archived at https://perma.cc/UD9F-9X3W); Google, sustainability.google/for-partners/ (archived at https://perma.cc/ENT9-JCL9)

12 Adidas, www.adidas-group.com/en/sustainability/managing-sustainability/partnership-approach/#/collaboration-and-memberships (archived at https://perma.cc/6RA8-DEW5); Cargill, www.cargill.com/sustainability/partners (archived at https://perma.cc/B6J7-M9V8)

13 www.nestle.com/csv/what-is-csv/partnerships-alliances (archived at https://perma.cc/L3S8-4XKJ)

14 www.shell.com/sustainability/our-approach/working-in-partnership.html (archived at https://perma.cc/2365-PBZD)

15 www.danone.com (archived at https://perma.cc/RN4Q-UL9M)

16 For example, B Lab UK, B Lab USA and Canada, B Lab Australia/New Zealand, B Lab Taiwan, B Lab East Africa, B Lab Europe, B Lab Asia or SYSTEMA for South America

17 MIT Sloan Management Review (2015) Joining Forces: Collaboration and leadership for sustainability, MIT Sloan Management Review in collaboration with The Boston Consulting Group and the United Nations Global Compact, January, sloanreview.mit.edu/projects/joining-forces (archived at https://perma.cc/Y6QD-HYG7)

18 There was an unfortunate example in 2021 where the EU Commission fined certain German automakers for colluding to not compete on above-legal standards technology for reducing fuel emissions

19 Sourced from: www.novartis.com/our-company (archived at https://perma. cc/L4U6-DMFJ); Novartis Annual Report 2020, www.novartis.com/sites/ www.novartis.com/files/novartis-annual-report-2020.pdf (archived at https://perma.cc/LDL6-U33K); Novartis in Society ESG Report 2020, www. novartis.com/sites/www.novartis.com/files/novartis-in-society-report-2020. pdf (archived at https://perma.cc/WYM7-GB4S); Novartis Q2 2021 ESG Update for investors and analysts, www.novartis.com/sites/www.novartis. com/files/environmental-social-and-governance-july-2021-update.pdf (archived at https://perma.cc/U5KS-FNEW); 50climateleaders.com (archived at https://perma.cc/MB4Q-ZN6Y), Sustainability and Climate Leaders

20 Source from: www.reckitt.com/about-us/who-we-are/ (archived at https://perma.cc/X474-YT4T); London Stock Exchange, www. londonstockexchange.com/stock/RKT/reckitt-benckiser-group-plc/company-page (archived at https://perma.cc/ED65-W6E2); Reckitt Annual Report 2020, www.reckitt.com/media/8728/reckitt_ar20.pdf (archived at https://perma.cc/ R4WY-3VEJ); www.reckitt.com/investors/annual-report-2020/ (archived at https://perma.cc/5C5M-RH72); Reckitt Sustainability Report 2020, www. reckitt.com/media/9261/reckitt-sustainability-insights-2020.pdf (archived at https://perma.cc/A6EZ-CYMS); authors' exchange with Miguel Veiga-Pestana, September 2021

13

Advocacy

What is it?

Companies calling for a price on carbon and for other businesses to follow their example in setting evidence- or science-based targets around carbon emissions reductions.[1] Businesses endorsing Black Lives Matter and speaking out about the urgency of racial justice after the brutal murder of George Floyd in May 2020.[2] Global businesses publicly endorsing the 'Open for Business'[3] campaign for LGBTQ rights in parts of the world with anti-equality laws. These are examples of corporate advocacy: speaking out and speaking up for social and environmental progress.

Some dismiss this as just marketing or PR. If that is all that it is, there are dangers for business. Any business taking a stand in sustainable development needs to be sure that its own core operations and behaviour will withstand scrutiny and prove consistent with what it publicly advocates. Otherwise, the public will quickly smell inauthenticity and spot inconsistency.[4]

Brands and businesses campaigning for causes are part of a much wider development in which companies and business leaders are speaking out and speaking up for sustainability issues. This new wave of advocacy can be headline grabbing but also strategic in driving the wider systemic changes required to achieve the transition to a sustainable society and economy. 'We are,' says the *New York Times* journalist David Gelles, 'looking to our CEOs for moral guidance in these troubled times.'

One powerful example of business advocacy in recent years is the annual letter to CEOs from Larry Fink, the founder and CEO of BlackRock, the world's largest institutional investor. These letters have been published since 2012 and have become increasingly urgent and insistent about the need for businesses to define their purpose and set long-term strategies that incorporate ESG factors.[5]

As we showed in our earlier book, *All In: The Future of Business Leadership*, advocacy by companies is not new. As referenced in that previous work, think of the great Quaker businesses of the nineteenth century, the pioneering work of Levi Strauss to desegregate its factories in the Deep South of the USA in the 1950s and the same company's campaigning for HIV / AIDS research in the 1980s. Think, too, of the outspoken campaigning of the late Anita Roddick, founder of The Body Shop, directly and through her global retail network.

What is different in the 2020s is both the number of vehicles for corporate advocacy and the range of topics being promoted, from action on climate change to mental health and well-being in the workforce. In *New Power: How Power Works in Our Hyperconnected World – and How to Make It Work for You* (2018), Jeremy Heimans and Henry Timms argue that a combination of a decline of deference, a loss of trust in established institutions, global connectivity and social media have combined to create 'New Power', which is more distributed and bottom up. We would argue that in an era of New Power there are more possibilities for corporate advocacy because of the potential to engage stakeholders in the course of it. At the same time, New Power also raises the stakes – it is easier for critics of any business, including disaffected current and former employees, to spot and ruthlessly publicize any inconsistencies or, worse still, hypocrisy, if the company's behaviour appears contrary to what the company is advocating.

Publications such as *The Economist* and *Harvard Business Review* have published articles focused on what they have termed 'CEO Activism'. CEO Activism has been defined as 'Senior leaders speaking out on social issues that are not directly related to their company's bottom-line but are often part of managing corporate reputation as well as positive public, employee, and other stakeholders' impressions.'[6] So defined, it aligns with advocacy.

In some instances, it is clear that a CEO is speaking as an individual rather than articulating a corporate position; what they say individually gets attention, however, because of the job they do as chief executives. Most of what is termed 'CEO activism', we consider to be part of advocacy. Richard Walker, Managing Director at Iceland Foods, based in the UK, champions sustainability. During the 2020 pandemic lockdowns he wrote a book about his approach: *The Green Grocer*. This includes an account of the Iceland 2018 Christmas TV advert: 'Rang-tan'. This re-used – with permission – an earlier Greenpeace advert about deforestation. Although the Iceland advert was banned from TV for being political, the ban itself generated intense publicity and raised the debate about sustainable palm oil.[7]

Advocacy is qualitatively and substantively different from traditional lobbying. Lobbying typically seeks changes in public policy (such as changes in tax policy, regulatory interpretations, subsidies, the awarding of public sector contracts or government grants, etc) to the direct benefit of the lobbyist. Advocacy, on the other hand, is identifying and speaking up for the behaviour, policies, laws, etc associated with advancing sustainable development more systemically, whether that is to the immediate and direct benefit of the company or not.

Sometimes, sustainable development advocacy is only indirectly in the interests of the advocate and, even then, perhaps more in the longer term – although this is changing as more companies use advocacy to help achieve their sustainability goals and commitments. Certainly, while the objects of lobbying will be governments and/or elected politicians, and public policy may be in play, the audience for advocacy may also be citizens, other businesses or other types of organizations like NGOs, since advocacy objectives are not limited to policy change but can also include persuading other businesses to adopt higher sustainability standards and nudging consumers towards more sustainable consumption.[8]

Why it matters

There are a good number of reasons why advocacy is a strategic part of corporate sustainability leadership:

- There are growing expectations of business to take a stand.
- There is substantial evidence now that, in many parts of the world, there is an expectation from both the general public and what the PR firm Edelman refers to as the 'informed public' (better educated, higher income, greater consumers of news) for businesses to speak out – although surveys vary as to what publics believe companies should prioritize in their advocacy. The 2021 Edelman Trust Barometer[9] reports that:
  - 86 per cent of people surveyed worldwide expect CEOs to speak out on controversial societal issues.
  - 66 per cent say that business leaders should take the lead rather than waiting for governments to act.
- Other recent Edelman Trust Barometers have identified equal pay, eliminating prejudice and discrimination, and training for the jobs of tomorrow as the top three issues for CEOs to advocate for.
- Advocacy can help bring a company's purpose and sustainability commitments to life for internal and external stakeholders:
  - The UK-based non-profit InfluenceMap has picked out 20 corporate leaders across a range of sectors and regions known for advocating ambitious climate policy, calling this the 'A-List of Climate Policy Engagement'.[10] To qualify, a company must exhibit sector leadership, sufficient support for ambitious climate policy and be strategically active.
- Advocacy can amplify the positive impact that a business can have on sustainability:
  - Even the biggest companies say they can only push the needle marginally alone, which creates need for collective action. Some sustainability leaders talk about the objective of their advocacy as inspiring other businesses to join in and help build a global

movement for sustainable development. We know there is a tendency for people and organizations to follow the leaders, which includes other businesses that they admire and respect.

- Urgency demands more and better advocacy:
  - Given the climate, biodiversity, health and inequality crises facing the world, there is wide recognition of the need for systemic change, which requires an enabling environment for sustainable development. Some argue that, given current stalemates in political structures in various parts of the world, there are fewer alternatives to companies taking a stand. Furthermore, global connectivity – the 'New Power' argument – makes advocacy by businesses more impactful.

Criticisms of advocacy include whether it is only for what might be termed progressive policies or only conducted when it feels safe and in line with public opinion. It is pointed out that not many companies have spoken up for migrants and refugees in Europe, for example, or for many other human rights abuses such as human trafficking. Others suggest some issues are matters of personal conscience and not the realm of business at all, challenging whether business has the legitimacy to be an advocate. Conversely, members of the Ipsos MORI Reputation Council firmly believe that businesses 'have a licence, or even an obligation, to speak out on the big socio-political and cultural issues of the day'.[11]

How to do it

Step 1: Determine if the business has the authority to advocate for sustainability

Would advocacy by the company generally or on a particular topic have credibility? This depends crucially on its track record, for example whether it has made clear public commitments on sustainability and whether these are being fulfilled. It's also crucial that the company's conduct and business performance (from sourcing and product development to corporate tax strategy and responsibility for product end of life) apply and advance sustainability best practice, ensuring that the company practises what it proposes to preach. Indeed, it would be prudent to conduct an overt 'practise what you preach' audit before starting out. In fact, that's smart PR – it is much more effective to say, 'we're falling short on x topic, here's how we are going to fix it and by when, here's why it matters to our business, and that's why we call on others to do x, y and z'.

Observers will also note whether there have been any recent scandals or failings by the business or egregious behaviour in the recent past that might compromise its credibility and undermine company positions. If there is doubt, it might be worth testing the waters with some key internal and external stakeholders. A further consideration is whether the business's recent operational and financial performance is sufficient to make any advocacy credible. A consistently profitable business that outperforms market expectations will be in a stronger position to fend off anyone questioning why they are spending time on advocacy.

There are also questions concerning the legitimate boundaries for multinational corporations operating outside their home countries and seeking to influence public policy agendas in host countries. Such activities can invite allegations of neo-imperialism. This is a key issue, for example, for many extractive sector companies that, since their businesses are geologically determined, cannot easily pick up their investment dollars and go somewhere else, and therefore have a particularly strong interest in seeing governance and service delivery (often largely funded by royalties and corporate taxes) improved.

This partly explains why the extractive sector has seen a cluster of multi-stakeholder, collaborative advocacy initiatives, most of which have been focused on improving transparency. They include the Extractive Industries Transparency Initiative (EITI), Publish What You Pay and the Voluntary Principles on Security and Human Rights. These all aim to help companies align with civil society and reformist elements in host governments around what constitutes good practice and use such alliances to build greater legitimacy for the use of corporate advocacy / influence. Still, in some countries, there are cultural or practical barriers to companies taking a stand – especially if this might bring them into conflict with governments. In any country, it is important to avoid the personal hobby horses of the owner or senior executives.

Step 2: Develop a framework or decision tool to help decide whether to speak out on a particular topic

Paul A. Argenti, Professor of Corporate Communication at the Tuck School of Business at Dartmouth College, suggests three tests for whether a business should advocate on a particular issue:

- Does the issue align with your company's strategy?
- Can you meaningfully influence the issue?
- Will your constituencies agree with speaking out?

Argenti argues that if a business can genuinely answer 'yes' to all three questions, it is appropriate to advocate on the topic. If it answers 'yes' to two questions, it may be better to support the advocacy of others or advocate in a partnership effort. And if there is just one or not even a single 'yes', then Argenti concludes the company should not speak out.[12]

It is particularly important that businesses proposing to speak up on a controversial topic discuss plans with their board – and, in some cases, with key investors. Boards and investors should rightly push for evidence that the proposed advocacy clearly links to sustainability strategy, commitments and performance.

Advocacy isn't the exclusive domain of large companies. Smaller businesses are getting involved too. In some cases, this involves endorsing an existing campaign from a big customer or a leader in its sector, or it may mean backing an advocacy campaign of a trade association, Chamber of Commerce or small business club in which the firm is involved. Some smaller companies also talk about 'inspiring others' rather than advocacy.

Many B Corps, for example, tell their own stories – especially during the annual B Corp Month campaign – in order to inspire and encourage other businesses to investigate B Corp certification for themselves in the hope that having more purpose-led businesses and more certified B Corps will advance sustainable development and social justice. The herbal teas business and early UK B Corp Pukka Herbs have inspired many farmers to switch to organic farming through a mix of their own example, passionate advocacy and the practical advice and help that they offer to farmers who decide to go organic.

Step 3: Define advocacy objectives

A business needs clear and transparent advocacy objectives. Objectives might include raising awareness on the sustainable development agenda, nudging public behaviour towards sustainability, recruiting more businesses for a collective sustainability goal or changing government policies.

It may be helpful to differentiate between:

- Short term, such as reacting to external events, which may be more akin to crisis management / crisis communications.
- Medium term, such as responding to invitations to join initiatives with other businesses, where there is more time to consult and to brief key stakeholders in advance.
- Longer term, such as proactively initiating an advocacy campaign as an extension of company purpose and sustainability strategy. This will be more analogous to long-term reputation and brand building. Typically, this may build on the company taking an increasingly visible leadership role in various sustainability forums and topics.

The Canadian sustainability expert Coro Strandberg suggests a number of potential benefits to a company from engaging in advocacy.

Achieving one or more of these benefits may constitute additional objectives for an advocacy campaign:

- Stimulate market signals and create incentives.
- Level the playing field and capitalize on early sustainability investments.
- Earn a seat at the table to shape future policy design and regulation.
- Build reputation, stakeholder trust and social licence to operate.
- Gain market share and attract customers by being seen as a proactive business working in the public interest.
- Increase employee attraction, retention and motivation.
- Generate earned media.[13]

If the business has a transparent and accountable culture (see Chapter 6), it should be automatic that it will be transparent and accountable in its advocacy. Openness should be a cardinal principle of advocacy. This means that the business publishes all its position papers and depositions to governments, parliamentarians and regulators. It lists out meetings held with power brokers in a timely and comprehensive fashion. And it is ready to explain how the business has arrived at the advocacy stances it is taking.

Step 4: Clarify the target audience(s) for advocacy and choose an appropriate mix of advocacy tools

Getting specific as to which stakeholder groups are most strategic for your company's advocacy is critical, as it will shape the content and approach to your campaigning. Target audiences may include other companies, elected politicians and governments, employees, suppliers, customers, end consumers and the public (to change societal attitudes and behaviours or to persuade the public to join in advocacy campaigns to other parts of society such as government).

Depending on the target audience, there is a range of advocacy tools and tactics to consider. These include:

- correcting any poor corporate behaviour and practice within the company;
- CEO speeches, op-eds, tweets and public statements;
- private representations to governments;
- advertising and campaigning;
- participating in sustainability coalitions;
- participating in government panels and councils (or withdrawing from such bodies in protest at government policies deemed to be inconsistent with the company's values);
- mobilizing action including petitions and/or encouraging employees and customers to sign petitions aligned with organizational positions, for example promoting voter registration and civic action;
- threatening to withdraw business from specific regions with discriminatory laws / practices;
- court action including supporting legal test cases;
- agitating for legislative change through representations to elected officials;
- working with government officials and parliamentarians in the detailed drafting of new legislation;
- commissioning and publicizing white papers and/or thought-leadership research on topical issues;
- endorsing and/or funding NGO campaigns around sustainable development.

Arguably, the most important things that companies can typically bring to the table for advocacy are a mix of knowledge and expertise, money (or to withhold money such as advertising spend), convening power and often having extra access to power including media, regulators, politicians and ministers, etc.

The best advocacy goes way beyond the CEO speaking out or the company taking a public stance or making a pledge. Some companies employ a highly sophisticated influencing strategy that includes a network of policy interventions, key powerbroker relationships across political, NGO and industry sectors, alliances, public campaigns, etc. This approach is based on having a core objective and set of plans to follow through on the action. For example, the advocacy goal might be to create a level playing field so that all companies need to pay a living wage through industry commitment in the first instance; then partnering with NGOs, trade unions, think-tanks, statistics' offices and academia to establish the infrastructure for calculating and socializing what a living wage would be in countries where there is no agreed definition; and only then securing legislation to enforce a living wage.

Some companies have consciously changed corporate practices to encourage other companies to follow suit. For example, the Peninsula Hotels (part of the Hongkong and Shanghai Hotels Group), committed to sustainable seafood and taking shark fin off menus, knowing this would influence other hotel chains. Based on very rough estimates from consultants, around 18,000 hotels around the world followed their lead, perhaps because they are listed in Hong Kong, which is the centre of this trade, and because they are an iconic, luxury hotel brand.[14] Nike's controversial 2018 advertising campaign, featuring the American football player Colin Kaepernick with the caption 'Believe in something. Even if it means sacrificing everything', was a bold stand for race equality. McDonald's is another example of a company that changed its practices with the full knowledge that it likely would lead to broader systemic shifts in agriculture. McDonald's committed to cage free eggs by 2025 knowing this would shift the marketplace more broadly and raise standards and practices across the egg industry.[15]

Whatever the mix of tools and techniques deployed, the advocacy should be:

- proportionate and not grandstanding nor deliberately distracting;
- embracing appropriate context and rooted in the best available scientific knowledge;
- consistent with advocacy positions of business coalitions and membership organizations of which the company is a member;
- tactful and respectful of alternative views;
- not associated with a particular political party.

Many companies that have committed to responsible business practices and to embed sustainability collaborate with other businesses to amplify their advocacy and to improve their prospects of success. The 2018 report Advocating Together for the SDGs looks at such collaborative advocacy.[16]

Some corporate sustainability leaders seek to involve other businesses in their sector by influencing the agenda and knowledge base of sectoral associations in which they are active. The consultancy PwC and the corporate responsibility coalition CSR Europe completed a study in 2018 to assess the Maturity and Integration of Sustainability in European Sector Associations. The study includes a survey of and interviews with 16 sector associations from 11 different industry sectors from manufacturing to retail. It concluded that sector associations have potential to raise sustainability impact through increased collaboration. This has been followed up by CSR Europe and Moody's with a European Barometer of Sustainable Industries, analysing 1,600 European companies in 40 industry sectors (October 2021).

Some companies such as Unilever are now explicitly asking all the trade associations of which they are members to confirm that the associations' own lobbying and advocacy are consistent with Unilever's commitments to policies in line with the Paris Climate agreement. Another approach involves publishing an account of how a company's own positions may differ from those of the associations they are part, an option modelled by companies such as Shell.[17] Similarly, businesses operating in countries where it is traditional for companies to donate to political parties and to the election campaigns of individual politicians must expect increased scrutiny if they are found to be funding politicians with points of view very different to what the business is advocating.

Step 5: Keep advocacy under review

Successful corporate advocates for sustainability maintain a degree of humility and listen carefully to criticisms and rebuttals, then reflect and amend their activities accordingly. This is not about backing down as soon as there is criticism; you cannot expect to please all of the people all of the time!

Advocates must be prepared for the reality that their positions may upset some stakeholders. This requires being both humble and willing to constantly reflect on whether the advocacy is right and whether the assumptions on which it is based still hold good.

In practice

Natura &Co

The Brazilian-headquartered Natura &Co, which, besides the original Natura founded in 1969 now also owns Avon, The Body Shop and the Aesop beauty brand, is the world's largest certified B Corp. The group had over $7 billion turnover in 2020 and operates in more than 100 countries.

Natura and the other companies in the group have long been pioneers of sustainability. In 2000, for example, Natura created a new business model – the Ekos line – with the idea of connecting its products with small local communities, most of them located in the Amazon region, sourcing ingredients from them in a respectful way. Ever since, Natura has 'been learning about how to contribute to the protection of the rainforest, aiming to connect and enhance the tradition and knowledge of these local populations, and introduce the richness of Brazilian biodiversity not only to Brazilian citizens, but to the world'.[18]

In 2020, the group announced its 10-year 'Commitment to Life' plan. 'The plan sets out 31 targets which will see Natura &Co step up its actions to tackle some of the world's most pressing issues, including the climate crisis and protecting the Amazon, the defence of Human Rights and ensuring equality and inclusion throughout its network, and embracing circularity and regeneration by 2030.'[19]

Drawing on its heritage and long-term commitments, the group's companies have become high-profile advocates for the creation of science-based targets for biodiversity that would correspond to those already defined for carbon emissions and water usage.

Natura is working through a number of multinational forums as well as trying to engage its value chain – suppliers, but also particularly consumers on the basis that by giving them visibility and access to the data, the company empowers them to make informed decisions and choose products that guarantee zero deforestation. 'If customers change their behaviour, companies will change theirs. That is one of the aims that we have, not only to advocate, but to mobilise,' says Keyvan Macedo, the Sustainability Director at Natura &Co.[20]

Timpson

Timpson is a family-owned and operated British retailer, that was established in Manchester, England, in 1865. Today it specializes in shoe repairs, key cutting, locksmith services and engraving, as well as dry cleaning and photo processing. The company also offers mobile phone repairs, jewellery and watch repair and custom-made house signs. It has an annual turnover of just over £200 million and employs around 5,000 employees in its own stores and through its franchisees.

For almost two decades, Timpson has been an advocate for the rehabilitation of offenders. According to an article in *The Guardian* newspaper, since 2008, when the company opened a shoe repair workshop in Liverpool prison, Timpson has 'employed more than 1,500 ex-prisoners. Just four have returned to jail. Many of those who turned their backs on crime – including some with drug and alcohol issues – have progressed to senior roles in the company, including a current board member.'[21]

Timpson works closely with the UK prison service and 70 individual prisons. Together, they identify prisoners with the right kind of personality to work with Timpson on release from prison. It is described as 'a closely managed process from selection, training and mentoring up to release, with the opportunity to secure employment with the company from walking out the gates. Ten per cent of Timpson colleagues were recruited directly from prison.'[22]

This commitment and track record has enabled the CEO James Timpson to be an effective champion of giving ex-offenders another chance in life. James has personally chaired the Employers Forum for Reducing Reoffending, which is a coalition of like-minded employers who offer a second chance to people with a criminal conviction. He now chairs the Prison Reform Trust. James is extremely active on social media and, through a weekly column in the *Sunday Times*, in promoting this cause, highlighting the moral and bottom-line business case for action.

In an August 2021 tweet, Timpson commented: 'It's great to hear many companies are so desperate to recruit they are now looking towards our prisons for talent. We've been doing this for years, even when we had very few vacancies, as it's a good way of finding amazing people.'[23]

Summary

There are growing expectations on companies to speak out, at least in some parts of the world. Corporate advocacy needs to be consistent with core purpose, strategy and performance. Advocacy should be proportionate and managed as professionally as any other part of the business. Businesses should apply four principles of responsible advocacy:

- Radical openness.
- Always practising what they preach.
- Clear legitimacy, only advocating where the business can show a direct link to achieving its purpose and sustainability.
- Humility, always listening and learning.

Depending on the company, topic or geographies, advocacy may be better handled in collaboration with others (other businesses, NGOs, etc). Done well, advocacy can inspire others and thereby scale impact.

Action checklist

1 Decide if the business would be a credible advocate for sustainability given its own financial and sustainability performance.

2 Clarify how advocacy fits into and amplifies overall sustainability strategy and objectives.

3 Be clear on overall advocacy objectives.

4 Develop a process for deciding whether to speak out on particular topics.

5 Define target audience(s) and goals for specific advocacy campaigns and choose an appropriate mix of tools and techniques.

6 Check for consistency between the company's own advocacy and that done on its behalf by trade associations and the like and be prepared to explain any actual or apparent inconsistencies.

7 Decide whether the business is going to advocate for and contribute to higher sustainability standards and performance within its own industry sector and trade association.

Further resources

- Chouinard, Y (2005) *Let My People Go Surfing: The education of a reluctant businessman*, Penguin
- Grayson, D, Coulter, C and Lee, M (2018) *All In: The future of business leadership*, Routledge, Chapter 7
- Heimans, J and Timms, H (2018) *New Power: How power works in our hyperconnected world – and how to make It work for you*, Doubleday Books
- Patagonia (2021) Volunteer your skills for action, www.patagonia.com/activism
- The Ceres Policy Network, also known as Business for Innovative Climate and Energy Policy (BICEP), was founded in 2009 on the understanding that the climate crisis presents tremendous

material risks but also offers economic and environmental opportunities for businesses, www.ceres.org/networks/ceres-policy-network

- The Valuable 500 is a global community of 500 business leaders committed to putting disability on their agenda and recognizing the value and worth of the 1.3 billion people globally living with a disability, www.thevaluable500.com

- Triple Pundit (2021) Brands taking stands, www.triplepundit.com/category/brands-taking-stands/59911

- Walker, R (2021), *The Green Grocer*, Dorling Kindersley

Endnotes

1 The Science Based Targets initiative, sciencebasedtargets.org/ (archived at https://perma.cc/6A96-HGGP)

2 Hsu, T (2020) Corporate voices get behind 'Black Lives Matter' cause: Major companies are often wary of conflict, especially in a polarized time. But some are now taking a stand on racial injustice and police violence, *New York Times*, 31 May (updated 10 June).

3 open-for-business.org/ (archived at https://perma.cc/MP2K-7USE)

4 Grayson, D (March 2019) Brands and businesses taking stands, *Impakter Magazine*

5 GlobeScan publishes a very helpful textual analysis of the Fink letters: (February 2019) From good governance to purpose and profit – GlobeScan analysis of Larry Fink's annual letters to CEOs, http://medium.com/@GlobeScan/from-good-governance-to-purpose-and-profit-45741e2450b5 (archived at https://perma.cc/LP4H-TCRE); GlobeScan (February 2021) Accelerating the tectonic shift to net zero: Analysis of Larry Fink's annual letter to CEOs, globescan.com/analysis-larry-finks-annual-letter-ceos-2021/ (archived at https://perma.cc/6XEQ-QC5G)

6 Chatterji, A and Toffel, M W (2017) Assessing The Impact Of CEO Activism, Harvard Business School Technology & Operations Mgt. Unit Working Paper; Brien, D (24 November 2020) 10 lessons from CEOs on how to manage corporate reputation in a new era of activism, Fast Company, www.fastcompany.com/90579293/10-lessons-from-ceos-on-how-to-manage-corporate-reputation-in-a-new-era-of-activism (archived at https://perma.cc/SY6R-E42B)

7 Walker, R (2021) *The Green Grocer: One man's manifesto for corporate activism*, DK

8 Grayson, D, Coulter, C and Lee, M (2018) *All In: The future of business leadership*, Routledge, p. 105

9 The Edelman Trust Barometer 2021, www.edelman.com/trust/2021-trust-barometer (archived at https://perma.cc/5DSK-Y44Q)

10 InfluenceMap (April 2018) The A-list of climate policy engagement: An InfluenceMap report, influencemap.org/report/The-A-List-of-Climate-Policy-Engagement-ba3251ef6c09b397ddec7c79de2c8565 (archived at https://perma.cc/2KJJ-44KA)

11 Ipsos MORI Reputation Council (2017) Taking A Stand – Do The Rewards Of Corporate Activism Outweigh The Risks?, reputation.ipsos-mori.com/taking-a-stand/ (archived at https://perma.cc/DX57-UDVT)

12 Argenti, P (2020) When should your company speak up about a social issue?, HBR [blog], 16 October, https://hbr.org/2020/10/when-should-your-company-speak-up-about-a-social-issue (archived at https://perma.cc/DFU4-3VJD)

13 Strandberg, C (2020) *Advocacy for Good: Corporate public policy advocacy for a sustainable future*, Conference Board of Canada

14 Shark fin goes off the menu at Peninsula hotels, *The Guardian*, 24 November 2011; globescan.com/recognizing-leaders-janice-lao-hsh/ (archived at https://perma.cc/8BN7-ZYFR)

15 Kelso, A (12 April 2019) McDonald's cage-free egg progress signals an industry sea change, Restaurant Dive, www.restaurantdive.com/news/mcdonalds-cage-free-egg-progress-signals-an-industry-sea-change/552588/ (archived at https://perma.cc/C7AL-T8LD)

16 businessfightspoverty.org/joint-civil-society-business-advocacy-is-emerging-as-a-powerful-tool-to-drive-policy-change-in-support-of-the-sdgs/ (archived at https://perma.cc/G6VG-Y3X6)

17 Shell press release (2 April 2019) Shell publishes reports on industry associations, sustainability and payments to governments, www.shell.com/media/news-and-media-releases/2019/shell-publishes-reports-on-industry-associations-sustainability.html (archived at https://perma.cc/F3JY-V788)

18 Payne, J and Sanchez, G (31 August 2021) *Mobilising the Value Chain to Act on Nature: Natura's approach*, Corporate Citizenship

19 Natura, 2021, Natura &Co gives first annual update on Commitment to Life 2030 Sustainability Vision, www.naturaeco.com/press-release/natura-co-gives-first-annual-update-on-commitment-to-life-2030-sustainability-vision/ (archived at https://perma.cc/GEG7-DC84)

20 Natura, 2021, Natura &Co gives first annual update on Commitment to Life 2030 Sustainability Vision, www.naturaeco.com/press-release/natura-co-gives-first-annual-update-on-commitment-to-life-2030-sustainability-vision/ (archived at https://perma.cc/GEG7-DC84)

21 Allison, E (2 August 2021) 'There is another way': Why Timpson boss hit out at PM's chain-gang plan, *The Guardian*

22 www.thersa.org/events/speakers/james-timpson-obe (archived at https://perma. cc/USL9-NMH9)

23 Timpson, J, Twitter: @JamesTCobbler, 22 August 2021

Conclusion

'We think they have the potential of being a multibillion-dollar African success story,' says Colin le Duc, Head of Research at Generation Investment Management, the sustainability-focused investment company established by former US Vice-President Al Gore and his business partner David Blood.[1]

'They' are M-KOPA. Founded in Kenya in 2011, M-KOPA's investors include Generation, the CDC Group, Triodos Bank, LGT Venture Philanthropy and the Gates Foundation.

M-KOPA (*Kopa* means 'to borrow' in Swahili) describes itself as 'a connected asset financing platform that offers millions of under-banked customers access to life-enhancing products and services'. Its Pay-As-You-Go (PAYG) platforms provide customers with everything from solar energy to lighting solutions to appliances and mobile phones.

M-KOPA's pioneering systems use solar energy to power lighting, flashlights, radios, TVs, fridges and more – all provided by M-KOPA – and support mobile phone charging. Eighty per cent of the company's customers live on less than $2 a day; three-quarters rely on small-scale farming for income, while the rest run small businesses – and energy therefore accounts for a significant amount of their spending.

M-KOPA's basic power system costs $200. It includes a solar panel, two LED bulbs, an LED flashlight, a rechargeable radio and adaptors for charging a phone. The kit comes with a two-year warranty, and its battery is designed to last at least four years.[2] For customers able to access these goods thanks to M-KOPA's financing, the products are life-changing.

'If you boil it down, what we are is a finance company,' says Nick Hughes, one of M-KOPA's founders. 'What we've done is to give the customers some collateral and a line of credit.'[3]

So far, M-KOPA has sold more than one million PAYG solar systems and provided $400 million in financing to millions of customers while raising over $180 million in equity and debt.

We chose to start the introduction to *The Sustainable Business Handbook* with anecdotes from Unipart Group, HAVI and MAS – well-established but not widely known businesses increasingly making sustainability part of the way they do business, particularly in response to the needs of their customers. We believe they represent a great wave of companies in every part of global value chains beginning or accelerating their sustainability journeys. Such broad participation in solving the greatest social, environmental and economic challenges is essential, and this handbook aspires to make it more common and more accessible.

The scale and gravity of the issues discussed at the start of this handbook, from climate and inequality to globalization and pandemic recovery, will not be solved quickly enough unless change in business models and practices is universal and able to embrace sometimes dramatic and disruptive innovations. In business, this involves incumbents such as Unilever, Patagonia, Natura &Co, IKEA and Interface, already recognized as leaders in rankings like the GlobeScan / SustainAbility Leaders Survey, but must now also include the thousands of other companies in value chains better represented by Unipart, HAVI and MAS. To play on the title of our last book, where we asked that companies go 'All In' on sustainability leadership, with *The Sustainable Business Handbook* we are inviting 'Everyone In' to help transition to a more sustainable and equitable future.

Change will also come from disruptive start-ups outside existing value chains, such as M-KOPA. We have been aware of M-KOPA for several years. It is exciting because its core business model is about sustainable development. It helps to address several of the UN Sustainable Development Goals (SDGs) such as improving health, tackling poverty, improving access to clean energy, addressing climate change and stimulating sustainable growth and jobs. It is exciting too because it is happening in Africa where access to solar power can transform lives and fortunes.

As we conclude this *Sustainable Business Handbook*, we want to leave you, the reader, with this parting advice and encouragement:

- Be ambitious. Be bold. See the possibility in sustainability.
- Engage and empower your colleagues.
- Learn from others. Indulge in what the long-term management guru Tom Peters calls 'creative swiping'!
- Collaborate to reduce risks and accelerate the transformation of your business.
- Enjoy the ride. Our experience, and the experience of all the people we have worked with over the years on sustainability, tells us that implementing sustainability is rewarding – and, dare we say, fun!
- Finally, speak up and speak out. Share your experiences, including your mistakes. Inspire other companies and entrepreneurs to join a global movement of sustainable businesses (and please tell us about your journey and your successes for our next edition of *The Sustainable Business Handbook*).

Yes, the challenges are daunting. The world is going through an enormous amount of change and disruption. Yet in the face of these challenges there are enormous opportunities, and we must be stubborn optimists and harness the power and ingenuity of business as a force for good.

Endnotes

1 Quoted in Grayson, D, Coulter, C and Lee, M (2018) *All In: The future of business leadership*, Routledge

2 Bloomberg (2 December 2015) The Solar Company Making a Profit on Poor Africans, www.bloomberg.com/features/2015-mkopa-solar-in-africa/ (archived at https://perma.cc/G9GQ-RYJQ)

3 Bloomberg (2 December 2015) The Solar Company Making a Profit on Poor Africans, www.bloomberg.com/features/2015-mkopa-solar-in-africa/ (archived at https://perma.cc/G9GQ-RYJQ)

ACTION CHECKLIST

Embedding sustainability in 40 questions

The *Sustainable Business Handbook* concludes with a summary checklist designed to help business leaders and owners assess how sustainable their business is now and what steps to take to make it higher performing and more resilient in the future.

1 PURPOSE:

   a. Does the business have a clear purpose that defines how it not only creates economic value but also social and environmental value?

   b. Is the purpose authentic, inspiring and practical in the eyes of stakeholders?

   c. Has the company engaged its stakeholders internally and externally on its purpose?

2 MATERIALITY:

   a. Does the business conduct a regular materiality analysis to identify its highest-impact sustainability / ESG issues?

   b. Are stakeholders engaged in the materiality process?

   c. Does the business consider how its materiality issues may change over time as a result of global megatrends including climate, biodiversity and inequality as well as technological, market and demographic shifts and disruptions?

3 BUSINESS CASE:

   a. Is there a robust process in place for developing and regularly updating the business case for sustainability specific to the company?

b. Does the business case clearly support the company's purpose and strategy?

c. Is the overall business case used to support specific business cases for sustainability initiatives and investments?

4 STRATEGY:

a. Is there an ambitious and comprehensive strategy for sustainability supported by a clear business case?

b. Does the strategy address all the company's material issues and meet stakeholder expectations?

c. Is the sustainability strategy aligned with the overall corporate strategy?

5 OPERATIONALIZING:

a. Is the sustainability strategy fully and effectively operationalized in all parts of the business?

b. Is the strategy reflected in company policies and processes?

c. Is sustainability performance considered in rewards and recognition?

d. Does operationalizing the sustainability strategy affect the product / service portfolio, including new product / service design?

6 CULTURE:

a. Have the board and senior management defined the desired culture of the organization and how it aligns with a sustainable business, and does it periodically check to ensure that desired and actual cultures align and act appropriately to close any gaps?

b. Does the desired culture reinforce the embedding of sustainability across the organization?

c. Does the culture facilitate innovation towards sustainability solutions?

7 LEADERSHIP:

   a. Has the business identified the leadership competencies required to incorporate sustainability across the organization?

   b. Are the necessary skills included in company leadership development programmes?

   c. Does the company encourage and support its social intrapreneurs?

8 REPORTING:

   a. Does the business regularly report its performance on its most material ESG issues honestly and transparently?

   b. Has the business adopted one or more of the recognized sustainability reporting guidelines or frameworks?

   c. Does the company participate in appropriate ratings and indices and use the results to benchmark its performance?

9 GOVERNANCE:

   a. Does the board participate in development and approval of the sustainability strategy?

   b. Are sustainability competencies and performance included in the board skills matrix and considered during individual director appraisals and overall assessments of board effectiveness?

   c. Is there strong board governance and oversight of the business's sustainability commitments and performance?

10 ENGAGEMENT:

   a. Has the business mapped its stakeholders and does it keep this picture up to date?

   b. Is the business responsive to stakeholder concerns and can it point to examples of where it has changed what it is doing, how it does it and with whom as a result of stakeholder dialogue?

   c. Does the business track new business opportunities that arise as a result of stakeholder engagement?

11 COMMUNICATIONS:

   a. Does the business regularly and effectively communicate about sustainability?

   b. Does the company's sustainability-related communication make use of both hard data and information and compelling storytelling?

   c. Are leaders at all levels of the business committed and confident in their ability to support the company's sustainability-related communication efforts?

12 PARTNERING:

   a. Does the business take a strategic approach to collaborating with others to advance ESG performance?

   b. Has the business identified gaps and blockages affecting the implementation of its sustainability commitments that could be addressed by working in partnership?

   c. Is there a capacity inside the company to capture and disseminate learning from involvement in different partnerships?

13 ADVOCACY:

   a. Is the business recognized as a credible advocate for sustainable development?

   b. Has the company established protocols for deciding whether it is appropriate to speak out on a particular issue?

   c. Are members of the board, the CEO and other senior executives equipped to advocate effectively?

GLOSSARY / JARGON BUSTER

Assurance: operational and reporting processes to give businesses and stakeholders confidence in the accuracy of statements, perhaps provided by an internal, independent perspective from internal auditors or, more typically, an external perspective from an external assurance provider such as an accountancy firm.

Board skills matrix: the skills required around the board table. Generic skills are the skills required of all board members. Specific skills are required of at least one member of the board.

Circular economy: where waste is eliminated, resources are circulated and nature is regenerated – in contrast with the linear economy 'Take, make, waste' approach.

Double materiality: a materiality process that not only showcases societal impacts but also financial impacts of each issue for an enterprise.

Dynamic materiality: the basic idea of dynamic materiality is that what investors consider to be the material environmental, social and governance (ESG) issues changes over time. This can happen slowly, as with climate change and gender diversity, or more quickly, as with plastics in the oceans.[1]

Enterprise risk management (ERM): in business this includes the methods and processes used by organizations to manage risks and seize opportunities related to the achievement of their objectives.

ESG: Environmental, Social and Governance refers to the three central factors (environmental, social, governance) used in measuring the sustainability and societal impact of an investment in a company or business.

GRI: the Global Reporting Initiative is an international independent standards organization that helps businesses, governments and other organizations understand and communicate their impacts on issues such as climate change, human rights and corruption.

Greenwashing:[2] hype or overclaim; when companies invest more of their time in marketing themselves as sustainable than in actually working on environmental or social inclusion initiatives. The term was originally used by the environmentalist Jay Westerfeld in 1986 when he criticized hotels that ran adverts to encourage guests to reuse their towels while neglecting sustainability in their general business practices.

Greenhushing: when businesses become so scared of being accused of greenwashing that they don't communicate their actual sustainability impacts and performance.

High-flyer: a person who is or has the potential to be very successful in an organization and who may have been identified as such.

Integrated reporting: brings together material information about an organization's strategy, governance, performance and prospects in a way that reflects the commercial, social and environmental context within which it operates.[3]

International Integrated Reporting Council: the IIRC is not a reporting standard but a framework for a process that results in communications by an organization about value creation over time.

Materiality: the process of identifying, defining and ranking the priority ESG / sustainability issues for a business. Can often lead to the production of a materiality matrix.

Pre-competitive collaboration: typically involves two or more companies within the same industry coming together to address a shared problem or pain point that doesn't impact direct business competition and is often focused on joint social or environmental impacts.[4]

Purpose washing: where a brand or business is accused of 'cashing in' – claiming to be purposeful in their marketing without making a real, meaningful contribution by changing their business practices.

Risk register: list of the risks identified by a board / Executive Team for their organization, typically with a summary of actions taken to mitigate the risk. It is a tool used as part of the risk management process to help identify, analyse and manage risks.

SASB: The Sustainability Accounting Standards Board is a non-profit organization, founded in 2011 to develop sustainability accounting standards to help investors, lenders, insurance underwriters and other providers of financial capital to better understand the impact of ESG factors on the financial performance of companies. It is now part of the Value Reporting Foundation together with the IIRC.

Social intrapreneur: an entrepreneurial employee who develops a profitable new product, service or business model that creates value for society and for their company. Social intrapreneurs help their employers meet their sustainability commitments and create value for customers and communities in ways that are built to last.[5]

Stakeholder: any group or individual who can affect or is affected by the activities of an organization.

Tier 1 and Tier 2 suppliers: Tier 1 suppliers are partners that a business directly conducts business with, including contracted manufacturing facilities or production partners. Tier 1 suppliers are often significant cost centres.[6] Tier 2 suppliers are those supplying Tier 1.

Endnotes

1 Eccles, R (2020) Dynamic materiality in the time of COVID-19, Forbes, 19 April; www.sasb.org/blog/double-and-dynamic-understanding-the-changing-perspectives-on-materiality (archived at https://perma.cc/5MPE-76P7)

2 See also Watson, B (2016) The troubling evolution of corporate greenwashing, *The Guardian*, 20 August, www.theguardian.com/sustainable-business/2016/aug/20/greenwashing-environmentalism-lies-companies (archived at https://perma.cc/GG4L-5URB)

3 Deloitte UK

4 www.resonanceglobal.com/blog/best-practices-to-harness-the-power-of-pre-competitive-collaboration-for-sustainable-supply-chains (archived at https://perma.cc/43M7-M93V)

5 ssir.org/articles/entry/cultivating_the_social_intrapreneur (archived at https://perma.cc/K7ZK-JBS8)

6 Source: Sustain.Life, www.sustain.life/post/tier-suppliers (archived at https://perma.cc/6NM7-2GH4)

KEEPING UP TO DATE
ON SUSTAINABLE BUSINESS

No book on the topic of sustainability can hope to keep up to date. As authors, we were pestering our editors up to the last possible moment to let us include some critical new development or resource!

If you want to stay current in sustainable business, you will need to build up your own intelligence sources and the capacity to analyse and make sense of all the available materials and insights and then to prioritize what is most material and important for your business. That might sound daunting, but we have some practical tips to make it easier.

1. Keep in touch with us

Each of us and our organizations regularly posts blogs, reports and news:

- Mark: The SustainAbility institute by ERM, www.sustainability.com
- Chris: GlobeScan, globescan.com
- David: Cranfield School of Management Sustainability Group, www.cranfield.ac.uk/som/expertise/sustainability, and the Institute of Business Ethics, www.ibe.org.uk
- David also has a personal website: www.DavidGrayson.net

We and our respective organizations are also active on social media, regularly posting news and views about sustainable business. We also have a podcast, the All In: Sustainable Business Podcast, where we interview leading figures in the field.

GlobeScan and the SustainAbility Institute by ERM also produce biannual expert surveys on the evolving sustainable development agenda.

2. Find your partners

We recommend that you try and persuade your business to join an appropriate sustainable business coalition, whether local or global, or, if they already belong, to maximize the value. Such coalitions have a lot of relevant knowledge and up-to-date insights – for instance newsletters and programmes of events such as round tables, workshops with experts and larger conferences. (See Chapter 12 for more.)

3. Make the most of what is freely available

Many coalitions, sustainability consultancies like ERM and Globe-Scan and the sustainability practices within consultancies such as Accenture, Deloitte, EY, KPMG, McKinsey & Co and PWC produce a regular flow of reports relating to different aspects of corporate sustainability, such as Deloitte's annual resilience reports and Millennial Surveys and KPMG's annual reviews of corporate sustainability reporting by the world's largest companies. Many of these reports are published in partnership with organizations like the UN Global Compact, for instance the triennial UNGC-Accenture CEOs' Survey and the World Economic Forum's annual Global Risks Survey with Marsh McLennan.

4. Follow the authors' authors

Between us, we have hundreds of books about sustainability on our respective bookshelves. There are a few authors that we actively track for their new books. These include John Elkington, Kirk Hanson, Peter Lacy, Judy Samuelson, Solitaire Townsend and Andrew Winston.

Among the recent business and sustainability books that have caught our attention are:

- Paul Polman and Andrew Winston (2021) *Net Positive: How courageous companies thrive by giving more than they take*, Harvard Business Review Press

- John Elkington (2020) *Green Swans: The coming boom in regenerative capitalism*, Fast Company Press
- Rebecca Henderson (2020) *Reimagining Capitalism in a World on Fire*, Portfolio Penguin
- Christiana Figueres and Tom Rivett-Carnac (2020) *The Future We Choose: The stubborn optimist's guide to the climate crisis*, Manila Press
- C B Bhattacharya (2019) *Small Actions, Big Difference: Leveraging corporate sustainability to drive business and societal value*, 1st edition, Routledge
- Bob Willard (2013) *The New Sustainability Advantage*, New Society Publishers

5. Get online

A happier by-product of the COVID-19 pandemic and lockdowns is that many more organizations are hosting webinars and virtual, online conferences, many of them free. Again, our respective organizations do this and so do many others, such as Bloomberg, BSR, CSR Europe, GreenBiz, Innovation Forum, Sustainable Brands, The Economist, UN Global Compact and the WBCSD.

6. Find your favourite sustainability conference

In non-COVID-19 times, there are hundreds or more in-person sustainability conferences each year. It will be interesting to see how many of them resume after the pandemic, how many stay online and how many go hybrid. In pre-pandemic times, the conferences we have found to be good places to get the latest news and views, reconnect with friends and colleagues and meet lots of new folk, include:

- Asian Forum on Enterprise and Society organized by Asian Inc Forum and the Asian Institute of Management.

- CSR Asia Summits, an annual gathering of practitioners and stakeholders on sustainable business from across Asia.
- BSR's annual conference, which alternates between the East and West coasts of the United States.
- CSR Europe, which in recent years has joined with other European business bodies for an annual Business Summit and runs its own sessions within the larger event.
- 3BL Forums.
- Reuters Sustainable Business's annual Responsible Business Europe Summit.
- Sustainable Brands annual conference and satellite SB conferences around the world in major centres such as Buenos Aries, Madrid, Paris, São Paulo, Seoul and Tokyo.
- GreenBiz's annual signature conference and the VERGE series.

7. Get into the podcast habit

An increasing number of people are listening to podcasts. Given the growth in interest in sustainability around the world, it is not surprising that there has been an explosion of sustainability-related podcasts.

GreenBiz, for example, has two weekly podcasts: GreenBiz 350, a weekly podcast about the people and companies behind the headlines in sustainable business and clean technology; and Center Stage, capturing the best of live interviews conducted on stage at GreenBiz and VERGE conferences.

On the GreenBiz website, contributor Holly Secon makes the following podcast recommendations:

- Sustainability Defined;
- Think: Sustainability;
- Sourcing Matters;
- Climate One;
- Stanford Social Innovation Review.

8. Engage your sustainability champions

If your business has a network of Sustainability Champions, get them to set up an online chat platform or forum and encourage them to share interesting sustainable business news items.

If you are a Chief Sustainability Officer, Head of Sustainability or part of a sustainability function, a news group can help you to populate a regular news round-up for your board and executive team.

You might encourage interested employees to set up a Sustainable Business Book Club or encourage them to join an external, existing one online, like the Green Swans Book Club hosted by the think tank and consultancy Volans.

9. Follow the news

Generally, you should pay attention to the news and absorb / analyse news through the lens of sustainability, sustainable development, sustainable business and sustainability for your business. Global business news outlets such as *The Financial Times*, *The Guardian* and *The New York Times* give extensive coverage to sustainable business news nowadays. There are also many more specialist offshoots from major media, like Bloomberg Green.

10. Build your network

You will want to build up a network of practitioners interested in sustainability, both within and outside your business. Make sure you make time to keep in touch and try and build this up as an informal, mutual help, brains trust.

If you need some insights in building your network generally, we heartily recommend the online course produced by the businessman and arch networker Oli Barrett: Build a Better Network.

INDEX

Printed in the USA
CPSIA information can be obtained
at www.ICGtesting.com
JSHW071137281223
54463JS00013B/177